ONE WORLD AND OUR KNOWLEDGE OF IT

PHILOSOPHICAL STUDIES SERIES
IN PHILOSOPHY

Editors:

WILFRID SELLARS, *University of Pittsburgh*
KEITH LEHRER, *University of Arizona*

Board of Consulting Editors:

JONATHAN BENNETT, *Syracuse University*
ALLAN GIBBARD, *University of Michigan*
ROBERT STALNAKER, *Cornell University*
ROBERT G. TURNBULL, *Ohio State University*

VOLUME 23

JAY F. ROSENBERG

University of North Carolina, Dept. of Philosophy

ONE WORLD AND OUR KNOWLEDGE OF IT

The Problematic of Realism in Post-Kantian Perspective

D. REIDEL PUBLISHING COMPANY

DORDRECHT : HOLLAND / BOSTON : U.S.A.
LONDON : ENGLAND

Library of Congress Cataloging in Publication Data

Rosenberg, Jay F.
  One world and our knowledge of it.

  (Philosophical studies series in philosophy ; v. 23)
  Bibliography: p.
  Includes indexes.
  1. Realism.   2.   Knowledge, Theory of.   I.   Title.
B835.R67   121   80-20437
ISBN-13: 978-94-009-9055-5   e-ISBN-13: 978-94-009-9053-1
DOI: 10.1007/978-94-009-9053-1

Published by D. Reidel Publishing Company,
P.O. Box 17, 3300 AA Dordrecht, Holland.

Sold and distributed in the U.S.A. and Canada
by Kluwer Boston Inc.,
190 Old Derby Street, Hingham, MA 02043, U.S.A.

In all other countries, sold and distributed
by Kluwer Academic Publishers Group,
P.O. Box 322, 3300 AH Dordrecht, Holland.

D. Reidel Publishing Company is a member of the Kluwer Group.

All Rights Reserved
Copyright © 1980 by D. Reidel Publishing Company, Dordrecht, Holland
No part of the material protected by this copyright notice may be reproduced or
utilized in any form or by any means, electronic or mechanical,
including photocopying, recording or by any informational storage and
retrieval system, without written permission from the copyright owner

DEDICATION

His father was a blacksmith and hers a shopkeeper. Both had come from Hungary in the early years of the century and had settled in Chicago, where opportunity promised.

Although his heart was never fully in it, he took his degree in business, for there was a Depression and then there was a war. For forty years he served with dignity and with skill as an executive of a corporation, the prospering of which was due in no small measure to his contributions to it.

She never made for herself a career beyond that of wife and mother, but in those capacities she served with equal dignity and skill, and with patience and with an unchecked liveliness of mind and diversity of interest.

They met and married late, but well, and, in the course of time, they had two sons. Both are university faculty. The younger became an art historian; the older, a philosopher — and wrote this book.

They're a little puzzled by it all, but they delight in their grandchildren. And, as for their sons — "Well, as long as they're *happy* . . . ", they say.

This one is for Mom and Dad.

MOTTO

I still think that the greater part of the world is mistaken about many things. Surely one may be sane and yet think so, since the greater part of the world has often had to come round from its opinion

— George Eliot
Middlemarch

Why, very well then: I hope here be truths.

— Shakespeare
Measure for Measure

CONTENTS

Preface   xi

0:	Introduction	1
I:	Epistemic Legitimacy: The Problematic of Empiricism	3
II:	Things: The Micro-Ontology of Realist Consciousness	22
III:	Time and the Self: The Limits of Idealist Consciousness	57
IV:	Correctness and Community: From the Individual to the Social	87
V:	Realism and Idealism: Evolutionary Epistemology	109
VI:	Attribution and Appraisal: Elements of a Theory of Conduct	129
VII:	Communal Norms: Steps Toward a Collective Pragmatics	156
VIII:	Explanatory Realism: The Convergence of Conceptual Schemes	170
IX:	Retrospect: The End of a Myth and the Future of a Discipline	188

Appendix I. Notes   193
Appendix II. Bibliography   201
Index of Names   203
Index of Subjects   205

PREFACE

Philosophy, Aristotle is well known to have said, begins in wonder. So, of course, does everything else. Astronomy begins in wonder at the moving lights in the sky; biology, in wonder at the living creatures of the earth; psychology, in wonder at the intricacies and eccentricities of our distinctively human form of life. So, at best, wonder is only a necessary condition for philosophy.

What is peculiar about philosophers is what we are inclined to wonder about. We wonder about everything. In particular, we wonder about astronomy and biology and psychology (and about philosophy) — about whether and how such disciplines are possible and, crucially, about whether and how such disciplines fit together. We don't just wonder about everything. We wonder about everything *all at once*. Philosophers are general practitioners.

Things stand ill with our discipline today. There was quite recently at large in America an occasional publication under the title *Jobs in Philosophy*. The title rested upon a confusion, and the publication furthered the confusion upon which it rested. For it did not, in fact, list jobs in philosophy. It couldn't. Philosophy is not a profession. Philosophy is a calling, a discipline. What *Jobs in Philosophy* in fact listed were jobs in *education*, for persons trained in the discipline of philosophy. (And there was an occasional anomaly, such as the job in law enforcement, advertised by the sheriff of Golden, Colorado, for a person trained in the discipline of philosophy.)

Education, of course, is a profession, and, like all professions, it fragments. It is practiced by a plurality of specialists. As medicine has its opthomologists and its orthopedic surgeons, as law has its experts on divorce and its experts on corporate taxation, so education has those who teach physics and those who teach philology — or philosophy. And such specializations divide and subdivide to form a structure wondrously intricate and fine.

Jobs in Philosophy reflected this fragmentation. The publication is now called *Jobs for Philosophers*, which is, to be sure, an improvement — but the fragmentation remains. Its positions are still listed by Area of Specialization (AOS) and Area of Competence (AOC). So there are courses to be staffed in philosophy of science and in philosophy of art, in ethics and in epistemology. And, alas, it seems that we have largely risen to the bait. Today in

America, the majority of my colleagues have confused their discipline with their profession. They think that it is *philosophy* which fragments, and they think of themselves as specialists — as philosophers of science or aestheticians, as moral philosophers or epistemologists. And they train their students in this confusion. They train their students to have an AOS and an AOC. And so, today, philosophy in America is largely without wonder — the wonder in which it properly begins and which remains the irrevocable root of its own internal dynamic.

Plato did not have an AOS and an AOC. Nor did Aristotle. Nor Aquinas, nor Leibniz, nor Hume, nor Kant, nor Mill, nor Hegel. Of course not. They were philosophers. Not philosophers-of-this or philosophers-of-that, not hyphenated philosophers, but *philosophers*. The real thing. The genuine article. They understood with perfect clarity the distinction between a discipline and a profession, between a calling and a job. And so of course they did what philosophers necessarily do. They wondered about everything, and about whether and how it all fits together.

This book is a study in philosophy. Consequently, it is a book about everything.

My last book (*Linguistic Representation*; D. Reidel Publishing Company; Dordrecht, Holland; 1974) was also about everything. By rights, then, this book ought to be about nothing — or about everything else. Well, enough thick books about Nothing have already seen the light, and, of course, there isn't anything else — so I wrote about everything again. It seemed like a reasonable thing to do. Nobody believed me the first time.

Which brings us to the question of how one proves a point in philosophy.

You tell a story that hangs together — and that diminishes the mysteries. You construct a synthesis which holds together under analysis. There is no other way. For philosophy is a discipline without data. What philosophy has, in place of data, is a history — the history of its own wonder. Its only phenomena are the puzzlements which evoke its practice, and its only successes the diminution of these puzzlements.

Success in philosophy grows continually more difficult. For the story which a philosopher tells about man and the world must accord with what, outside of philosophy, we otherwise know about man and the world — and we continually know more. And so, if Lobachevski and Riemann, Einstein and Planck, and Heisenberg and Darwin have altered our understandings of ourselves and our world, then our philosophers' stories must perforce accommodate the lessons of Lobachevski and Riemann, Einstein and Planck, and Heisenberg and Darwin.

This demand would seem to militate against an historical approach to philosophy. Oddly enough, however, it has quite the opposite effect. For, in the face of all such burgeoning understandings, only our own shared history remains to serve as our common language — and thus as the indispensible medium of an inquiry that is moved by a sense of the problematic which fresh knowledge alone can transform but never alleviate, for both the possibility of what is known and the very possibility of our knowing it forever fall within the scope of what properly elicits philosophical wonder.

The story which I tell in this book attempts to accommodate the lessons of Lobachevski and Riemann, Einstein and Planck, and Heisenberg and Darwin. But it begins with Kant and it ends with Socrates, and my problematic throughout is structured in terms of, and conditioned by, an understanding of the history of a specifically *philosophical* inquiry. In consequence, this is neither an easy book nor a fashionable one. I apologize neither for its difficulty nor for its unfashionability. The problematic which moves it is quite real, and still very much alive — and our own history is still our only authentic access to it.

Too many of us seem all too ready to adopt what is facile. What is facile is, after all, easily accessible, and we are all too eager to mistake such easy accessibility for the clarity of thought and perception which our natures evidently unrelentingly demand. The tendency is manifest in our art and in our politics — and, regrettably, in our philosophy as well. A spurious clarity of facile accessibility obscures our true problematic like a glittering icy veneer, which enchants the eye as it distracts the mind. But authentic clarity in philosophy (and in art and politics as well) does not arise from easy accessibility. Authentic clarity comes from penetration. It emerges at the end of inquiry, not at its beginnings, and then only if the problematic which moves that inquiry has been pursued relentlessly through all its obscurities and complexities to the point of laying bare the root posits upon which the whole of an intricate and protracted dialectic ultimately rests. And such fidelity to the true complexities of a problematic does not make for easy accessibility. Good philosophy is hard reading.

This book may or may not be good philosophy. But it *is* hard reading. So there is, at least, a chance.

This is not quite the book which I originally set out to write. The book I set out to write, under the auspices of a Guggenheim Fellowship during academic 1976–77, had as its theme "the pragmatic justification of regulative principles". Some of what would have been the substance of that book has found its way into Chapters VI through VIII of this one. You will notice that it comes along rather late. That is because I discovered some other business that needed to be attended to first.

The quickest way to describe this book is that it is what the *Critique of Pure Reason* would look like were it to be written today — in the light of the lessons of Lobachevski and Riemann, of Einstein and Planck, of Heisenberg and Darwin, and, of course, of Kant. Such a reincarnative enterprise may well strike you as neither possible nor necessary. In answer to reservations of this general sort, I shall largely allow the book to speak for itself. It is worth remarking, however, that there are enough reincarnations of Descartes and of Hume and, lately and especially, of Hegel now wittingly or unwittingly abroad in the philosophical world to lend the exercise more than a little point and immediacy. If an authentic clarity is indeed our aim, we must be particularly careful not too hastily *aufzuheben* what is not yet fully *begriffen*.

In philosophy, as in science, there are no crucial experiments. A thesis which is refutable in isolation by counterexample is a thesis not worth bothering about. There are, indeed, black swans in Australia — but what responsible ornithologist had ever professionally committed himself to the contrary opinion? Like a scientist's theory, a philosopher's story stands or falls as a whole. And what defeats it, if and when it is defeated, is always and only a *better* story — better, that is, at hanging together, at accommodating what we otherwise, outside of philosophy, know about ourselves and our world, and at diminishing the mysteries.

This book is like that. It is *one long story*. It stands or falls as a whole. Success in philosophy grows continually more difficult. It will be for others to judge whether or not this book will be numbered among the philosophical successes. But if it is not, what will *show* that it is not will not be "counterexamples" but a better story. For my problematic is quite real. And so the question always remains: What is the *alternative*?

In the telling of such a long and complicated story, of course, I have inevitably said some things which are just plain *stupid*. Everybody does. *Those* claims, needless to say, I am quite happy to renounce in advance, promptly and completely.

This book owes its contemporary being, of course, to others besides the distinguished historical personages whom I have had occasion to mention. Particular gratitude is due the John Simon Guggenheim Memorial Foundation and the *Zentrum für interdisziplinäre Forschung* (ZiF) at the University of Bielefeld, West Germany, each for affording me an uninterrupted year 1976–7 and 1978–9, respectively) of research to stand in the place of customary sabbatical leave which the legislature of the Sovereign State of North

Carolina, under the misguidance of an ill-conceived and petty miserliness, has not *yet* seen fit to grant its otherwise overworked and undercompensated university faculties.

Beyond such indispensible contributions to its mere existence, however, this book owes, as well, substantial elements of its theme and character to the influences of various non-institutional persons, among whom should be numbered: Wilfrid Sellars, who taught me how to do it; Daniel Dennett, whose work illuminated the essential continuities between our cognitive capacities and the lesser competences of our non-human animal and vegetable companions; Richard Smyth, who shed new light on Descartes and on Peirce; David Falk, who thinks that I underestimate the complexities of practical reason; Barry Stroud, who didn't believe what I said about transcendental arguments; Richard Burian, who didn't believe what I said about theoretical convergence; Jonathan Bennett, who didn't believe what I said about intersubjectivity; Thomas Wartenburg, who didn't believe what I said about Kant's analogies. and, especially, Richard Rorty, who didn't believe what I said about *anything*, and who still doesn't, and who advocates surrender. To these persons, and to others whose influences I have doubtless overlooked, my thanks.

This is the first of my books which I did not type myself. Ms. M. Kämper, of the ZiF, typed it. Ms. Kämper types fluently in several languages. To my great good fortune, one of them is English. I am in her debt. This is also the *longest* of my books to date.

It had to be. It is an ambitious book. But then, philosophy is an ambitious discipline. The mysteries which it aims to diminish are *big* mysteries – and it aims to remove them *all*. I make no such claim for this book. It accomplishes as best it can the task which it sets for itself – but that is *not* to set philosophy on "the secure path of a science". *Science* is on the secure path of a science, and if philosophy has a task in this connection it is only to make sure that it *stays* there. That, indeed, *is* part of the task of this book.

And as for the rest, it is time to let the book begin to speak for itself. The conversation has been going on for over 3000 years. This book is only a remark. The most I can realistically hope for is that it is a remark which, as the conversation continues, others will, from time to time, find worth repeating. In that spirit, I commend it to its audiences.

Bielefeld, West Germany, 1979   JAY F. ROSENBERG

INTRODUCTION

Socrates taught us to be suspicious of answers. It was not until the twentieth century, however, that we learned to be properly suspicious of questions. The concept of a pseudo-question, of *Scheinprobleme*, may, in the end, be the one lasting legacy of the Positivistic aspirations that shaped our discipline in the early 1900's.

That there are, and have always been, pseudo-questions in philosophy was, indeed, worth saying. But, like all truths in philosophy, this truth, too, has bred its excesses. That there are, and have always been, *only* pseudo-questions in philosophy is an expression of one such excess. The thesis is not without its adherents. I am not among them. But I recognize, too, the temptation of the view which I have branded excessive. So I shall try to be as cautious about asking my questions as I am about answering them. This, in turn, however, makes it difficult for me to tell you what this book is about.

This book is about realism, in the sense of that term which contrasts with 'idealism'. In particular, this book is a (pragmatist's) defence of a systematic ontological realism in the setting of a naturalistic empiricist epistemology. That is (almost) how I should have been able to put it a hundred years ago. Today, alas, that will no longer do. Our own meta-philosophical taxonomies — all those lovely crisp 'ism's — are among the things of which we have, quite properly, been taught to be suspicious. But how, then, am I to proceed?

The Positivists had a vision — the vision of a truly scientific philosophy, an a-historical philosophy, a philosophy without *Verstehen*, conducted wholly in the austere canonical idiom of the new mathematical logic. It was a glorious vision — but it was only that. For the logical idiom, like all mathematics, yielded by itself only form without content. The content, of course, remained — it could hardly do otherwise — although it was now relegated to the commentary. And fifty years later, when the concept of a *Scheinproblem* had ceased to be used simply as a bludgeon to sweep the field clear, what we found was that our questions had not gone away. The questions endured, and with them so did the history — for the proper questions of philosophy are human questions, and we humans are cultural beings. We are products of our history and we are embedded in that history.

It is with that history, then, that I shall begin. The recorded thinkings of my predecessors will be the conceptual medium in which I shall embed my own thinking and out of which both my questions and my answers will grow. So, although this book is still about realism, I shall not begin by talking about realism, by telling you what realism is. I shall begin by talking about Kant and Hume, about Berkeley and Locke and Descartes, and (later) about Peirce and Strawson and Wittgenstein. Perhaps when I am finished you will know what I mean by 'realism'. Perhaps not. But, if I talk long enough and carefully enough, you should, at least, know when I am finished what question I have been asking and how I propose to answer it — however you would yourself choose to frame the question and its answer. And that is probably the best one can hope for at this point in the twentieth century.

CHAPTER I

EPISTEMIC LEGITIMACY: THE PROBLEMATIC OF EMPIRICISM

The basic theme of Kant's Analytic is the epistemic legitimacy attaching to certain concepts, judgments and principles. His model is not logical but legal. He speaks of "deductions", but his term 'deduction' derives not from logic but from *Rechtsphilosophie*. It alludes not to entailment but to juridical defences of claims of right or of legal entitlement. What Kant explicitly intends (A84 = B116ff.) is that the conclusion of what he calls a "transcendental deduction" state, not a matter of fact, but a matter of right. It is to say, in other words, that something may be done, for all rights are, at base, conduct rights. (Rights of ownership – property rights – are no exception. What the legal owner of a particular item or good possesses are rights to the exclusive use and disposition of that item or good.) A Kantian transcendental deduction thus articulates and secures a principle of permission. If successful, it establishes or legitimizes our right to employ certain concepts, to make certain judgments, and to apply certain principles. It establishes or legitimizes our right to a family of cognitive *acts*.

On even this schematic an understanding of Kant's project, there are two questions which need immediately to be raised. We should ask, first: our right to employ *which* concepts? (to make *which* judgements?, etc.) Here the suggestion is that there is something special about the concepts (or judgments or principles) which raises a question concerning our right to employ *them*. But we should also ask, second: our right to employ concepts (apply principles, etc.) *in what way*? And the suggestion now is that there is something special about the manner or mode of employment which raises a question about our right to *so* employ concepts. A proper understanding of what Kant proposes to accomplish by constructing a "transcendental deduction" can be obtained only if we can answer both of these questions. Kant, of course, supplies his own answers – and it is to these which we should next turn.

The concepts which Kant regards as standing in need of a transcendental deduction are what he calls "*a priori* concepts". He characterizes these as concepts "independent of and not derivable from experience" (A2; B2). The judgments whose legitimacy is at issue he calls "synthetic *a priori* judgments".

CHAPTER I

> The proper problem of pure reason is contained in the question: How are *a priori* synthetic judgments possible? (B19)

Kant contrasts his intended transcendental deduction with what he calls an "empirical deduction"

> ... which shows the manner in which a concept is acquired through experience, and which therefore concerns, not its legitimacy, but only its *de facto* mode of origination. (A85 = B117)

What Kant is adverting to here is a project proposed by Hume. Hume suggests that one can only legitimize an "idea" by showing it to be "derived from impressions". The giving of an empirical deduction would consist in showing, for an "idea" *from what* "impressions" it may be "derived" (*ENQ*: II).

Like Kant, Hume recognizes several species of judgment, several different ways in which the class of judgments may be subdivided. Corresponding to Kant's class of "analytic judgments", we find Hume's "abstract reasonings". They concern, he tells us, only "relations *among* ideas" (*ENQ*: IV, i). The key feature of such "abstract reasonings" is that — like Kant's "analytic judgments" or Locke's "trifling propositions" — they are not ampliative. They are concerned exclusively with what is "contained in" ideas (concepts) already possessed, but they cannot serve as a source of new ideas, nor can they somehow legitimize the possession and employment of the old. In a somewhat more modern terminology (which should not, on that account alone, be judged more transparent), such judgments are purely *formal*. Analytic judgments, abstract reasonings, or trifling propositions are ones in which — to put it Quinewise — "descriptive terms occur vacuously". Only the syncategoremata count. To sound yet another note, their epistemic authority derives from a *logical warrant*. They possess apodeictic necessity. One denies them on pain of formal inconsistency or self-contradiction.

"Matters of fact" (Kant's "synthetic judgments", Locke's "ampliative propositions"), in contrast, are "derived from experience", and the descriptive concepts employed in expressing them are legitimized by exhibiting the manner in which experience gives rise to them (*ENQ*: IV). Hume pictures us as finding in complex "impressions" the originals of certain "simple ideas" and as *abstracting* them to obtain the raw materials from which new complex ideas could then be synthesized. Conversely, every *legitimate* complex idea can be broken down ("analyzed") into ingredient simple ideas, each of which could then be traced to an original appearance in an impression ("immediate experience").

It is this last task which Kant speaks of as supplying an empirical deduction. On Hume's account, it is the sole means of legitimizing our possession and employment of an idea, and a necessary precondition of the legitimacy of any judgment in which such an idea (concept) is mobilized.

Hume's dramatic philosophical discovery was that most or all of the key concepts which had figured in classical metaphysics — self, substance, causation, space and time — could not be *thus* legitimized. With respect to the notion of causation, for example, Hume asks us to

Suppose two objects to be presented to us, of which the one is the cause and the other the effect; it is plain that, from the simple consideration of one or both these objects, we never shall perceive the tie by which they are united, or be able certainly to pronounce, that there is a connection betwixt them. It is not, therefore, from any one instance, that we arrive at the idea of cause and effect, of a necessary connection, of power, of force, of energy, and of efficacy. (*THN*: I, iii, 14)

It follows, Hume concludes, that there is no single impression of necessary connection and, thus, that there is no way of deriving an idea of such a connection from impressions at all (since the mere diachronic repetition of similar impressions adds nothing more in the way of experiential content). No representation of a causal connection as something more than a mere constant conjunction and temporal succession, then, can arise from or be grounded in experience.

Similarly, Hume argues that the notion of a (substantial) self cannot be "derived from original impressions".

If any impression gives rise to the idea of self, that impression must continue invariably the same, through the whole course of our lives; since self is supposed to exist after that manner. But there is no impression constant and invariable. (*THN*: I, iv, 6)

Since "derivation from impressions" is, on Hume's view, the only way in which any idea could be legitimized, by his criteria the putative concepts of causation and self at issue here are illegitimate. His full-dress official position, indeed, is that these are merely ostensible ideas which we *do not in fact have*, for the simple reason that, by Hume's lights, we *cannot* have them. Officially, Humean illegitimacy amounts to non-existence, and he consequently often speaks of us as "mistaking" something else for the idea of a necessary connection or a substantial self. Unofficially, however, (and admittedly less explicitly) Hume recognizes that these are more than mere metaphysical conceits, and so we find in Hume's writings also the rudiments of a theory of "habit" or "custom" — and of an active "faculty of imagination" — which does yeoman service in providing somewhat *ad hoc* surrogate notions to fill the resulting gaps in our impoverished conceptual resources.

Now against this Humean picture, Kant proposes to move in several ways. Most fundamentally, by divorcing sensibility from understanding, he abandons the tacit identification of representation with resemblance common to all concept empiricists. In Hume's thought, for example, the notion of an impression plays two quite different roles. Hume sometimes thinks of an impression of a ϕK — for instance, of a red rectangle — as a ϕ and K *particular* — as something red and rectangular. It is something like a patch of mental pigment in an iconic mental picture. On other occasions, however, Hume speaks of such an impression as an ur-knowing — a *conviction* that something is (or that there is something) ϕ and K (red and rectangular). An impression, on this understanding, is something suitable to serve as a premiss in inference and to enter into logical relationships with other impressions, rather like a mental sentence in a language of inner speech. (Hume, of course, does not invent this ambiguity. He inherits it. Its ancestors are the uses of 'idea' by Berkeley and Locke — and also by Descartes, about whom we must shortly say a great deal).

From the outset of his project, Kant proposes rigorously to separate the two roles which Hume thus conflates. He assigns one of them, the first, to the sensibility — providing the matter or content of experience — and the other, the second, to the understanding — providing the (categorial) form. What Kant calls an "experience" itself, however, is a kind of resultant vector sum of these two components — one of the things which he speaks of as a "synthesis" (A92 = B125ff.). An "experience" is "an empirical cognition (*Erkenntnis*), that is, a cognition which determines an object through perceptions" (B218), where "perceptions" (*Wahrnehmungen*), in turn, are to be understood as "*representations accompanied* by sensation" ("*mit Empfindung begleitete Vorstellungen*", B147; my emphasis). An experience is a perceptual *taking*, where this is explicitly to be contrasted with the mere (passive) *having* of sensations.[1]

On Kant's view, then, in any experience we are to distinguish two aspects: one of sensation, pure receptivity or affectedness (in which humans are continuous with other animal species); and one which is judgmental, a bringing under concepts which we ourselves supply. On Kant's view, the world is not given to us conceptually structured. Rather it acts on us, and we structure it. We bring concepts *to* sensations; we do not extract concepts *from* them.

The primary Kantian unit of "experience", thus, is not the atomistic and particulate "impression" or "idea" of concept empiricism but the perceptual *judgment*. The question of the legitimacy of a concept, on this account, is the question of the legitimacy of such judgments in which the concept at issue is mobilized, that is, employed in the structuring of our (perceptual) experience (i.e., our ostensible empirical knowledge) of the world.

This answers, in passing, the second of our two questions: our right to employ concepts in what way? Kant's answer: in application to possible experience. And here "experience" is not an unstructured passive sensory having but an empirical cognition (a candidate for ultimate endorsement as empirical *knowledge*) already internally structured in terms of the very concepts at issue.

Like Hume, then, Kant is proposing an epistemic impossibility. But where Hume concluded that there are concepts which one cannot have unless one has (*per impossibile*) the requisite experiences (i.e., impressions!), Kant inverts the order and proposes that there are *experiences* which one cannot have (i.e., perceptual judgments which one cannot make) unless one already legitimately possesses and can apply certain concepts. This is the point of Kant's observation regarding the outcome of a transcendental deduction that, although it needs proof,

> ... it should be entitled a *principle*, not a *theorem*, because it has the peculiar character that it makes possible the very experience which is its own ground of proof, and that in this experience it must always itself be presupposed. (A737 = B765)

For a transcendental deduction is to be a justificatory argument legitimizing our employment of a family of concepts in the having of certain experiences — that is, in the making of certain synthetic (perceptual) judgments — which themselves couldn't be had — that is, be *made* — were we not already legitimately in possession of and able to deploy just those concepts.

This inversion is the first methodological outcropping of Kant's "Copernican revolution" in philosophy, which can thus be seen as having its roots precisely in Kant's theory of experience. It is this inversion which lies at the base of the "Copernican revolution" in its more usual presentation as well. For where Hume *posits* a standard of conceptual legitimization and finds, upon measuring them against it, that the categorial conceptions of classical metaphysics fall short of it, Kant begins with the *fact* of experience thus conceptually structured and proceeds to inquire into those conditions by reason of which its actual legitimacy — never problematically or skeptically at issue — is made possible. That is, he proceeds to inquire in what manner the legitimacy of categorial concepts and synthetic *a priori* judgments may be demonstrated or (perhaps better) exhibited. Thus while Hume's dialectical viewpoint is always prospective — seeking a justification for that which, in the absence of appropriate legitimization, is otherwise to be foregone — Kant's is retrospective — seeking a *post facto* demonstration of the legitimacy of that which is in fact (and, he will argue, inescapably) legitimately done. Hume's question is: *Have* we any legitimate idea of causation (self, substance, etc.)? Kant, however, begins with the fact of experiences which are so structured, and argues that they could not in fact *be* our experiences unless we were already legitimately in possession of the relevant categorial concepts. His question is: How are *a priori* synthetic judgments *possible*? Our actual possession of the categorial concepts mobilized in such judgments is never called into question.[2]

I have been speaking quite casually for some time now of "categorial concepts" but, despite my informal gestures in the direction of a perennial metaphysical tradition, we have still not effectively isolated the class of concepts (and the family of judgments) at issue in Kant's program. We know them to be concepts which fail of Humean legitimacy, which cannot be afforded an "empirical deduction", but we still stand in need of a positive complement to this, essentially negative, characterization. What are the marks by which the relevant family of concepts may be demarcated and identified?

Kant proposes two such marks: unrestricted universality and unqualified necessity.

Necessity and strict universality are ... sure criteria of *a priori* knowledge, and are inseparable from one another. (B4)

Here too, it turns out, Kant is simply following out lines sketched by Hume. The notion of a self which engages Hume's critical attention, for example, is the notion of a something which must (necessity) accompany every (universality) representing which is mine. Again, the causal concept which Hume finds lacking legitimacy is that operative in what he calls "a general maxim of philosophy", that "whatever (universality) begins to exist must (necessity) have a cause of its existence", (*THN*: I, iii, 3). Viewed from a broader historical perspective, in fact, we can see in Hume's denials of conceptual legitimacy simply the remorseless endorsement of the consequences of a fundamentally Platonic thesis: that experience can yield knowledge of what *is now* and what *has been*, but not of what *is always* or *must be*,[3] when that thesis is coupled with Hume's empiricist view that "all knowledge is derived from experience" *and* his account of *experience* as consisting in the having of (original) impressions.

It is worth observing in this connection that, even at best, a Humean "empirical deduction" could establish no more than a relative or derived right to concepts. A description of "the manner in which a concept is acquired through experience and through reflection upon experience" (A85 = B117) could be justificatory only against the background of a posit or argument which established that concepts which originate in a certain way *are* legitimate, that is, against a *presumption* of legitimacy for the sources of the concepts at issue.

This observation has a strict counterpart in the juridical setting which Kant takes as his model for a "transcendental deduction". My establishing that I have a legal right of ownership in some item, for example, normally proceeds by demonstrating that certain states of affairs obtain or have obtained. Money and goods changed hands; signatures were affixed to certain documents; the participants were sane and sober; and so on. But all of this would go no distance toward establishing my legal rights of ownership unless it were somehow *independently* settled that by doing such things, and in virtue of having done them, I acquire certain exclusive rights to use and dispose of some item.

Now it can certainly be the case that the lawbooks in fact so specify. But this still establishes at best only a derivative or relative right. The claim which I have in the item is then legitimate *if the laws are*. The authority or bindingness of law, in other words, may be transmitted to me vis-a-vis the disputed item through the performance of certain acts specified in the legal codes, but that authority or bindingness itself is, in the context of this sort of demonstration, simply a posit or a given.

A Humean "empirical deduction" is like that. It concerns the *transmissibility* of a presumptive original legitimacy through certain logical or mental operations — abstraction and synthesis (combination). The epistemic authority of the resultant conceptions is derivative from, and no more secure than, the epistemic authority attaching to its experiential sources.

For Hume, and for empiricists generally, the epistemic authority of sensory experience is little more than a blind posit — an epistemological given, embraced out of a taste for desert landscapes or for want of a convincing alternative. A Kantian "transcendental deduction", in contrast, aims at establishing just such an *original* legitimacy. Its legal counterpart would be the question of the original authority or bindingness of law, that is, the question of the justification of our *practice* of vesting conventional juridical rights of use and disposition in persons vis-a-vis certain items on the basis of certain (arbitrary) interpersonal performances. Looked at from this perspective, then, what Kant proposes to offer us is a strategy for legitimizing epistemic *first principles*, that is, for securing *non-derivative* epistemic authority for certain concepts and judgments. And this observation, in turn, allows us to make contact with a broader epistemological dialectic.

From the standpoint of traditional epistemology, the problem of epistemic first principles emerges as the problem of certainty. The philosophical spectre which looms should the problem remain unsolved is skepticism, in one or some of its many incarnations. The *locus classicus* for this family of considerations is, of course, Descartes' *Meditations*. A brief but careful look at his argumentation should consequently be our next order of business.

"Certainty" is an elastic term-of-art, and so it is important, in any discussion of certainty and skepticism, to be clear about which of the many possible interpretations of the term is at stake. What Descartes intends by "certainty", he tells us, is *indubitability*, and he proposes to disqualify as certain any belief for which he can isolate even the least "grounds for doubt" (*MED*: I). When we look carefully at what Descartes is prepared to entertain as constituting a "ground for doubt", however, what we discover is somewhat at odds with standard accounts of the matter.[4] Cartesian exegesis typically has it that, since doubt is a rational attitude — that is, an attitude which can be well- or ill-supported by appeal to reasons — Descartes' concern is with the quality of our *reasons for* beliefs. What is wanted of an indubitable or certain belief, on this interpretation, is that it be supportable and supported by *logically sufficient* reasons, that is, by reasons of such a character as to insure that the belief in question can be abandoned only at the price of contravening logic, of a formal incoherence.[5] The primary Cartesian contrast is thus taken to be one between certainty and *revisability*. Regressive arguments of the familiar sort then lead inevitably to the conclusion that what is needed to defeat the skeptic encamped outside our epistemological gates is that we secure a family of *indefeasible* beliefs (whether indefeasible by virtue of being "self-warranting" or for some other, equally arcane, reason) adequate to serve as points of anchorage for the balance of our empirical representations. Knowledge is supposed to need a foundation, and what is characteristic of foundations is that, come what may, they stay put.

But a close reading of the fundamental Cartesian texts does not, in fact, bear out this interpretation. When we look at his considerations concerning grounds for doubt, what we in fact find Descartes attending to is not the quality of our reasons for beliefs but rather the nature of the (possible) *sources of* beliefs. Each of his ostensible "grounds for doubt" takes the form of an hypothesis concerning the possible sources of belief. The culmination of this concern, of course, comes with the hypothesis that all our representations are the consequences of acts of an "evil demon".

Descartes operates with a bimodal, Scholastic, ontology of formal and objective being, upon which he constructs a classical, "ontological", theory of truth. A thought (representing) is true if what has objective being in the representation also has formal being in the world. What troubles Descartes about representings issuing from the agency of a *genie malign* is not that they would *ipso facto* be false (for, indeed, they needn't be — for that reason alone). What troubles him is that they would be *arbitrary*. Even if our beliefs were true, there would in such a case be no *connection* between the fact that they were true and the fact that they were ours, i.e., that we held them. Our having a certain world-picture would be explained wholly in terms of demonaic caprice — and the character of what existed *formally* in the world would have no part in that explanation.

It is just such a connection between formal and objective being which God's benevolence is intended to secure and mediate. Our having of a clear and distinct conception is to supply an *epistemological* guarantee of the formal being of what exists objectively in our representation precisely because God, guided by his benevolent non-deceptiveness, so *ontologically* structures the world as to guarantee the correspondence. The *explanation* of a clear and distinct conception thus moves from the formal being of what is represented through God's mediating benevolence to its objective being in the representing.

The primary Cartesian contrast is thus not — as it is standardly taken to be — one between certainty and revisability but rather one between certainty and *arbitrariness*. What is needed to answer Cartesian demonaic skepticism, then, are not considerations which imply that our representings are irrevisable, in whole or in part, but rather an argument to the effect that — even *if* defeasible — our ways of thinking about the world are not arbitrary but determinate, and, indeed, are so determined as to ensure *some* connection between our *having* a particular world-picture and its being a *correct* world-picture.[6]

In recent epistemological theorizing, the challenge posed by Descartes has emerged as a question regarding what are called "criteria". Here, too, the problem is that of securing a connection. Since, however, contemporary thought has largely abandoned Descartes' bimodal ontology, the sought connection is no longer one between two ostensible modes of being but rather one between — to put the issue most generally — what is encountered (that is, observed or observable) and what is imputed or ascribed. The issue can, in fact, be set out quite broadly, in terms of an argument concerning forms of epistemic warrant for judgments.

This argument departs from a posit which is central to all epistemologies fairly called "empiricist" — that there are only two species of epistemic warrant possible for any judgment: logical and evidential. Logical warrants are (analytic) entailments. An observation (or family of observations), O, provides a logical warrant for a judgment, J, just in case O entails J or, equivalently, just in case one affirms O and denies J only at the price of formal incoherence (self-contradiction). If a judgment is warranted, but not, in this sense, logically warranted, then it must be adequately supported by evidence. This is just the fundamentally "empiricist" claim that all (synthetic) knowledge is "derived from experience", in one of its most general instantiations. The point of the argument which I have in mind, however, is to demonstrate that the possibility of *any* evidential warrant presupposes the existence of just such logical warrants.

The argument has one, very simple, additional key premiss: *Evidence* is correlational. Some candidate phenomenon, E, in other words, counts as *evidence* for the truth of a judgment, J, just in case J is in fact true, always or often, when E obtains (or is present). It follows immediately that one can *warrantedly judge* that E is evidence for the truth of J if and only if one can *warrantedly judge* that the truth of J is thus regularly correlated with the obtaining (or presence) of E. But this latter judgment, in turn, will be possible only if one can warrantedly judge *both* that E obtains *and, independently* of that judgment, that J is true.

Now an appeal to ostensible evidence E, however elaborate, could only *warrant* acceptance of a judgment that J if one could independently establish (or, at the very least, have good grounds for believing) that E is not merely ostensibly evidence for the truth of J but that E is *in fact* evidence for the truth of J. But from this observation it immediately follows that no ostensible evidence E, however elaborate, could be the *sole* ground for an epistemically-well-founded judgment that J. There must be at least one other warranted route to the judgment that J is true to which one can appeal in certifying the ostensible evidence E as actual evidence.

But if this other warranted route itself appeals to ostensible evidence, of course, the question of whether this new ostensible evidence is itself actually evidence will again arise. On pain of circularity or infinite regress, then, we can conclude that one can warrantedly judge that J on evidential grounds only where one can be warranted in judging that J on *non*-evidential grounds. *Ex hypothesi*, however, the only form of non-evidential warrant is logical. (If one admits "the light of nature" or "divine revelation" or some other *tertium quid*, it seems fair enough to conclude that one is no longer entitled to call oneself an "empiricist", at any rate). And this secures the desired conclusion: The possibility of *any* evidential warrants presupposes the existence of logical warrants. It follows as a corollary, of course, that if some family of judgments cannot be based on a logical warrant of the appropriate sort, acceptance of those judgments cannot be epistemically warranted *at all*.

It is this last corollary, combined with appropriate denials of the possibility of logical warrant for various classes of judgments, in fact, which forms the core of all traditional skepticisms. Since exact qualitative similarity of two objects is logically possible, for example, no finite set of observations (analytically) entails the truth of any judgment of diachronic numerical identity. Thus we arrive at (Humean) skepticism concerning the continuing existence of things unperceived, for, if such judgments cannot be thus logically warranted, it follows from the argument which we have just constructed that they cannot be warranted at all.

The "problem of other minds" arises in an identical fashion. The fact of possible pretence stands in the way of there being a relation of entailment between statements describing the observable behaviors of a person and the judgment that, for example, that person is in pain. Applying the line of reasoning developed above, we arrive at skepticism with respect to ascriptions of sensations, thoughts, and the like to other persons in general (See Chappell, *PM*).

The traditional "problem of induction" fits the model as well. Here the key step consists in the observation that no set of statements about what *has* happened can *entail* any statement about what *will* happen. Applying the general argument, we reach the immediate conclusion that no judgments about the future can be epistemically well-founded (warranted).

Indeed, even Cartesian demonaic skepticism should be cast in this logical mold, for it precisely moves from the premiss that no set of observations concerning the contents of representings can *entail* any proposition concerning the sources of those representings to the conclusion that judgments concerning the sources of representings cannot be warranted at all.

From this perspective, then, we can appreciate Kant's problematic as addressed to no mere historical anomaly but rather to a general, perennial, and characteristically "empiricist" predicament: How can one provide an epistemic well-founding for families of concepts and judgments which, in the appropriate sense, are "non-observational"? What varies from time to time and from skepticism to skepticism is only what counts as "observable". If one limits "observation" to "sense-data" in the now-familiar way, claims about everyday physical objects will be counted "non-observational". If one allows that such ordinary objects are in fact "observed", then it is claims about electrons, protons, and other such "theoretical entities" which are deemed "non-observational". And if one admits only the bodily behaviors of persons as "observed", claims about their "mental states" will be classed as "non-observational". Through all such variations, however, the underlying epistemological principles and line of reasoning remain the same.

Such philosophical theories as phenomenalism, instrumentalism, and behaviorism should be properly viewed as parallel responses to this predicament. Each of them represents an attempt to parse the desired connection as *in fact logical*. Indeed, each of them proposes exactly the same strategy for accomplishing this parsing: Understand the *sense* (meaning) of the "non-observational" claims to be given by a complex set of *conditional* "observational" claims. But each of these "Conditional" theories fails in the same way, as well. Each of them runs up against the fact that no finite set of "observational" conditionals *can* be logically equivalent to (or even entail) the "non-observational" claims at issue. In each case, the "non-observational" claims turn out to have what is sometimes referred to as "surplus content". This story is by now a familiar one, and there is, on that account, no need to retell it here. What is important for our purposes is the invariant pattern of argument underlying and motivating all such Conditional philosophical theorizing – the common epistemological predicament and the shared set of "empiricist" epistemic presuppositions.

Such Conditional proposals, of course, are not the only possible response to this underlying epistemological predicament, but the more recent alternative – what I call the "Criteriological" solution – fares no better. Strawson, for example, offers (in *IND*) an argument from "descriptive metaphysics" for the conclusion that there must be "logically adequate criteria" both for diachronic re-identifications of objects and for ascriptions of *P*-predicates ("mental states") to others. We *do possess*, he claims, a conceptual scheme containing these features, and, since we could not possess such a scheme unless our *warrantedly* engaging in the corresponding epistemological practices were possible, it follows that there must exist "criteria" which are in fact "logically adequate" to warrant our so doing. Strawson's response thus takes the form of a *reductio* of various skepticisms, but it is what mathematicians would call a "non-constructive existence proof", for he offers no instances or examples of such "logically adequate criteria".

Alas, this procedure engages the position of the skeptics without engaging their arguments – and so it leaves Strawson vulnerable to a reply in kind.

Although we may *seem* to possess a conceptual scheme instantiating the disputed features, the skeptic may argue, in actuality we do *not* – because, as the epistemological argument shows, we *cannot* possess any such conceptual scheme. (Recall Hume's imputations of "mistakes" – and Berkeley's insistence that, *contra* Locke, we do not in fact have *any* contentive concept of "matter".)

Now Strawson characterizes such a reply as "revisionary metaphysics" and quite properly refuses to trade our ostensible conceptual scheme for a mere melange of metaphysical promissory notes. But it is, of course, open to the skeptic to reply in turn that Strawson is practicing an epistemological revisionism no less schematic and promissory than the metaphysics which he imputes to his antagonists. Failing a convincing critique of the skeptic's epistemological *arguments*, and lacking any developed and articulate epistemological alternative to classical empiricism, the confrontation between Strawson's "descriptive metaphysics" and his opponents' "descriptive epistemology" – for so they shall characterize it – remains an unresolved standoff.[7]

What "logically adequate criteria" were intended to supply was some third species of epistemic warrant – one weaker than analytic entailment and not comparably arguable on considerations of meaning or syncategorematic form alone, yet at the same time stronger than probabilistic evidence and knowable without inductive appeals to an observed correlation of experiential elements.

But it should now be obvious that such a Criteriological connection between "observables" and "non-observables" would just *be* Kant's "synthetic *a priori*". It would be synthetic precisely in being weaker than entailment, and it would be *a priori* in its possessing "logical adequacy", and is, in its being stronger than mere evidential correlations. While not being itself an analytic or logical truth, a judgment expressing such a Criteriological connection would need to possess some species of epistemic indefeasibility or, to put the matter bluntly, some species of *necessity*. For, in order to be "logically adequate", the connection between whatever phenomena would function criteriologically as warrants and whatever is imputed or ascribed by the judgments thereby warranted would have to be thought as universal and exceptionless. It would, in other words, be a synthetic and necessary connection, and its obtaining would thus be expressed precisely in Kantian synthetic *a priori* judgments. The question which remains, then – the question with which the skeptic confronts Strawson and which, as we have seen, Strawson does *not* answer – is just the question which Kant asks: How are synthetic *a priori* judgments *possible*? Until this question has been answered, the Criteriological response to the epistemological predicament of classical empiricism remains nothing more than the expression of a pious hope.

Kant's problematic, then, turns out to be nothing less than the basic problematic of a consistent empiricism, that is, of an adequate empiricist epistemology. Knowledge of the world as we customarily conceive it — that is, our *warranted* possession of a conceptual scheme incorporating diachronic continuities, other minds, subatomic fine-structures, inductive regularities, causal connections, and their epistemic like[8] — is possible only on the condition that we represent at least some synthetic correlations as necessary. That is the upshot of the epistemological reasoning in the present chapter.[9] But the rejection of such a synthetic *a priori* has traditionally been taken to be the very hallmark of empiricism. The would-be empiricist thus confronts a dilemma: He can hold fast to his epistemological presuppositions — at the price of abandoning his representations of our customary world-picture as epistemically ill-founded (lapsing either into a Humean or Cartesian skepticism or into some species of idealism — Berkeley's or Hegel's or one of their more recent phenomenalistic variants). Or he can hold fast to the customary conceptual scheme — the route of "descriptive metaphysics" — at the price of abandoning empiricism (lapsing either into a classical rationalism of self-warranting beliefs or innate ideas or into one of its more recent Criteriological variants).[10]

On the face of it, embracing the Kantian route of "transcendental deductions" seems to be a surrender of the second sort, for Kant apparently proposes to supply us with a "third way" — a new form of epistemic warrant which is neither logical nor evidential. But while there is certainly something right about this interpretation, it incorporates a fundamental mistake. For it tempts us to suppose that Kant is proposing to supply something which stands alongside formal (analytic) deduction and classical (instantial) induction — "some unique and heretofore undiscovered form of argument" (Stroud, *TAEN*). It tempts us, in other words, to anticipate "canons of transcendental validity", paralleling those of deductive and, perhaps, inductive validity (e.g., the "Requirement of Total Evidence"). If this were so, if Kant were in fact proposing to supply such a new form of argument, then he would indeed be abandoning anything which could properly be called "empiricism". But this is not what Kant is up to.

What Kant proposes instead is a new *strategy* for demonstrating or establishing epistemic legitimacy. What he sketches is not a new form of *argument* but rather a new form of *reasoning*, that is, a new way of bringing reason to bear on questions of justification. What Kant intends to do, in fact, is to demonstrate the legitimacy of categorial concepts and the epistemic authority (warrantedness) of synthetic *a priori* judgments neither by constructing them from concepts possessing prior legitimacy nor by deriving them – deductively or inductively – from judgments possessing prior authority, but instead by *embedding* them in broader contexts the legitimacy or authority of which is then independently arguable on grounds compatible with the fundamental epistemological posits of empiricism.

There is a nice analogy in biological theorizing which not only brings out the logical point currently at issue but also has the additonal virtue of proving useful to us at several later junctures. Consider a traditional biological *functionalism*. While causal explanations were supplied to account for the "how" of biological processes, functional explanations of the sort which I have in mind were classically offered in answer to "why" questions. The circulation of an animal's blood, for example, was afforded a causal explanation in terms of the action of its heart: The blood circulates *in consequence of* the contractions and relaxations of the heart. When, however, a "why" question was addressed to one aspect of this explanation – "Why does the heart beat?" – the answer was framed as an explanation which looked to be some sort of converse to the first, causal, account: The *function* of the (beating) heart is the circulation of the blood. Even more typically, in fact, this "why" question was interpreted as requesting an account of the *existence* of something – in this case, of hearts – and the functional explanation supplied as an answer was set in a *teleological* mode: The heart exists *in order to* circulate the blood.

Such naive teleology, of course, engendered a family of philosophical puzzlements of its own – and, with them, a family of philosophical solutions. As in the case of epistemic warrants, the dialectic produced two major camps, strictly analogous to the Conditional and the Criteriological proposals in epistemology. The "reductivist" camp viewed functional explanations as being *really* causal explanations, unperspicuously expressed. Like their Conditionalist epistemological counterparts, however, such Reductivist proposals ran aground on the issue of "surplus content". To say that the function of the heart is the circulation of the blood is to say more than that the blood circulates in consequence of the action of the heart. *Many* phenomena result from the contractions and relaxations of the heart – rhythmic sounds, for example – but only *some* of these are properly regarded as being among its functions. Something more is intended by a functionalist claim than its mere causal converse, then, but the Reductivist views offered no elucidation of this conceptual surplus.

The classical alternative, of course, was to endorse the ostensible teleology as real. Like the Criteriological epistemologies, such Teleological proposals invoked a mechanism of *special connection* – thus, for example, "final causation". The difficulty with this alternative is that it proposes to dissolve a

18   CHAPTER I

puzzle by affirming a mystery. The only available, moderately plausible, model for such "final causation" is volitional human action consequent upon the *representation* of a desired end. This, however, leaves the would-be Teleologist with the unpalatable choice between populating the organic tissues with spirits — that is, imputing to the heart, for example, a (rudimentary) cognitive awareness of the blood which circulates through it and of the body's need for such circulation — and advancing the notion of final causation as an "unexplicated primitive" — that is, as a mere enigma which offers no authentic explanatory advance on the original question. The history of philosophy has seen both of these alternatives embraced, of course — as well as the Humean or Positivistic course of castigating the original *question* as "illegitimate" or "metaphysical" ("Science can only ask *how*, never *why*"), that is, of "committing it to the flames".

The correct solution to the problem of a functional explanation's "surplus content" is provided by the theory of evolution. The evolutionary perspective successfully supplies the requisite content by showing how the causal relationship between blood circulation and the action of the heart can itself be caught up in an explanatory account of how *organisms* so structured came to exist and persist in the present terrestrial environment. We explain the circulation of the blood causally by appealing to the action of the heart, but the existence of the heart is explained in turn not by a further appeal to either synchronic or teleological causality but by *embedding* that question in a broader, diachronic, theoretical context. We explain the existence (now) of hearts (that is, of the *organs*) by explaining the emergence (by random mutation) and the persistence (by environmental selection and genetic transmission) of creatures with hearts (that is, of the *organisms*). It is such a diachronic evolutionary account which is in fact unperspicuously encoded by the teleological vocabulary: "The heart exists *in order to* circulate the blood". The sought "surplus content" is an implicit appeal to the contributions of blood circulation to the biological integrity and adaptability of organisms so structured (efficient internal transport of oxygen and nutrients, thermal homeostasis, and so on) — an appeal which becomes both explicit and explanatory in the context of an evolutionary account of the origin and proliferation of organisms possessing such cardio-vascular systems.

The theory of evolution shows us how we can fund functional explanations without appeal to explanatory principles different in *kind* from those structuring causal explanations. Analogously, Kant proposes to secure epistemic legitimacy for categorial concepts, and for the synthetic and necessary judgments in which such concepts are mobilized, without appeal to any species of epistemic warrant different in *kind* from the logical and evidential warrants endorsed by the empiricist tradition. His strategy is likewise to *embed* the original question of legitimacy in a broader context. In a brief and radically simplified form, what Kant proposes to do is this: to analyze the notion of a *world*, and then to demonstrate that *meta*-judgments of the form:

"The synthetic *a priori* judgment *J* is true of the world" or
"The categorial concept *C applies to* the world"

are themselves *analytic*, that is, are themselves *logically* warranted.[11]

Kant's operative notion, of course, is not precisely that of a world but rather that of an "object of possible experience". But we have already seen that what Kant intends by "experience" (*Erfahrung*) is "an empirical cognition" (B218). Its key characteristic is that it is a *unitary synthesis* of representations. Kant's starting point is that "one single experience in which all perceptions are represented in thoroughgoing and orderly connection" (A110). What sets Kantian experience apart from *mere* representations ("impressions and ideas") is just this "thoroughgoing and orderly connection". An object of experience is represented *as* an element in such a single, unified, integrated synthesis. More compactly put, an object of experience is represented as *in a world*. Experience, in the full-dress Kantian sense, is thus experience *of a world* (that is, of things as universally in a single world). And what Kant is claiming is that — *in point of logic* — such an experience will be *possible* only if our representings are structured in terms of the problematic categorial concepts which we have surveyed or, equivalently, if the corresponding synthetic necessary judgments are endorsed as true.[12]

Considered in this light, Kant's arguments are fundamentally addressed neither to the legitimacy of individual categorial concepts nor to the epistemic authority of specific synthetic and necessary judgments but rather to our warranted employment of a complete *system* of representations in which such concepts are applied and such judgments endorsed. What Kant recognizes is that whatever considerations *directly* warrant the espousal or adoption of such a total conceptual system will then *derivatively* warrant those judgments expressing synthetic and necessary connections, and those concepts mobilized in such judgments, the representations of which are logically inseparable concommitants of the possession and employment of that system.

What Kant primarily rejects, then, is not the epistemological principles of classical empiricism but its tacit commitment to an epistemological atomism — the conviction that concepts are to be legitimized and judgments to be warranted, if at all, individually and in isolation from any broader conceptual setting. And what, in the first instance, he puts in its place is a species of representational holism. The primary question of legitimacy is to attach not to individual concepts or judgments but to a larger conceptual structure in which they are embedded as logically indispensible features or aspects. Having secured epistemic legitimacy for the system as a whole, no special problem concerning categorial concepts or synthetic *a priori* judgments remains. Their legitimacy will be an immediate consequence of the demonstrable analyticity of the relevant meta-judgments in which they are embedded — demonstrable, if such analyticities are indeed themselves demonstrable, in accordance with wholly logical warrants, that is, with principles of epistemic warrant which are entirely compatible with the basic presuppositions of classical empiricist epistemology.

These last remarks highlight two outstanding problems. First, of course, there is the question of the relevant analyticities, the problem of establishing that the applicability of categorial concepts and the truth of synthetic *a priori* judgments are indeed *entailed* by the notion of a world, that is, of a "thoroughgoing and orderly" synthetic unity of experience. This, in fact, will be our project in the next chapter. But second, and more important, there remains the question of the warrants for adopting or espousing any conceptual system, even taken as a whole, at all. For the epistemological predicament of empiricism is not so much resolved by the Kantian strategies which I have been discussing as defused or transposed into another key. Our justificatory work will still not be finished. We will still need to understand how the adoption of a conceptual system as a whole can itself be legitimized.

On the face of it, we will confront here a predicament no different from the one which we have been exploring. We will require a form of reasoning which will yield as a conclusion that the adoption of some specific conceptual scheme or system is epistemically warranted. But we can immediately see that such a form of reasoning can be neither deductive nor correlational, in any straightforward sense. Both the logical and the evidential modes of justification operate only *within* the context of such a representational system and so presuppose its epistemological well-founding. So, although it now attaches to entire systems of descriptive concepts rather than to individual judgments, the problem of epistemic first principles, it appears, will still very much be with us. Will we not then *still* require a "third way" — a form of epistemic warrant is neither logical nor evidential?

The proper course at this point is not to recapitulate the classical dialectic in yet another form but instead to press our investigations in other directions. That is what I propose to do in the balance of this book. In particular, we shall need to take seriously an observation which I expressed at the beginning of this chapter but then allowed to lie dormant: that justification concerns not a matter of fact but a matter of right, and that all rights are at base *conduct* rights. What we need to do is to examine a conceptual scheme from a perspective which views it as a system of conducts or practices. We need to develop a general account of cognitive *doings*, and of the forms of reasoning which bear on questions of right with respect to such doings. This enterprise will occupy the major part of the book's later chapters.

But before we can undertake this investigation, there is an even more fundamental question which must be raised. The conducts at stake here are *our* conducts, and our aim — you may recall — is to isolate and secure some connection between the correctness of a conceptual scheme and *our* espousal of it. We must, of course, press the question of in what the "correctness" of any conceptual scheme might consist. But there is another, subtler, question here too, and it is a major part of Kant's genius that he succeeded in focusing our attention upon it as well: Who are *we*?

Kant's answer is as difficult as it is ultimately insightful. But is has significant consequences for the puzzles which now confront us, and so it must be expounded and explored in detail. And that will be my main task in the central portions of this book.

But all this stage-setting only serves to delay the onset of the intricate work which confronts us. The proper thing to do now is to begin. The centerpiece of a Kantian "transcendental deduction", I have suggested, consists in the demonstration of a family of analytic entailments, which collectively secure a logical warrant for meta-judgments expressing the applicability of categorial concepts to — and the truth of the corresponding synthetic *a priori* judgments of — a world, thought of as a synthetic experiential unity. It is to that demonstration which I now turn.

CHAPTER II

THINGS: THE MICRO-ONTOLOGY OF REALIST CONSCIOUSNESS

Where there is a thing, there is also what is not that thing. A thing is distinguished from, and contrasts with, its environment. There must, consequently, always be something in which a thing and its environment differ. I shall call it their *contents*. Where thing meets environment, there is a boundary. A boundary is a difference in content. How a thing is bounded in its environment I shall call its *form*. The content of a thing is what it is made of or consists of. Its form is how that content is arranged in the environment. A thing, then, is form plus content. It is so-much thus-arranged (form) such-and-such stuff (content).

I shall illustrate this abstract discussion with two models, which will be with us throughout the balance of this chapter. The first model is something like the traditional picture of "visual sense-data": variously-shaped color patches — in this case all of uniform saturation and brightness, varying only in hue — arrayed against a uniform, let us say black, background. This will be the Visual Model.

The second model I owe to Strawson. It is a simplification of his "No-Space world", a world in which all experience is auditory.

> ... sounds or sequences of sound of various degrees of complexity are heard. Some of the sequences may be supposed to have the kind of unity which pieces of music have. (*IND*: 54)

The environment in Strawson's No-Space world takes the form of a *master-sound*, "a sound of a certain distinctive timbre ... at a constant loudness, though with varying pitch" which is heard continuously (and which is unique in being thus continuous).

> It may be compared with the persistent whistle, of varying pitch, which, in a wireless set in need of repair, sometimes accompanies the programmes we listen to. (*IND*: 68)

This will be the Auditory Model.

More precisely, my Auditory Model will be Strawson's No-Space world subject to a certain restriction. To think of a unitary sound sequence *as a sequence* is to think of it as not one thing but as a succession of things. I, however, want to begin synchronically. How a succession of things can, in another sense, be one thing — that is, in what the *unitariness* of a "unitary sound sequence" consists — is, in fact, among the topics which I wish to investigate. So I shall not begin by supposing that we understand it. Instead, I shall restrict my Auditory Model, to begin with, to single pure tones. This is the "simplification" of which I spoke when I first mentioned the No-Space world.

In the Visual Model, a thing is a color patch. Its content is its color (hue); its form is its (relative) size and (geometrical) shape. It is important that we be clear that, in this model, colors are not qualities of things. They are the stuffs of which things consist. The grammar of color terms, in other words, is here the grammar of "mass terms". A thing in this model might, for example, be a small round patch of red. As we customarily think and speak, the term 'red' in such a construction is an attributive adjective with a suppressed or tacit nominal — a small round patch of red cloth, ink, paint, tape, or just *stuff*. But in the Visual Model, a small round patch of red is made or consists not of cloth, ink, paint, tape, and so on, but of *red*. 'Red' is itself a nominal expression with a logical and grammatical behavior of our customary 'cloth', 'ink', and so on. The expression "small round patch of red" should thus be thought of in grammatical analogy to the customary construction "small cubical piece of sugar".

I want to *count* things in the environment at a given time by counting closed, bounded contents in that environment at that time. I lay it down as a principle — applicable to both my models — in other words that every difference of content implies numerical diversity (that is, a plurality of things). The immediate consequence of this principle for the Visual Model is that its things cannot have *spatial parts*.

What we might describe from our customary perspective as a square patch whose left half is green and right half red (i.e., as a bicolored square patch) does not properly admit of such a characterization in this model. The green-red interface is a boundary between differing contents and therefore, according to my principle, a boundary between two things. To put the same point differently, my principle is equivalent to the stipulation that each thing consists of a *single* content. To employ our customary description of the ostensibly bi-colored square, we should need thus to be able to specify of what *the square* consists *in contrast to* the contents of each of its "halves". The "left half" consists of green and the "right half" of red, but the only contents in this model are colors and there is no further, single, color of which *the square*, in contrast to its "halves", consists. The proper description of this situation, then, is as a rectangle of green adjoining a rectangle of red — but the specified situation contains no square things at all.

To put a sharper edge on the point, a thing cannot have parts *which are things*. For, of course, a thing can have, for example, a left half and a right half. It can have edges and corners. But the left half of a red square, its bottom edge, its upper right corner, and so on are not themselves *further* things. They are not themselves closed, bounded patches of color. These "virtual parts", as I shall call them, have no ontological standing apart from the thing to which they "belong". The easiest way to highlight this fact, although it gets us momentarily ahead of our story, is by noting that reference to such a "virtual part" is always relativized to a *time*.

Imagine the red square rotated through 180° in the plane. What was its left half is now its right half; what was its bottom edge has become its top edge; what was its upper right corner is now its lower left. The full-dress form of reference to a virtual part is thus, for example, "the upper right corner *of* the thing *at a given time*", and what we have here is not talk about another thing but rather a way of talking about the one thing by talking about its form. A paradigm sentential context incorporating such reference to virtual parts is something like this: "At time t, the upper right corner of the red square is closest to the green circle". But what this says is simply that, at time t, the green circle is *above and to the right of* the red square. "Reference to virtual parts" will always be dispensible in this way in favor of talk about the *spatial relations of things*, that is, the spatial relations of closed, bounded color patches. Since this is so, in fact nothing is lost by adhering to the principle of single contents, the principle that every difference of content implies numerical diversity, and I shall continue to do so. Virtual parts of things, then, are not themselves further things.

Similar points obtain for the Auditory Model. A thing in this model might be a short loud burst of A-above-middle-C. Its content is its tone (pitch-timbre); its form is its (relative) loudness and temporal duration. The virtual parts of such a thing would be, for example, its beginning, its middle, and its end (or specifications of these, e.g., the first 1/2 second of A-above-middle-C). As was the case with our color patches, talk "about" such virtual parts will be dispensible in favor of talk about the relations of things (sounds), either to each other or to the master-sound.

The rudimentary notion of a thing in an environment, then, requires form and content. Form and content themselves, however, are correlative notions, and it makes no sense, on that account, to propose such a notion as "pure form". The point is of historical interest, in fact, for just such a notion is

THINGS   25

embodied in certain 16th Century accounts of substance. Descartes supplies us with one example:

> The truth of the matter ... is that this wax was ... only a body which a little while ago appeared to my senses under these forms and which now makes itself felt under others. But what is it, to speak precisely, that I imagine when I conceive it in this fashion? Let us consider it attentively and, rejecting everything that does not belong to the wax, see what remains. Certainly nothing is left but something extended, flexible, and moveable. (*MED*: 29–30)

Extension, flexibility, and moveability are the modalized counterparts of size, shape, and (relative) position — the monadic and relational forms of the things of our Visual Model. But when we ask *what it is* which "occupies space" (is extended), has such-and-such a shape and size, and moves from position to position, what we discover is that Descartes' metaphysical picture supplies no answer. All sensory contents are systematically excluded as candidate contents for "the real wax", and no alternative content is proposed. We are left only with "pure form" — but that is not an intelligible notion.

Just this point is tellingly scored by Berkeley's Philonous against his Hylas. Midway through the first *Dialogue*, Hylas arrives at the Cartesian picture. *Primary* qualities, he holds, are independently real, while *secondary* qualities are mere appearances, in sensations only. The dialogue continues:

> *Phil.* Can you ... separate the ideas of extension and motion from the ideas of all those qualities which they who make the distinction term "secondary?"
>
> *Hyl.* What! is it not an easy matter to consider extension and motion by themselves, abstracted from all other sensible qualities? Pray how do the mathematicians treat of them?
>
> *Phil.* I acknowledge, Hylas, it is not difficult to form general propositions and reasonings about those qualities without mentioning any other, and, in this sense, to consider or treat of them abstractedly. But how does it follow that, because I can pronounce the word "motion" by itself, I can form the idea of it in my mind exclusive of body? ... Mathematicians treat of quantity without regarding what other sensible qualities it is attended with, as being altogether indifferent to their demonstrations. But when, laying aside the words, they contemplate the bare ideas, I believe you will find they are not the pure abstracted ideas of extension. ... but, for your further satisfaction, try if you can frame the idea of any figure abstracted from ... other sensible qualities.
>
> *Hyl.* Let me think a little — I do not find that I can.
>
> *Phil.* And can you think it possible that should really exist in nature which implies a repugnancy in its conception?
>
> *Hyl.* By no means.
>
> *Phil.* Since therefore it is impossible even for the mind to disunite the ideas of extension and motion from all other sensible qualities, does it not follow that where the one exist there necessarily the other exist likewise?
>
> *Hyl.* It should seem so. (*TD*: 34–5)

CHAPTER II

Philonous' thought-experiment is exactly this: to conceive of a form without (a difference in) content. And its upshot is consistent with my results so far. A form is demarcated by boundaries which are constituted by differences in content. Where there is a form, then, there *must be* contents to differ. Form and content are logically correlative notions. We understand them by understanding how they contrast with one another and conjointly contribute to the elucidation of the notion of a thing.

These discussions of Descartes and Berkeley show, too, that the distinction between form and content which I have been exploring corresponds, at least roughly, to the traditional distinction between "primary" and "secondary" qualities (although we should remind ourselves again that contents are not qualities but rather stuffs). As Hylas' remarks suggest, the primary qualities were precisely the parameters treated of by the then-new mechanics, that is, dealt with by "mathematicians" who "treat of quantity": shape, size, number, motion, rest, and "gravity" (i.e., mass). The balance of the sensible qualities inherited the classification "secondary", a label which was reinforced by the emerging appreciation of the physiology of perception, in particular, of the fact that the perceiver is passive in perception — not acting but rather being acted upon.

In Kant's thought, form and content become "magnitudes". These make their appearance in his systematic exposition of the "synthetic principles of pure understanding", the "rules for objective employment" of the categories (A161 = B200). His first group of such rules are the Axioms of Intuition, and "Their principle is: All intuitions are extensive magnitudes" (B202; cf. A162). His second group are the Anticipations of Perception, and they are governed by the principle: "In all appearances, the real that is an object of sensation has intensive magnitude, that is, a degree" (B207; cf. A166).

Kant's reference here to "the *real* that is an object of sensation" corresponds to our notion of a *content*. "The real" is the real *in* space or time, that is, in an environment. (See A173 = B215 and A241 = B300.) The real is what *fills* space or time; it is the real *content of* a region of space or time. The question of extensive magnitude, then, is the question of *how much* of the environment is filled; the question of intensive magnitude, that of *with what* it is filled. Kant's "intuitions" or "appearances" are thus, near enough, our "things-in-an-environment", and what Kant is telling us is that any such thing must be *so much* (form) of *such-and-such kind of stuff* (content).

The Axioms of Intuition (extensive magnitude) correspond to Kant's category of Quantity; the Anticipations of Perception (intensive magnitude), to his category of Quality. Their connection with the traditional classes of "primary and secondary qualities" is relatively straightforward. "Primary qualities" answer questions of quantization. They address a "How much?" of extensive magnitude in a conceptual system which represents things as composita of points or instants (i.e., *ideal* virtual parts) amenable to the mathematics of the calculus. But a loud sound is not a compositum of many soft sounds, nor is a bright red a sum of a multiplicity of dim reds. The question here is not a question of quantity but of intensity; not "How much?" but "How strong?", and its answer is given not in quantitative but in qualitative terms: loud or soft, severe or mild, bright or dim. Thus Kant concludes that an intensive magnitude cannot be conceptually dissected into analogues of the points and instants of the calculus but is rather

... apprehended as a unity, ... in which multiplicity can be represented only through approximation to negation = 0. (A168 = B210)

Kant's way of expressing these points is, perhaps, not completely felicitous, but we can get an intuitive grasp of the distinction he has in mind by contrasting two possible modes of *vanishing* for a thing in our Visual Model. Should it disappear by *shrinking*, there is continually less and less of the same stuff. But if it vanishes by *fading*, there is, so to speak, a constant amount of continually weaker and weaker stuff. Shrinking is a loss of extensive magnitude and fading a loss of intensive magnitude.[1] (See A174 = B216)

Any system of *concepts* which embodies the notion of a thing in an environment, then, must contain some form/content disinction, a family of terms with the grammar of "mass terms" for singling out the contents of which the things consist, and a "mathematics" of quantity, intensity, and relation for characterizing the forms of those things and their (relative) positions within their environment. This, in summary, is our — and Kant's — first group of analytic entailments. That the concepts of form and content apply to the represented world is entailed by the premiss that the world is represented *as* containing things in an environment. I shall call such a representational system a *Minimal Core*, retaining, too, the restriction that every difference of content implies numerical diversity. What I want next to consider is what happens when the conceptual resources of a Minimal Core are mobilized *diachronically* in an effort to provide descriptions of various forms of *change*.

Let me begin with the Auditory Model. Let 'T_1', ..., 'T_n' indicate the various pure tones which are the things of this model, a difference in subscript signaling a difference in content. I shall use superscripts to indicate differences in *loudness*, ranging from 0 (where the tone is not heard at all) through some maximum value, T_i^{max}. The "master-sound" will be designated 'M'. Subscripts will indicate its continuously-varying pitch (the higher subscript corresponding to the higher pitch), but, since it is stipulated to be a sound of constant loudness, 'M' will carry no superscripts. Finally, the arrow '$\Rightarrow$' will be read as "changes to", so that, for example, '$M_a \Rightarrow M_b$' represents the pitch of the master-sound changing from a to b, and '$T_i^j \Rightarrow T_i^0$' represents the "fading out" of a tone of pitch i from loudness j to inaudibility.

There are only two ways in which a change in a thing can be *systematically related* to the master-sound. Expressed in the notation which I have just introduced, they are:

(α) $\quad T_i^j \Rightarrow T_i^k$ while $M_a \Rightarrow M_b$

and

(β) $\quad T_i^j \Rightarrow T_i^k$ while M_a remains constant.

I shall call these α-changes and β-changes.

The need to attend to such relationships arises directly from the question which I wish to set. It is this: We have equipped ourselves with a rule for counting things in an environment *at* a time. Every difference of content implies numerical diversity. What would it take to be similarly equipped with a determinate rule for counting things *across* time? In terms of our Auditory Model, the question concretely amounts to this: If a tone of pitch i is heard at t_1 and then, later, at t_2, what must be the case if there is to be a non-arbitrary distinction between having heard *two similar* (i.e., indistinguishable) *tones* on these two occasions and having heard *one tone twice*?

What makes this "mathematical" question of more than passing interest is that it contains the whole nisus of a *realist ontology*. Let me take a moment to explain why I make this claim, for it is not, on the face of it, transparently true.

Negatively viewed, classical realism, as it is contrasted with idealism, is the denial of the thesis that the *esse* of things is *concipi*. Positively put, realism proposes to distinguish the *existence* of a thing from its being perceived or thought of (that is, from its *being represented*). But this distinction is precisely equivalent to a difference in arithmetic — a distinction (at least potentially) between a *count* of the number of things which exist (in an environment at a time) and a count of the number of things which are represented (as being in that environment at that time). For an idealist, these two counts necessarily coincide. An idealist can only count existing things by counting representings of things, since for a thing to exist just *is* for it to be represented. (Its "mode of being" is "objective being".) A realist, in contrast, countenances in his ontology things which exist *un*-represented. Thus for a realist – but not for an idealist – there can be a determinate distinction between *two* (exactly similar) existing things and *one* existing thing twice represented. The count of things existing need not, for a realist, coincide with the count of things represented.

Our customary system of concepts contains both realist and idealist elements. A straightforward example of "things" whose *esse* is *concipi* is provided by *pains*. For a pain to exist just *is* for it to be felt, and the notion of "unfelt pain" is customarily regarded as being internally incoherent. What this comes to in "arithmetic" terms is not that each occasion of feeling a pain (of a certain character in a certain bodily place) *entails* the existence of a new pain, numerically distinct from any other. For we can and do speak of "feeling the same pain twice". But what it does amount to is that there is no *determinate distinction* between feeling the same pain twice and feeling two exactly similar pains. Our "idealism" with respect to pains, in other words, manifests itself arithmetically through the *absence* of any determinate rule for the diachronic counting of pains. How, for example, we choose to answer the question "Is the sharp pain which I felt in my left ankle upon awakening Thursday the *same pain* as the sharp pain which I felt in my left ankle when I stepped off the curb Tuesday afternoon?" is wholly arbitrary. Neither answer – "yes" or "no" – is rationally contestable. And I can report the periodic (re-) occurrence of an ache in my abdomen to my doctor indifferently by "Doctor, that pain is back again" (one pain, multiply experienced) and "Doctor, those pains are back again" (many pains, experienced in succession).[2]

To *be* a realist, then, – as I propose to use the term – is just to *have* a representational system which embodies a *determinate, non-arbitrary* distinction between two similar (indistinguishable) things and one thing twice encountered. It is, in other words, to have precisely what the "idealist" necessarily lacks: a rule for counting things *across* time, from encounter to encounter, which can determinately issue in different results from the simple counting of encounters (representings).[3]

To return to our Auditory Model, then, the question which I am asking is: What would it take to *be a realist* with respect to the things of that model?[4] We need there to be a determinate, non-arbitrary distinction between *a* T_i at time t_1 followed by *a* T_i at time t_2, on the one hand, and, on the other, *a* T_i at t_1 followed by *the same* T_i (again) at t_2. But, *ex hypothesi*, the T_i at t_1 is indistinguishable from (exactly similar to) the T_i at t_2. There is nothing about the *thing*(s), considered in isolation, in other words, to *be* this determinate, non-arbitrary distinction. We need, thus, to ask what *else* is going on at t_1 and at t_2, and what goes on between t_1 and t_2. We must, in other words, look, not at the thing(s) in isolation, but at the *relations* of the thing(s) to the environment. And, in the Auditory Model, the master-sound is (the whole of) that environment. That is why we shall need to attend to α- and β-changes.

If any thing could occur in any environment at any time, there could be no basis upon which a distinction between the occurrence of a new thing and the re-occurrence of an old thing could be erected. What we would have would be a random play of sounds, and the only possible diachronic counting rule would be idealistic: every temporal discontinuity implies numerical diversity. If there is to be any hope of securing the desired realist counting rule, then, it is clear that there must be determinate *regularities* of relation between things and their environment. Let me, therefore, supplement the Auditory Model with several diachronic regularities.

What we need, in fact, are regularities to suggest an analogue to our customary concept of *local motion*, a change of position. The reason, to put it very crudely, is that, for a thing to exist unperceived (unrepresented), we need someplace for it to *go*, some place where it can *be* without being perceived. Now the only "places" in our Auditory Model are the pitch-levels of the master-sound, M, so let me first assign some things to some pitch-levels. What this amounts to phenomenologically is the stipulation of certain *regularities of co-occurrence*, for example:

$$T_i^{\max} \text{ whenever } M_a$$

This is a tone of pitch-content i "stationed" at master-sound level a. One can "approach it":

$$T_i^j \Rightarrow T_i^{\max} \text{ whenever } M_x \Rightarrow M_a$$

and one can "recede from it":

$$T_i^{\max} \Rightarrow T_i^0 \text{ whenever } M_a \Rightarrow M_x, x < a-\epsilon \text{ or } x > a+\epsilon.$$

Such movement "toward" or "away from" a "stationed" tone thus manifests itself as a family of regularities of succession — in particular, as a family of α-changes.

Of course, there may be more than one tone of pitch-content i. Another might be "stationed" at master-sound level c, for example, giving rise to an analogous set of regularities of co-occurrence and succession. And still other

THINGS

elaborations and refinements of the model are possible. But we already have enough in these brief posits on which to go to work.

If α-changes supply our analogue to local motion, what should we say about β-changes? In terms of our intuitive manipulations of the model, a β-change, for example

$$T_k^0 \Rightarrow T_k^{\max} \text{ while } M_e \text{ remains constant}$$

could be the manifestation of either of two occurrences. It might represent the *coming into being* of a tone with pitch-content k at master-sound level e, or it might represent the *movement of a tone* (thing) "toward" the perceiver "stationed" at master-sound level e. Similarly, a diminution of loudness from a maximum to 0 with constant master-sound pitch-level could be a manifestation either of the passing out of existence of a k-tone or the movement of a k-tone away from a stationary perceiver.[5]

If we allow coming into being and passing out of existence into our enlarged representational scheme, we will never be able to construct the desired *determinate* realist counting rule for the things of our Auditory World. The reason, quite simply is that there would then be nothing to fund a distinction between the emergence (coming into being) of a *new* thing and the re-emergence (return) of an *old* thing. Once again, in fact, we would have a situation in which any thing *could* occur in any environment at any time.[6] It follows that the things of a *realist* Auditory World must be *permanent*. "In all change of appearances substance is permanent; its quantum in nature is neither increased nor diminished" (B224; cf. A182, A187 = B230).

A change in phenomenological loudness in the Auditory World is what I shall call a "change of ontological consequence". It represents an ostensible *loss of content*, a diminution in the amount of "sound stuff" existing in that world, that is, a passing out of existence. The Kantian "Principle of Permanence" is grounded on the recognition that any conceptual system in which such passings out of existence (and their correlative comings into being) are represented as *possible* cannot be a system which also contains a determinate diachronic counting rule for its things. Realism with respect to things, in the sense in which I have elucidated the term, is incompatible with the admission of such "generation and corruption". That is, realism *entails* permanence.

An equivalent way to put the point is this: Changes of ontological consequence must be represented as *appearances* merely. In the Auditory Model, what this amounts to is that the things of that model change only in *apparent* loudness. The *real* amount of "sound stuff" remains constant. A determinate realist diachronic counting rule for the things of that model can be supplied, if at all, only on the supposition that *all* β-changes, if any, are apparent changes of loudness which result from real changes of (relative) position, that is, from tone movements relative to a stationary perceiver. Realism, thus, entails as well the introduction of a distinction between *real and apparent change* with respect to the forms of the contents of the things of the world and, derivatively, a distinction between the *real and apparent forms* which undergo the ostensible changes.

But can we admit β-changes into our model at all, even on the supposition that they be *interpreted* as tone-movements, and still construct a determinate realist counting rule for that model's things? The surprising answer is that we cannot. We wish there to be a determinate and non-arbitrary distinction between two encounters with one thing and encounters with two indistinguishable things, and we must construct this distinction wholly from the resources available within the model — pitch-content, phenomenological loudness, and relations to the master-sound. The possibility which we must now guard against is this: that on our "return" to an M-pitch-level at which we formerly found *a* T_i "stationed", we indeed find there *a* T_i, but one different from the one which was there when we left.

Suppose that there were T_i stationed at M_a and M_c. At t_1 we encounter *a* T_i at M_c. We then "move" to M_k (that is, the pitch-level of the master-sound increases from c to k) and "return" to M_c at t_2 (that is, the pitch-level of the master-sound decreases from k to c). But suppose that, while we are thus "moving about", the T_i at M_c and the T_i at M_a "change places". During the interval t_1-t_2, the T_i which was at M_a at t_1 moves to M_c and the T_i which was at M_c at t_1 moves to M_a. Had we remained at M_c, in other words, we *would have* experienced two β-changes:

$$T_i^{\max} \Rightarrow T_i^0 \text{ while } M_c \text{ remains constant}$$

(when the first T_i "departed"), and

$$T_i^0 \Rightarrow T_i^{\max} \text{ while } M_c \text{ remains constant}$$

(when the second T_i "arrived").

If these β-changes are *possible*, our encounter with a T_i at M_c at t_2 could be an encounter with a second *thing*. But it could also be a re-encountering of the *original* thing, if the two T_i had, instead, stayed put. Since we were "away", "visiting" M_k, there is nothing in the resources of the model phenomenologically available to us to which we could appeal in order to choose between these counterfactual descriptions. It follows that whether we represent our experiences of a T_i at M_c as encounters with one thing or two things is wholly arbitrary. And this is just to say that, if the β-changes sketched above are *possible*, we cannot have a *determinate, non-arbitrary* realist diachronic counting rule for things. Turning the point on its head: a determinate realist counting principle is possible only if such β-changes are represented as impossible.

But representing such β-changes as impossible is exactly equivalent to representing the regularities of co-occurrence between individual things (tones) and specific pitch-levels of the master-sound as *necessary*. A tone "stationed" at a particular M-pitch-level, we must hold, not only does not "depart", but *cannot*. We can have our diachronic realist arithmetic only on the condition that we posit *necessary connections* between auditory things and pitch-levels of the master-sound.[7]

What emerges from these reflections on the Auditory Model, then, is a sort of "conceptual package" — a group of notions, distinctions, and posits which go together, in the sense that a consistent, determinate representational system which embodies any one of them must embody them all:

(R1) a determinate distinction between two indistinguishable things, each once encountered, and two encounters with a single thing;

(R2) the diachronic persistence (perdurance) of things unencountered (unperceived);

(R3) the permanence of contents (substance);

(R4) the representation of certain sorts of phenomenological successions (i.e., of β-changes) as impossible;

(R5) the representation of certain regularities of co-occurrence and succession (i.e., of families of α-changes) as necessary;

(R6) the representation of a distinction between real and apparent form and change of form;

and, although I did not stress these points in my exposition,

(R7) the locatability of the perceiver (experiencer) in the environment occupied by things (i.e., at specific pitch-levels of the master-sound at given times);

and

(R8) an explanatory system in which apparent changes of ontological consequence (i.e., of tone-loudness) are accounted for as resulting from real changes of relation (i.e., of the relative position of thing and perceiver).

Now this is a fairly elaborate package. It is so elaborate, in fact, that one may well wonder whether the logical inter-dependencies among these notions, distinctions, and posits are indeed genuine or rather instead mere artifacts of the model, relationships arising from the peculiar limitations of the Auditory World, rather than from any authentic logical connections obtaining among a realist arithmetic, perdurance, permanence, necessary connections, perceiver locatability, and the distinction between real and apparent form and change of form. I want to argue that these conceptual interdependencies are indeed genuine, that (R1) through (R8) are indeed, as I have presented them, analytic co-implicates. That is why I have two models. It is to the Visual Model which I now turn.

In order to determine the consequences of introducing one or another of the members of our "conceptual package" into the Minimal Core representation of the Visual Model, it will be necessary to scale down the model's complexity a bit. Instead of allowing an unlimited diversity of shapes, let me, to begin with, limit the model to *circular discs* of uniform and invariant spectral hues and constant intensities. The things of this model will then be monochromatic discs of various sizes in motion against a uniform black background. There will thus, to begin with, be two sorts of changes which a *single* thing could manifest:

(Π)   changes of position

and

(Σ)   changes of size (expansions and shrinkages)

Let us first dispose of a small problem posed by these Σ-changes. In the limit of expansion, a thing loses its boundedness. Its color supplants black as the content of the environment. In the limit of shrinkage, the thing vanishes entirely. And a thing may ostensibly come into being by expanding from a "dimensionless point". Ultimately, I should want to accommodate such Σ-changes, but let me begin by excluding them. I shall thus stipulate that the size of any disc varies, if at all, only between a maximum and a minimum, although these maxima and minima may themselves be different for different things.

I begin by thinking of these things as registered on a flat "Visual Plane". As before, to fund any realist counting principle, we shall need some regularities.

The potential occurrence of any thing in any part of the environment at any time would again yield only a random play of appearances. In the absence of determinate regularities, any departure from the idealistic diachronic counting rule: Temporal discontinuity implies numerical diversity, must be deemed wholly arbitrary. But even in so stripped-down a model, there is an amazing diversity of possible regularities which we might introduce. We have first, for example, what I shall call "regularities of manifestation". A disc of a given color may *periodically* come into being in a certain region of the Visual Place, traverse it in some determinate direction, and pass out of existence in another region of the Plane. That is, a disc of a given color may manifest itself along a given "track" at (and for) regular intervals.

Supposing the Visual Plane to be roughly rectangular, for example,[8] a red disc may "enter" in the upper right corner every m time-units, and then take n time-units to traverse the Plane diagonally downward and to the left until it "departs" in the lower left corner. All red discs may do this, or there may be various points of "entry" (coming into being) and "departure" (passing out of existence) for red discs, and various "tracks" as well, each with its own periodicity. Since, however, I have temporarily outlawed limiting Σ-changes, I shall suppose that all discs, of whatever color, will "enter" and "depart" only at the *edges* of the Visual Plane.

Correlated with such regularities of manifestation, there may be, second, what I shall call "regularities of waxing and waning". Thus, for example, a disc of a given color might regularly "enter" at its maximum size, shrink continuously along its "track", and "exit" at its minimum − or it might regularly do the opposite. It might "enter" and "depart" at minima (or maxima), waxing to its maximum (or waning to its minimum) midway along its "track". Or, alternatively, it might maintain a constant size from entry to departure.

Finally, there is the possibility of what I shall call "regularities of interaction". The most striking example would be an "ostensible occlusion". Phenomenologically, an ostensible occlusion offers the following show: One disc approaches another until they are in tangential contact at a point. One or the other then undergoes a continuous alteration of *shape* − changing from a full disc into an increasingly-thinner waning crescent − until it vanishes. Subsequently, a thin crescent appears on the opposite edge of the single remaining disc and waxes until it becomes a second full disc in tangential contact with the other. Finally, the newly-grown disc moves away from the other. Some time-lapse photography should aid in envisioning the process:

36   CHAPTER II

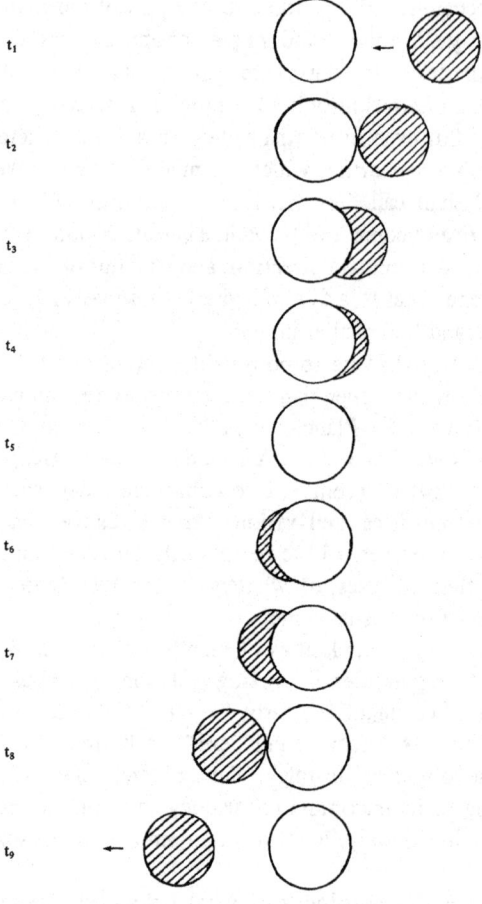

Fig. 1.

This, of course, is not the only possible form of an interaction between two discs. We might, in addition, find "partial occlusions", Figure 2, and "annular occlusions", Figure 3. All of these forms of interaction, however, manifest a sort of change which we have not yet had occasion to mention:

   (Θ)   changes of shape

Like Σ-changes, Θ-changes are "changes of ontological consequence". Each involves an ostensible diminution in the quantity of "color stuff" existing

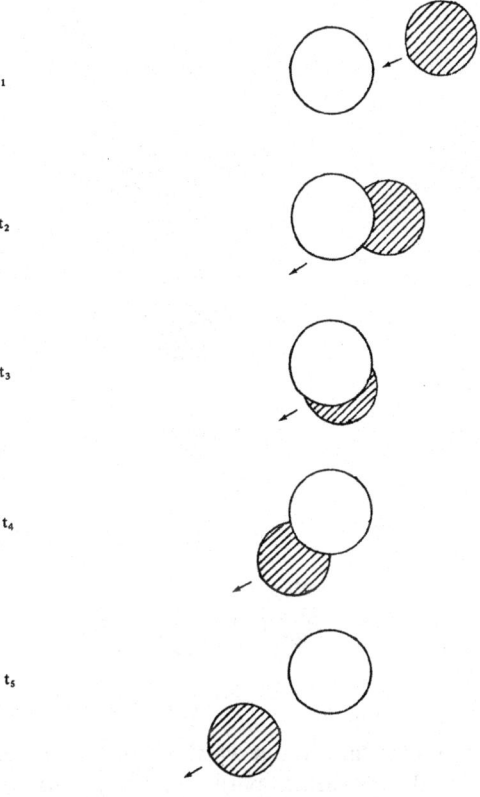

Fig. 2.

in the (visual) world. Π-changes, in contrast, have no ostensible ontological consequences. What we should expect to find, then, is that when we attempt to introduce a realist diachronic counting principle for the things of this Visual Model, both Σ- and Θ-changes will emerge as *merely apparent*, to be *explained* in terms of Π-changes, in particular, in terms of Π-changes relative to a perceiver who will be located in the environment occupied by our visual things. And this is indeed the case.

Consider the question of whether the small dark disc pictured as present at t_9 in Figure 1 is numerically the same as that pictured as present at t_1. Were we counting idealistically, according to the principle that temporal discontinuity implies numerical diversity, the answer would be that it is not,

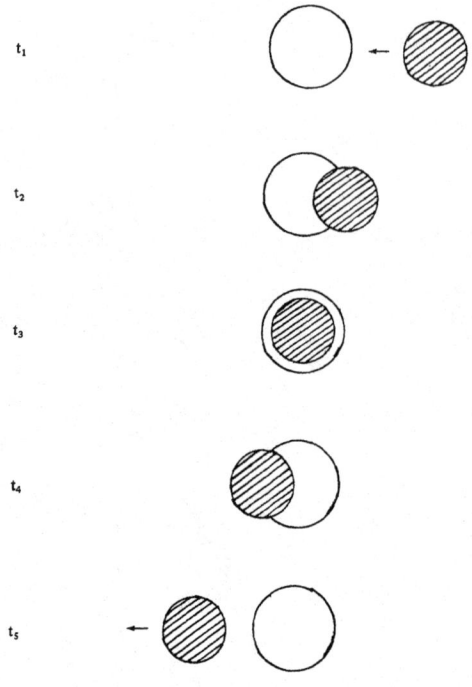

Fig. 3.

for there is an intervening time, t_5, at which no such disc is present. In such a case, however, we should need to posit a passing out of existence for the disc manifest at t_1 and a coming into being for the disc manifest at t_9, and, as we have seen, a system of representations which admits such creations and annihilations as real possibilities cannot contain a determinate realist diachronic counting rule.

But suppose we try to introduce such a rule into our conceptual scheme. Suppose, in other words, that we take the experience of the small dark disc at t_1 and the experience of the small dark disc at t_9 to be two encounters with a single thing. (R1) What conclusions might we then draw?

To begin with, if one thing has been twice encountered at different times, we must represent it as persisting (perduring, continuing to exist) between those times. So we have (R2). In particular, however, it must be represented as existing at t_5, when it is not perceived. So we need someplace for it to *be* at that time. It follows that we must re-conceptualize our space. We need "places" *not in* the Visual Plane, for at t_5 the Visual Plane itself contains no small dark disc. What we say, of course, is that the small disc is *behind* the larger one at t_5. We introduce into our representational system, in other words, the notion of a dimension "perpendicular to the Visual Plane", as we would customarily put it. By adding such a notion, we come to represent our space as *three*-dimensional. And this immediately gives us an alternative account of the Θ-changes manifested by the dark disc at t_3, t_4, t_6, and t_7. We now have the conceptual *resources* to represent such changes as merely apparent. (R6) We may, in other words, do so. But must we?

So far, the content of a thing remains its color, construed as a sort of stuff. A Θ-change thus has ontological implications. It is the coming into being or the passing out of existence of more stuff. But if the content of a thing – the stuff of which it consists – can come into or pass out of existence, then so can things themselves, for a thing is nothing but a (closed, bounded) quantity of stuff. And, as before, if things can be created and annihilated, a *determinate, non-arbitrary* realist diachronic counting principle is impossible. Here, too, then it must be the case that "In all change of appearances substance is permanent; its quantum in nature is neither increased nor diminished" (R3). And thus, just as we needed to represent the changes in loudness for things of our Auditory world as merely apparent, so too we must represent the changes in shape (and size) for things of our Visual World as merely apparent (R6).

It follows, then, that only Π-changes are real – and that Σ- and Θ-changes are to be *explained* in terms of them (R8). But explained now? An ostensible (monadic) change in shape or size is to be explained in terms of an actual change in relative position. In the relative positions of *what*? Of the two discs, to be sure – but of the *perceiver* as well. For the *apparent* ceasing to exist of the small dark disc at t_5 is, on this conceptual scheme, accounted for as a manifestation of its *real* occlusion by the larger light disc which lies, at t_5, *between* it *and the perceiver*. The perceiver thus receives a relative location within the new three-dimensional space (R7). Similarly an apparent change of *size* must also be accounted for as manifesting a real change of relative position. Since a single disc can change in size, we must again represent the perceiver as in spatial relation to it in order to supply the other term requisite for a change in relative position. Apparent Σ-changes thus come to be explained by representing them as resulting from real changes in the distance of things from the perceiver, along a dimension perpendicular to the Visual Plane. The positing of a realist diachronic arithmetic for the Visual World thus demands at least the rudiments of a "geometrical optics".

We discover in the Visual Model, too, then, that the elements of our "conceptual package" (R1), (R2), (R3), (R6), (R7), and (R8) "go together" as mutual co-implicates. But what of (R4) and (R5), our impossibilities and necessities? Well, it turns out that they too are consequences of our realist arithmetic, but here the argument is just a bit more complicated.

Our explanatory account of apparent Σ-changes embodies a posited correlation between (apparent) size and (relative) position. What this amounts to phenomenologically is a correlation between two families of *regularities*: regularities of waxing and waning, and regularities of manifestation. What I wish to argue is that these correlations must themselves, in our new conceptual system, be represented as necessary.

The reason, to put it briefly, is that, once we have reconceptualized our space as three-dimensional, regularities of manifestation alone do not define a unique path through that space for a thing relative to the perceiver. A disc "entering" at the upper right corner of the Visual Place and "departing" at the lower left which wanes from its maximum apparent size at entry to its minimum at departure may follow the same *two*-dimensional track as one which waxes from its minimum at entry to its maximum at departure. But our new explanatory system requires that we represent the distance between the waning disc and the perceiver, in *three*-dimensional space, as continuously increasing as the disc traverses the Visual Place, while the distance between the waxing disc and the perceiver must be represented as continuously decreasing. It follows that if we ever do identify a waning disc of a given color entering along a given track at t_i with a waxing disc of the same color entering along the same track at t_j — that is, if we treat the second encounter as our reencountering of a single persisting thing — we shall be employing a conceptual scheme which allows that the paths of a thing through *three*-dimensional space can vary arbitrarily.

But to allow this is to abandon our realist diachronic arithmetic! If the spatial paths of unperceived things can vary arbitrarily, then there will be no determinate distinction between a re-encounter with the same thing on a different path and a first encounter with a numerically distinct thing on that different path, a thing which was "substituted" for the original while it was "out of view". In order to secure a determinate, non-arbitrary realist counting principle, we must represent it as *impossible* that a thing thus arbitrarily alter its path through three-space. But this is just to say that a *waning* entry along a given track *cannot* be succeeded by a *waxing* entry along the same track. It is, in other words, precisely to represent certain sorts of phenomenological successions as impossible (R4) or, equivalently, to represent certain regularities of co-occurrence (of manifestation and of waxing and waning) as necessary (R5).

Our situation here, in fact, is very much the converse of that in the Auditory World. There, to secure a determinate realist count, it was necessary to represent tones as *necessarily stationary*. We needed to posit that only the perceiver "moved" — and that posit manifested itself as representations of impossibility and necessity: the impossibility of β-changes (certain phenomenological successions) and the necessity of specific families of α-changes (certain regularities of co-occurrence and succession).

In the Visual World, however, it is the perceiver who is stationary. Thus, in order to secure a determinate realist count, we must represent things (discs) as having *necessarily fixed orbits* (paths through three-space) relative to the perceiver. And this posit, too, manifests itself as representations of impossibility and necessity: the impossibility of certain sequences of Σ- (and Θ-) changes (that is, of certain phenomenological successions) and the necessity of specific correlations among Σ-, Θ-, and Π-changes (that is, of certain regularities of co-occurrence and succession), for only the *combination* of regularities of manifestation with regularities of waxing and waning and regularities of interaction uniquely fixes a determinate orbit for a thing through the three-dimensional, perceiver-containing space. But just such determinate orbits are required if we are to be able to explain ostensible changes of ontological consequence as merely apparent, which in turn we *must* be able to do to secure a determinate, non-arbitrary realist diachronic counting principle.

Our investigations of the Visual Model, then, bear out the conclusions drawn from the Auditory Model. (R1) through (R8) are, indeed, logically interdependent. Any consistent representational scheme which embodies one of these elements must embody them all. Such a conceptual scheme is realist in that it represents things as independent in their existence of their being encountered (perceived). It thus represents things as persisting unencountered (perduring), and it must, in consequence, incorporate — at least schematically — the representation of a system of "locations" and "relative positions" in which a thing can be (exist) without being presented (encountered) and in terms of which ostensible changes of ontological consequence can be explained as merely apparent. Such a system of "locations" is, of course, a "*space*", in the broadest sense of the term. It is, in fact, to sound a Kantian note, a "form of outer sense".[9]

One salutary byproduct of the Auditory Model, however — an insight which we owe to Strawson — is that it shows us how "unspacelike" such a "form of outer sense" can be. Our customary conception of space is the conception of a three-dimensional continuum, amenable to the mathematics of a geometry, which is not itself an object of encounter. The master-sound, however, is not like that. It is uni-dimensional, experiencable (and experienced), and, indeed, there is nothing in our arguments which requires that its pitch-variability be continuous rather than quantized, that is, proceeding in discrete (sufficiently small) distinct steps. Yet *functionally*, the master-sound fulfills the same conceptual demands in our representation of the Auditory World as does the space of our customary conception in our representation of our customary world.

Both our customary space (and its analogue in the Visual World) and the master-sound emerge functionally as elements of certain explanatory accounts. In the Auditory Model, the hearing or not-hearing of a particular thing (tone) "stationed" at a given pitch-level of the master sound is explained in terms of the "location" of the mobile perceiver along the master-sound relative to the "location" of that thing. The tone is represented as permanent and thus as available for encounter by any *suitable positioned* perceiver. Similarly, in the Visual Model, the seeing or not-seeing of a particular thing (disc) is explained in terms of the perceiver's spatial location relative to it (and to other things – recall the occlusion pictured at t_5 in Figure 1). The disc itself is again represented as permanent (that is, unchanged in its existence) and thus as available for encounter for any suitably positioned perceiver. And in both the Auditory and Visual Models, ostensible changes of ontological consequence (changes in loudness; changes in size or shape) are represented as merely apparent and are explained in terms of the relative locations and changes in the relative locations of things and perceiver.

What both the master-sound of the Auditory Model and the three-space of the Visual Model supply, in other words, is, in the first instance, a family of *relations* defined over both the things of the model *and* the perceiver, which figure in explanations of the "modes of sensible appearing" *of* things *to* the perceiver. It is the relations of "distance" and "direction" (*relative* position) among things and the perceiver, thus, and not the (monadic, "absolute") locations of things or the perceiver, which carry the functional load of a "form of outer sense".

Our *customary* mode of representation of such relations is as functions of a family of *loci* "occupied" by things and by the perceiver in what I shall call an *arena*. We assign to things and to the perceiver sequences of loci-at-times (that is, paths within the arena), and we formulate our explanations in terms of "Laws of Appearing" (e.g., "auditory thresholds" in the Auditory Model;

our rudimentary "geometrical optics" in the Visual Model) which represent modes of appearing (i.e., apparent *forms*: loudness; size and shape) as *functions* of relative arena-loci of things and perceiver, and ostensible changes of ontological consequence as *functions* of the arena-paths of things and perceiver. The arena itself is represented as if it were a "thing" to which perceivers and things-proper stand in determinate relations across time.

But while this mode of representation is customary, nothing in our "conceptual package", (R1) through (R8) demands it. For, as we have seen, it is the relations among things-proper and the perceiver to which we appeal in our explanatory accounts, and hence references to the arena itself, represented as "thing-like", serve functionally only to *mediate* inferences of possible from actual encounters and of apparent from real form in accordance with the "Laws of Appearing". The whole *content* of such laws, however, is, as we have also seen, already embodied in the representation of certain phenomenological successions as impossible and of certain regularities of co-occurrence and succession as necessary. Indeed, the *having* of a "form of outer sense" just *is* the representation of such regularities *sub specie necessitatis et impossibilitatus*, and the arenas themselves, thus, are nothing more than artifacts of a particular, customary, mode of representation for such necessities and impossibilities. Arenas are, in other words, (to frame it in a recently fashionable vocabulary) "logical constructions", or, as Kant put it, they are *Undinge*.[10]

I shall call a representational system embodying the elements (R1) through (R8) a *Realist Core*. What I have been arguing so far, then, is that the conceptual advance from a Minimal Core to a Realist Core is *unitary*. It cannot be taken piecemeal by the incremental grafting of individual elements drawn from the collection (R1) through (R8) onto a Minimal Core for the reason that each member of our "conceptual package" *logically* implicates all the others. The transition from synchronic minimality to diachronic realism constitutes, and must be taken as, a single conceptual quantum jump.

This is the point at which we can say something about the traditional problem of universals and particulars. The ontology of a Minimal Core is not yet an ontology of particulars and qualities but, as we have seen, an ontology of form and content or, as we might alternatively put it, of *structured stuffs*. Any representational system which incorporates a distinction between a thing and its environment must, I have argued, embody such a Minimal Core and thus any particular-and-universal ontology must be founded on an ontology of structured stuffs.[11]

What is needed for an ontology of qualified particulars is a conceptual shift from the representation of, for example, the color of a thing (disc) in our Visual model as a *content* of which the thing *consists* to its representation as a *quality* which the thing *instantiates*. We need, in óther words, to represent color not as a content but as a *mode of appearing*. And what this amounts to concretely is a distinction with respect to change.

Real changes in a content are changes of ontological consequence. Changes in a mode of appearing are not. To represent an ostensible contentive change as real is to represent it as a creation or an annihilation and such a posit, we have seen, is incompatible with the having of a consistent determinate Realist Core. To represent some phenomenological aspect as a quality, then, we should need to represent changes of ostensible ontological consequence with respect to that aspect as apparent merely.

To transform color from content to quality in our Visual Model, then, we should first need to introduce into that model a family of color-*changes*, and then to so structure our representational scheme as to allow, for example, the diachronic reidentification of a white disc at t_1 with a red disc at t_2 ($t_1 \neq t_2$). In such a case, since we would represent the thing as persisting unchanged in its existence from t_1 to t_2, it would follow that the existence of the *thing* could consist neither in the existence of a quantity of white (stuff) nor in the existence of a quantity of red (stuff), but rather must consist in the existence of some permanence variously *determinable* as white or as red.[12] What are contents in our current Visual Model would thus come to be represented diachronically in a manner paralleling our treatment of size and shape — as phenomenological modes of sensible appearing, and as actual states of or relations among things determinative of such modes. Like shape and size, color would become dichotomized into real color and apparent color, and our re-conceptualization would not be *complete* until we could represent, and thus explain, phenomenological changes in color as apparent merely and as *consequences* of changes which (like changes of relative position) our revised scheme posited as indeed real.

The transition from an ontology of structured stuffs to an ontology of qualified particulars then just *is* the transition from a Minimal to a Realist Core, conducted with respect to the *contents* of things of the Minimal Core. But, since any representational system which embodies a distinction between a thing and its environment must *incorporate* an ontology of structured stuffs, our new representational scheme must posit some *new* (real, natured) contents to figure in the explanatory accommodation of qualitative changes as being *not* of ontological consequence. Bare potentialities or principles (of unification or individuation for quality-clusters) will not do here, for, as we have noted, such Lockean "somethings" are representationally indistinguishable from nothings and, so, conceptually idle.

It follows that the ontology of particulars-and-universals which emerges from such a reconceptualization is not problematically Platonistic. On the Platonistic account (for which see, e.g., Russell *ORUP*, Bergmann *passim*, and Strawson *IND*), universals are "thinglike" subsistents, joined to particulars by a *relation* of prediction (participation, etc.), The particulars themselves are bare substrata. They are nothing in themselves (have no natures) but serve only as principles of unification for various clusters of quality-instances and as grounds of individuation for similar clusters variously presented in space. Predication (exemplification) is a subsistent *tertium quid* ("nexus", "non-relational tie") which serves to bind such substrata together with the qualia which they exemplify.

But the shift from structured stuffs to qualified particulars not only does not demand such Platonic separation and reification, but is, in fact, incompatible with it. A round white disc does not become a bare particular related (tied) by predication (exemplification, etc.) to roundness and whiteness but rather a round white particular (see Long, *PTQ*) which, in turn, consists of some *new* content variously determinable as really or only apparently round and really or only apparently white. To represent a color as a quality is to represent it not as a content but as a mode — and this, indeed, is not separation and reification but in fact its opposite (a sort of "de-reification") for it deprives phenomenological color-*changes* of the ontological consequences which, when represented as changes of content, they ostensibly had.

It is now time to relate the "conceptual package" which I have developed under the rubric of a Realist Core to the Kantian transcendental deduction as we are familiar with it from the first *Critique*. As the forms and contents of a Minimal Core corresponded to Kant's extensive and intensive magnitudes, the things of a Realist Core are Kantian *objects of possible experience*. Kant, in fact, reserves the term "experience" for encounters under the conceptual structuring of a Realist Core. Experience, we will recall, is "an empirical cognition, that is, a cognition which determines an object through perceptions" (B218), where perceptions, in turn, are "representations accompanied by sensation" (B147). Kant is prepared to admit as intelligible, if only speculatively, such *outré* constructions as "intuition without thought" in which appearances (*Erscheinungen*) would "crowd in upon the soul, and yet ... be such as would never allow of *experience*" (A111; my emphasis). Indeed, what would set such encounters apart from experience proper would be precisely their lack of any "thoroughgoing and orderly connection" (A110). Without such connectedness, appearances "would not then belong to any experience, consequently would be without an object, merely a blind play of representations (*Vorstellungen*), less even than a dream". (A112; cf. B136–7, B143, and A156–B195.)

The keynote of Kant's notion of experience, then, is the unitary synthesis of representations. To connect diverse representings occurring initially only under the conceptual structuring of Minimal Cores into the unitary experience of a world in "thoroughgoing and orderly connection", we must bring them under a system of concepts embodying the representation of an inclusive and pervasive field of relations, universally defined over all such individual representings. That is, we must represent our diverse individual Minimal representings as occupants or elements of a single arena.[13]

For us, it is *time* which functions as such an inclusive and pervasive arena, as a "form of inner sense".

There is only one whole in which all our representations are contained, namely, inner sense and its *a priori* form time. (A155 = B194)

I stress "for us" here since, although we cannot properly *imagine* it, there is no logical incoherence in the notion of an intelligence which is discursive without being — as is our own — successive. But our Minimal representations are diverse in the order of their existing, and their plurality is a plurality in time. For Kant, this observation is simply a brute fact: "It may be that all finite thinking beings necessarily agree with man in this respect, although we are not in a position to judge" (B72). But it is a fact which establishes the identity of his project with ours.

For the unity of synthesis which is required for Kantian experience must thus be a *diachronic* unity, a synthesis of representings across time. And from this it follows directly that Kant's "objects of a possible experience" are precisely our "things of a Realist Core", for it is by being represented as successive encounters with a single thing that diverse Minimal representations are brought together into a "thoroughgoing and orderly (diachronic) connection". To make the same point from a more straightforwardly Kantian perspective, the persisting (perduring) thing posited in a Realist Core has the logical function of serving as a *mediating third*, bringing two (or more) Minimal representations into conceptual relation to *each other* by positing them as in relation to *it*.

It should now be easy to recognize here the Kantian notion of an Analogy of Experience. Kant's prototype is drawn from mathematics:

(In mathematics, analogies) are formulas which express the equality of two quantitative relations, and are always *constitutive*; so that if two members of the proportion are given, the third is likewise given, that is, can be constructed. (A179 = B222)

Kemp-Smith, following Mellin, would read 'three members' for 'two' here and 'fourth' for 'third', but this is an error. The mathematical operation upon which Kant patterns his philosophical notion of an analogy is what we nowadays call the construction of the *geometrical mean* of two quantities. Given, for example, the two quantities a and c, this operation consists in the production of a third quantity, b, such that the ratio of a to b is identical to that of b to c. Here we have precisely the construction of a third member from two givens by an appeal to "the equality of two quantitative relations", that is, the equality of the ratios $a:b$ and $b:c$.

But a philosophical analogy, on Kant's account, is not quantitative but *qualitative*, and, consequently,

... from two given members we can obtain *a priori* knowledge only of the relation to a third, not of the third member itself. The relation yields, however, a rule for seeking the third member in experience, and a mark whereby it can be detected. An analogy of experience is, therefore, only a rule according to which a unity of experience may arise from perception. (A179-80 = B222)

Recall the ostensible occlusion pictured in Figure 1. If we take the "two given members" to be the qualitatively similar Minimal representings of a small dark disc pictured as occurring at t_1 and t_9, the sought "relation to a third" will be found in their posited (objective) *substantial identity* — the ontological counterpart of the temporal relation of continuous duration. The two Minimal representings are brought into relation with each other by being represented as two presentations of a single perduring thing, two appearings of a single object. It is this "object itself" which is the sought third term, the that-which-twice-appears and which unites the two representings through the *a priori* (that is, posited) relation of substantial identity.

Given our earlier discussions, the point of Kant's talk of *rules* here is also relatively straightforward. As we have seen, an appeal to the notion of a perduring thing in explanatory accounts of, for example, the phenomenological similarities of the Minimal representings pictured as occurring at t_1 and t_9 is *equivalent* to our representing families of regularities — of manifestation, waxing and waning, and interaction — as necessary. But to represent a regularity of succession or co-occurrence as necessary, in turn, is nothing more than to lay it down as a *rule* (of inference) that *whenever* one element of the regularity is presented, the other is (will be) similarly available. In driving a conceptual wedge between the existence of a thing (disc) and its being presented, we posit the thing as unchanged in its existence at such intervening times as t_5 and thus as *available* for encounter by any subject suitably positioned in the relevant arena — the three-space of our new representational scheme. It is in this sense that our Realist Core supplies a "rule for seeking the third member in experience". It brings our actual Minimal representings into relation with each other by positing them in relation to a single object of actual *and possible* encounters — that is, it warrants our reasoning to *counterfactual* conclusions about the encounters which a perceiver *would* have under conditions whose descriptive specifications are themselves provided by the enlarged diachronic representational scheme. And it is in this sense, too, that an Analogy of Experience "is not a principle *constitutive* of the objects, that is, of the appearances, but only *regulative*" (A180 = B222–3). In adopting a Realist Core, we are not provided with new contents — a new phenomenology — but undertake only a new conceptualization, one which allows for the diachronic integration of a discursive plurality (manifold) of Minimal representings into a single synthetic unity, the representation of a world in "thoroughgoing and orderly connection".

Where the Axioms of Intuition and the Anticipations of Perception were *a priori* requirements of even the synchronic distinction between a thing and its environment and thus "referred to the possibility of appearances (*Erscheinungen*)" (A178 = B221) — to what I have been calling Minimal representings — the Analogies of Experience pertain to experience (*Erfahrung*) in the full Kantian sense of the term. Kant isolates, correctly as we have seen, the key to a consistent and determinate Realist Core in the representation of phenomenological regularities under the aspect of modality, as necessary or impossible.

The principle of the analogies is: Experience is possible only through the representation of a necessary connection of perceptions. (B218) [14]

Kant proceeds to supply a trio of analogies in accordance with the principles of his architectonic (corresponding to "the three modes of time" — duration, succession, and co-existence). But his divisions have about them a certain air of artificiality — and understandably so. His First Analogy, the "Principle of Permanence of Substance":

In all change of appearances substance is permanent; its quantum in nature is neither increased nor diminished. (B224) [15]

corresponds to our (R3), but we have already seen that such a posit — while ostensibly addressing only duration — is logically inseparable from the representing of a distinction between real and apparent form and change of form (R6) and that this, in turn, already demands the representation of temporal relations of both succession and co-occurrence (co-existence) among Minimal representings under the aspect of modality (R4 and R5). Kant's putatively three analogies thus grade off smoothly into one another to form a single indissoluble conceptual package of analytic co-implicates. And when we turn from Kant's architectonic to his argument, in fact, that is exactly what we find.

Kant reserves the term "change" (*Wechsel*) for an absolute coming to be or ceasing to exist of substances (contents), employing "alteration" (*Veränderung*) to mark a succession in the *ways* in which a perduring thing successively exists or in which its existence is "positively determined" — in its "accidents" (A186–7 = B229–30). The distinction corresponds to our own between real and apparent change. A real (Kantian) change (*Wechsel*, in an *appearance*) is, in our terms, merely apparent (i.e., not in the *thing*) and, in Kant's terms, a real alteration (*Veränderung*, in the *thing*), that is "a way of existing which follows upon another way of existing of the same object" (A187 = B230). The gist of his argument is the same as the one which I offered earlier: Real change (*Wechsel*) in a *content* is inconsistent with a determinate Realist (diachronic) ontology:

... the unity of experience would never be possible if we were willing to allow that new things, that is new *substances*, could come into existence. (A186 = B229)

All ostensible "changes of ontological consequence", in other words, are to be merely apparent, that is, *alterations*.

Kant frames his reasoning, however, in a way which brings out its intimate connections with the Second Analogy:

If we assume that something absolutely begins to be, we must have a point of time in which it was not. But to what are we to attach this point, if not to that which already exists? For a preceding empty time is not an object of perception. But if we connect the coming to be with things which previously existed, and which persist in existence up to the moment of this coming to be, this latter must be simply a determination of what is permanent in that which precedes it. (A188 = B231)

While the ostensible appeal here is only to the unperceivability of time, it is clear that the operative notion is the discursive successiveness of representations, the need to secure a connection, for example, between the representings of the dark disc pictured at t_1 and t_9 of Figure 1 in the face of its phenomenological absence at t_5. To represent the occluded disc as permanent, and thus as existing unpresented (unperceived) at t_5, is just to represent its change of shape and subsequent vanishing (from t_2 through t_5) as merely apparent, and as explained by its state of motion in three-space relative to the lighter (occluding) disc and to the perceiving subject at t_1. It is, in other words, just to represent its apparent ceasing to be (and its subsequent apparent coming into existence) as an *objective consequence* of its real prior determinations.

But this is just *causality*! — "that order of the manifold of appearance according to which, *in conformity with a rule*, the apprehension of that which happens follows upon the apprehension of that which precedes" (A193 = B238). The connecting of "the coming to be with things which previously existed, and which persist in existence up to the moment of this coming to be" which, according to Kant, *constitutes* the positing of a permanent in perception (i.e., of substance) is thus simply a special case of "referring" something which is "apprehended as following" to "something else which precedes it and upon which it follows in conformity with a rule, that is, of necessity" (A194 = B293). It is a special case, in other words, of the Principle of Succession in Time, in accordance with the Law of Causality, which is Kant's *Second* Analogy:

All alterations take place in conformity with the law of the connection of cause and effect. (B232) [16]

Kant enforces an architectonic separation of the two analogies by structuring his exposition of the Second in a manner which presupposes the conclusion of the First. Thus he takes an objective distinction between the being (existence) of a thing and its being apprehended (presented) to be fully secured by the argument of the First Analogy. *Given*, then, that "all appearances of succession in time are one and all only *alterations*, that is, a successive being and not-being of the determinations of a substance which abides" (B232), Kant proposes to isolate and take up a further dimension of conceptual slack concerning the objectivity of temporal succession. As the First Analogy drove a wedge between being and being apprehended, the Second is to ground the distinction between (merely) being apprehended successively and (actually, objectively) being successive — that is, between real and apparent sequentiality.

This is the point of the famous examples of the house and the ship (A190 = B235ff.). In viewing the house, for example, I see the foundation before I see the roof. In the object, however, foundation and roof co-exist. Here the locus of everything successive is in the representings, not in the world (A191 = B236). In viewing the ship, however, I see, for example, the ship opposite the dock before I see the ship opposite the tree. And here we would like to find a basis for locating a real succession in the world — the ship *is* opposite the dock before it *is* opposite the tree, the one determination of location objectively preceding the other.[17]

The problematic of the Second Analogy is set by the observation that the two cases are phenomenologically indistinguishable. Each consists simply of a succession of perceptions:

Every apprehension of an event is ... a perception that follows upon another perception. But ... this likewise happens in all synthesis of apprehension ... (A192 = B 237)

We seek a way of distinguishing (a) the perception of a succession from (b) a succession of perceptions. But, since we are intelligences discursive in time, every instance of (a) *is* an instance of (b), and so "the apprehension of an event (i.e., of an *objective* succession) is not yet thereby distinguished from other apprehensions" (A192 = B237).

I am conscious only that my imagination sets the one state before and the other after, not that the one state precedes the other in the object. (B234)

But if *this* is the problem of the Second Analogy, then it is clear that Kant's architectonic separation of it from the First is simply sleight of hand, for we cannot even entertain the question of the diachronic connectability of Minimal representings unless we correlatively set those representings in a determinate order in time. The *topology*, at least — if not the directedness — of temporal succession plays a crucial role in our positing of substantial permanence. It is necessary, for example, that the ostensible occlusion pictured at t_5 in Figure 1 be represented as falling objectively *between* the representings at t_1 and t_9, for, if we allowed instead the possibility that the Minimal representings at t_1, t_5, and t_9 were of states all of which objectively co-exist — as do roof and foundation in the case of the house — we would not even have an *ostensible* coming to be (in contrast, for example, to a coming to be *noticed*) to explanatorily accommodate in a diachronic synthesis.

We ought to expect, then, that — architectonic considerations notwithstanding — Kant's *argument* for the Principle of Causality will make no essential use of the posit of permanence. And, indeed, just this is what we find. Abandoning the universal posit of causality renders it impossible, Kant argues, to tell *any determinate diachronic world-story at all*:

CHAPTER II

Let us suppose that there is nothing antecedent to an event, upon which it must follow according to rule. All succession of perception would then be only in the apprehension, that is, would be merely subjective, and would never enable us to determine objectively which perceptions are those that really precede and which are those that follow. We should then have only a play of representations, relating to no object; that is to say, it would not be possible through our perception to distinguish one appearance from another as regards relations of time. For the succession in our apprehension would always be one and the same, and there would be nothing in the appearance which so determines it that a certain sequence is rendered objectively necessary. I could not then assert that two states follow upon one another in the (field of) appearance, but only that one apprehension follows upon the other. That is something merely subjective, determining no object; and may not, therefore, be regarded as knowledge of any object, not even of an object in the (field of) appearance. (A194–5 = B239–40)

What Kant is doing in this passage is providing an account of what it is for a being to *have* (the concept of) a unitary objective time. The having of (a concept of) unitary *space* — a "form of outer sense" — we have seen, consists in the representation of certain phenomenological regularities of co-occurrence and succession under the aspect of modality, or, equivalently, in the having of a representational scheme embodying "laws of appearing", principles governing the explanation of ostensible changes of ontological consequence in terms of the modes of sensible appearing of things to a perceiving subject in that space. Similarly here, the having of (a concept of) unitary objective *time* will consist in the possession of a representational system embodying "laws of succession", principles governing the explanations of ostensible precedence in terms of a posited *objective history*, that is, an order of objective successiveness. Such a representational scheme, in other words, must embody rules governing the relations of actual to ostensible precedence or, what is equivalent, rules relating the order of *possible* to the order of *actual* presentations (perceptions, apprehensions) — for objectively co-existent things must be represented as available for experience in *arbitrary* sequence by, so to speak, any "suitably attending" subject.

The objective succession will therefore consist in that order of the manifold of appearance according to which, *in conformity with a rule*, the apprehension of that which happens follows upon the apprehension of that which precedes. (A193 = B328)

Putting the same point with a different emphasis, the representation of a pair of *apprehendings* (= Minimal representings) as *non*-arbitrary in their order of precedence and succession is equivalent to the representation of that *order* as itself necessary, *relative to a posited objective history*. We posit the represent*ed* things (appearances) as independent in their existence from our

(Minimal) representings and, indeed, as determining the (phenomenological) ordering of those representings. The things themselves then (e.g., the successive modes or determinations of a substance) must be determined in their *existence* as predecessor and successor by something other than that (phenomenological) order of apprehension, that is, by something objectively in the world. But this is just to say that we must represent the predecessor state of the world *as* containing an objectively necessary condition of the existence of the successor state, that is, as containing something of which the successor state is an objective consequence.

> The situation, then, is this: there is an order in our representations in which the present, so far as it has come to be, refers us to some preceding state as a correlate of the event which is given; and though this correlate is, indeed, indeterminate, it none the less stands in a determining relation to the event as its consequence, connecting the event in necessary relation with itself in the time-series. (A198–9 = B243–4)

The outcome of this line of argument is the conclusion that any representation of a unitary diachronic world containing principles allowing for a distinction between (merely) apparent and actual (real, objective) *precedence* will necessarily be a representational scheme which brings diverse occurrent states of the world under a family of relations of objective *consequence*, that is, a scheme which embodies a set of temporally-conditioned descriptions of world-states relating predecessors to successors under *some* set of principles of necessitation.

That the structure of conceptual demands imposed by the problem of determinate time-order thus supplies a solution to Hume's problem of causality as well is an example of Kant's "Copernican revolution in philosophy" at its finest. While Hume sets the problematic of causation in the form of a "failed deduction" of necessitation from objective succession, Kant argues, instead, that a family of objective causal relations is already necessarily presupposed in the very representation of an objective determinate ordering of occurrences in time, that is, in the distinction between ostensible and actual sequentiality of states or events. Any world represented as having a *history* will necessarily be represented as a world subject to causal law. But the fact of this causality will not, as Hume would have it, be inferred from the specifics of that history — the regularities of succession and "constant conjunction" — but rather is a demonstrable precondition of the positing of any objective history at all. (See A199–200 = B244–5.)

That is how much the demand for a determinate ordering of occurrences in time establishes. But, in another sense, we should be cognizant, as well, of how little it establishes. Earlier I remarked that one salutory byproduct of the Auditory Model is that it secures the distinction between a form of outer sense — that is, whatever in representation has the logical *function* of bringing things and the perceiving subject into synchronic relations allowing for the explanation of modes of sensible appearing of those things to that subject — and space as we customarily conceive it — that is, an unperceivable three-dimensional Cantorean continuum of points, amenable to the mathematics of a geometry.

We are now in the position to make a similar point concerning causation. As we have seen, the argument genuinely available to Kant here has as its conclusion only that a Realist Core must be a representational scheme which brings diverse occurrent world-states under *some* family of temporally-conditioned relations of objective consequence. But, just as a form of outer sense is to be distinguished from space as we customarily conceive it, so also these relations of objective consequence may be distinguished from causation as we customarily conceive it, for there is nothing in the argument to limit such relations to reversible Laplacean state-determinacies. All that is demanded of a representational scheme adequate for a consistent and determinate diachronic Realist Core is that it embody *some* set of temporally-conditioned descriptions of world-states linking successors to predecessors under a family of principles of necessitation. To sound a contemporary note, however, there is nothing in this result to demand that these descriptions be framed in terms of "macro-observables" or "classically conjugate property pairs". The *Kantian* notion of causality, then, is fully compatible with those current redescriptions of the world which incorporate such theoretical arcana as Planck's quantum jumps, Schroedinger's psi-function, and Heisenberg's uncertainties.

That Kant mis-set the level of generality of his conclusions has been an exegetical commonplace since the emergence of non-Euclidean geometries and a non-Newtonian physics. But we must take care that his undeniable historicity does not blind us to the overall cogency of his reasoning. The key to a proper understanding of Kant's "transcendental deductions" lies in taking their mediate conclusions *functionally*, that is, in their logical and explanatory relations to the fundamental arithmetic posits of a diachronic Realist Core. When we do so, we discover that the basic posit of a *determinate* diachronic synthetic unity analytically implies each of a package of conceptual features which can appropriately be termed "categorial": not matter but *substance* (compatible with the interconvertibility of mass and energy); not space but a *form of outer sense* (compatible with Riemannian or Lobachevskian geometries — or worse); not causation but *principles of objective consequence* (compatible with quantum-theoretical indeterminacies); and even, to frame a logical point somewhat paradoxically, not time but *principles of objective succession* – or, even more generally, a form of inner sense – (compatible with the relativistic denial of absolute simultaneity).[18] Such features are *meta*physical not in the sense of being "transcendent" but in the sense that they isolate a set of conceptual invariants necessarily characteristic of *any* descriptive system adequate for the representation of a determinate unitary world.

There is another, more radical, sense in which Kant may be said to have mis-set his level of generality. It is arguable that he thought of himself as providing a set of most-general *descriptive contents*, common to all representational systems adequate to depict a unitary world. But it is less misleading to look at his arguments as in support of the conclusion that such a world must be represented as instantiating some determinate *mathematical form*. Our "functionalistic" interpretation of Kant's "categorial concepts" amounts to the result that any representation of a world as a determinate diachronic unity is necessarily a representation of a world answering to a determinate mathematics – "geometries", in the broadest sense, of its "inner" and "outer" arenas, and a "mathematical physics" of objective consequence (recall the "geometrical optics" of the Visual Model) in terms of which the mathematics of these arena-representations becomes caught up in explanatory accounts of what are thereby represented as appearances merely (that is, as phenomena). In this light, Kant's Analytic can be seen as, in part, supplying an answer to the same question for which Plato (or Socrates) designed the Theory of Forms – the question of the relationship of mathematics to the phenomenal world.

Even more broadly drawn, however, this question is nothing less than the question of the relationship of the ideal or conceptual order to the real – and that brings us once again conveniently around to the issue of realism and idealism. The upshot of the present chapter is only this: that *if* we are to be realists, then we must be *Kantian* realists. The "categorial" features of our "conceptual package" (R1) through (R8) are mutual co-implicates, and are severally and collectively analytically entailed by the having of a determinate diachronic arithmetic which initially *is*, I have argued, precisely in what *being* a realist consists.

But this is an "iffy", conditional, result. We now know what *kind* of a representational system we must adopt or espouse if we are to be realists, but it remains open to us to ask whether we must or should be realists *at all*. *If* we are to be realists, we must adopt or espouse a Kantian representational scheme. That, in detail, is in what being a realist consists. But are we *justified* in adopting or espousing such a representational scheme? What speaks in favor of realism? And what is the alternative?

Kant's surprising answer is that there is no alternative — for us. We *must* be realists. Or rather, to put the emphasis in a way which brings out the logical point at stake, *we* must be realists. For Kant's claim is precisely this: the fact that our representational system is a Realist Core is *entailed* by the fact that it is *our* representational system. To secure this striking result is the aim of my next chapter. And, of course, in the process, it will be necessary to say something rather more definite about who, in fact, *we* are.

CHAPTER III

TIME AND THE SELF:
THE LIMITS OF IDEALIST CONSCIOUSNESS

Who, then, are *we*? Part of the answer has already been given in the course of the last chapter. We are, at least, *temporally discursive intelligences*. The characterization has three parts. Separately and conjointly, these parts all have consequences.[1]

To say that we are intelligences is to impute to us the ability to employ *concepts*. Without being contentious, it is difficult to say very much about what a concept might be. Fortunately, I shall not need very much. The essential minimum characteristic of a concept is that it can have *instances*, that diverse items can "fall under" a single concept. A concept thus imposes an arithmetic on the items which "fall under" what it is the concept "of". To be an intelligence, then, is at least to be a being which can represent a plurality of items and to represent that plurality *as* determinately arithmetically partitioned into subgroups according to the concepts which the items are represented as "falling under".

To be a *discursive* intelligence is to be an intelligence which can represent such a plurality (a manifold) only by representing its elements *as standing in relations*. In particular, if two items are represented as "falling under" all the *same* concepts, then to be nevertheless represented as two, they must be represented as standing in some relation to each other (and in different relations to whatever other items are represented as well).

Finally, to be a *temporally* discursive intelligence is for at least some of the represented plurality of items to be represented as standing in relations of before and after, as being predecessors and successors to one another.

That is *at least* who *we* are. But we are also, crucially, something more. What I propose to do in this chapter is two things. I shall, first, argue that, if that were all there was to the story of who *we* are, our representational system could consistently be through-and-through idealist. But, second, I shall proceed to consider what else *we* in fact are — and to argue that, if *that* is who we are, then *our* representational system *must be* a Realist Core.

My expository strategy will be to consider the situation of an hypothetical individual *idealist* temporally discursive intelligence. In honor of two of his illustrious predecessors (Berkeley and Hegel), I shall call him 'George'. George possesses a representational system or conceptual scheme which embodies an *idealist* world-picture. I want to look at the inner workings of that representational system. What we need to consider first, of course, is what about it makes it the conceptual scheme of an *idealist*.

The investigations of the preceding chapter give us an idea how to proceed here. The thesis of classical Idealism is that the *esse* of things (to use my neutral term) is *concipi*. Realism, in contrast, proposes contentively to distinguish the existence of a thing from its being represented (perceived, apprehended). What we saw in the last chapter is that this contrast in ontology is equivalent to a difference in arithmetic. An idealist can count existing things only by counting representings of things. For a realist, however, there can be a determinate distinction between two (exactly similar) existing things, each once encountered, and one existing thing twice encountered. A realist, then, is a being who possesses a representational system which embodies a distinction which that of any idealist lacks.

To say of George's conceptual scheme that it is idealist, then, is to say that it lacks any distinction between the existence of a thing and its being encountered (perceived, apprehended), or equivalently, that it lacks any diachronic contrast between "numerical identity" and "exact similarity". But how is the *absence* of a distinction or contrast manifested in the inner workings of a representational system?

To answer this question, it is simplest to focus on yet another distinction which our reflections in the last chapter show us to be a co-implicate of the contrasts which we have just been surveying — the distinction between the real or actual and the merely apparent. For an idealist, but not for a realist, there will be no distinction between a thing's *actually* being and its (merely) *seeming* to be.

For a realist, in fact, my last sentence is incomplete and ambiguous. The verb 'to be' may be read "existentially" or "predicatively" or as "the 'is' of identity". Correlatively, then, there will be a *trio* of distinctions which our idealist may be said to lack:

(i) the distinction between a thing's actually *existing* and its merely seeming to exist;
(ii) the distinction between a thing's actually *being* ϕ and its merely seeming to be ϕ; and
(iii) the distinction between a thing's actually *being identical to* some (specific) otherwise-represented thing and its merely seeming to be thus identical.

What our earlier investigations of a Realist Core have shown us, in fact, is that (i), (ii), and (iii) are elements of an indissoluble "conceptual package". Any coherent determinate conceptual scheme which embodies one of them necessarily embodies them all. What is more to the immediate point, however, is that any Realist Core embodies all of these distinctions in part by embodying the distinctions *among* them as well.

The most economical characterization of an idealist conceptual scheme, then, is that it lacks any distinction among these three distinctions which are necessary co-implicates of any Realist Core. And now we can see how such idealism can be manifested *within* a representational system: Whatever is the functional counterpart within that system of our verb 'to be' will be *univocal*. It is such a conceptual scheme, then, which, to begin with, I shall impute to George.

Before settling down to work, however, there is an objection which needs to be faced, for it will surely arise at just this point and it threatens to undermine my enterprise at the very outset. The objection I have in mind runs something like this:

> You claim that *the* characteristic feature of idealism is the absence of any distinction between reality and appearance, between being and seeming. But who has ever actually advocated such a position? Berkeley, for example, was certainly able to give an account of illusions, hallucinations, dreams, and the like — an account which sharply distinguished these experiences from veridical perceptions and, *a fortiori*, distinguished the objects of such experiences and the characteristics of those objects from the objects and characteristics presented in veridical perception as (mere) seemings from (actual) beings. By your criterion, then, Berkeley was apparently a realist! But if *Berkeley* was a realist, then there never was an idealist — and your hypothetical opponent is a phantom, less even than a straw man.

Now this objection is well-taken and, indeed, deserves a response — on a variety of levels. The *first* thing that needs to be said is that *of course* Berkeley was an idealist — or, more accurately, that Berkeley was a *professed*, a *self-proclaimed* idealist. That is, Berkeley did explicitly endorse the *thesis* that the *esse* of all things (apart from minds) is *concipi* (of which his '*percipi*', following the broad uses pioneered by Descartes' '*cogitatione*' and Locke's 'ideas', was but a special case). Berkeley, in other words, purported to adhere to the view that the ontological status of *all* things (other than minds) is the same as the ontological status which *we* (currently) assign to, e.g., pains or afterimages.

The *second* thing which needs to be said, however, is that I am about to argue at some length (following Kant) that, if *this* is the thesis of idealism, idealism is a view which *cannot* be coherently espoused. To put my conclusion somewhat paradoxically, I propose to show that the only possible *sense* which we can give to the thesis of idealism is not, in the end, a *possible* sense — i.e., not possible *for us*. If I am right about this, however, it follows that "idealism" is a philosophical position which *necessarily* fails of any authentic historical instantiation. It should follow, too, that Berkeley was able to sustain his own idealistic pretensions only by engaging in some sort of double-think or self-deception. Berkeley, in short, that historical paradigm of idealism, must, if I am right, despite all contrary protestations, have been a crypto-realist, an idealist *manqué*. And so, I believe, he was. Although I am about to argue my point abstractly and in general, I think it is consequently worthwhile digressing for a moment to examine the particular case of Berkeley in some detail, in order to run the objection I sketched above fully to ground. In the process, I shall also try to highlight a number of historical considerations which I hope will have the additional effect of showing that the readings I have given to "realism" and "idealism" are neither perverse nor, in fact, especially idiosyncratic. To Berkeley, then.

Our hypothetical objector reminds us that Berkeley was able to offer an "account" of illusions, hallucinations, dreams, and the like. Indeed he was. The notion of an "account" here, however, is importantly ambiguous. An "account" of such "non-veridical experiences" may be either ontological or epistemological. That is, one may propose to "distinguish non-veridical from veridical experiences" by answering either (or both) of two *prima facie* different questions: "*What is* the distinction between non-veridical and veridical experiences?" (ontological), or "*How can we* distinguish non-veridical from veridical experiences?" (epistemological). Berkeley offers answers to both.

Epistemologically, Berkeley's answer is, broadly speaking, coherentist. Our only *test* for the veridicality of an experience – our only useable criterion or ground of judgment – is its fitting or failing to fit together in an orderly and systematic way with *others* of our experiences. This is a hallmark of Berkeley's *empiricism*. It contrasts, for example, with Descartes' appeals to the "clarity and distinctness" of ideas. Where Descartes held that some experiences might, so to speak, be *self*-warranting – testifying to their own veridicality by reason of their own *intrinsic* features – and thus serve as an indubitable foundation for all knowledge, Berkeley held all warrant or justification to be diachronic, extrinsic, and relational. For Berkeley, no experience is *self*-warranting. The veridicality of any single experience is testified to only by *other* experiences, by that one experience fitting together with those others to form an orderly, lawful, coherent system of experiences. Although Berkeley himself claimed otherwise – and saw that as an advance on the position taken by Locke – his epistemology thus allows for a standing skepticism regarding the veridicality of any *one* experience. Indeed, by eschewing Cartesian *intrinsic* certainty or indubitability, Berkeley, as we shall see, opened himself to a skepticism as universal as that which plagued his rival Locke.[2]

But while this coherentist epistemology is a hallmark of Berkeley's empiricism, it is entirely disconnected from his *idealism*. Berkeley is no phenomenalist. While coherence constitutes the only way in which we can *confirm* the veridicality of an individual experience, the veridicality or non-veridicality of the experience is only indicated by and not constituted by such methods of confirmation. Epistemologically, in other words, the "idealist" Berkeley is in perfect agreement with the "realist" Locke. For Locke, the veridicality of an experience *consists* in its being suitably "backed" by "matter". But since Lockean "matter" is not itself an object of encounter, and since, in consequence, there can be no question of confronting or comparing an experience with the "matter" which ostensibly "backs" it, any *judgment* of veridicality can only be grounded in and justified by coherentist considerations.

Ontologically, however, the issue apparently stands quite differently. For Berkeley, as for Locke, the distinction between veridical and non-veridical experiences *consists* in the correspondence or lack of correspondence of those experiences to something else. Locke's "something else" is what he calls "matter". Berkeley calls his "God's ideas". One of our experiences *is* veridical, on Berkeley's view, just in case its object corresponds to an "archetype" in the "Divine Mind". This correspondence, in turn, when coupled with God's perfection, is what *explains* the orderliness and systematicity upon which we ground our *judgments* of veridicality and non-veridicality.

The difference between Locke and Berkeley here thus lies neither in their epistemological views concerning the warranting or justification of judgments of veridicality, nor even in the fact that the veridicality of an experience consists, for one but not for the other, in its correspondence to some "*secundum quid*". The difference lies, rather, in the ontological status which Locke and Berkeley respectively assign to their *secunda quid*. To invoke a Scholastic/Cartesian terminology, we may say that Locke holds his "matter" to have *formal* being, while for Berkeley, the "archetypes in the Divine Mind" (like the "accusatives" of the "ideas" in our own) possess only *objective* being. For Berkeley, indeed, *nothing* apart from minds (and ideas in minds) possesses formal being. And that is to say that the ontological status of those *secunda quid* in the correspondence to which the veridicality of our experiences consists is *for God* the same as the ontological status of, e.g., our pains and afterimages *for us*. The existence of these "archetypes" consists in their being perceived (experienced) *by Him*. And here we find the ultimate nexus of difference between Berkeley's "idealism" and Locke's "realism". For Berkeley, the distinction between veridical and non-veridical experience is not, as it was for Locke, founded on a difference in *esse* between two (ontological) kinds of *objects*. It rests, rather, on the difference between two kinds of *subjects* — the finite, receptive, and mundane, on the one hand, and the infinite, creative, and Divine, on the other.

So much, then, for Berkeley's official position. What we need to ask now is: Is the *professed* difference between Lockean "realism" and Berkelean "idealism" any *genuine* difference? Is *this* distinction between "realism" and "idealism", in other words, one which we can make coherent sense of, one which can be intelligible to us?

The distinction between reality and appearance, between being and seeming, classically tracks together with the distinction between truth and opinion. The real is what has its being (existence) and its character (nature) apart from and independently of opinion. It is that, indeed, upon which the rightness of opinion depends. In a somewhat later terminology, reals (real things) are things which are as they are independently of how they are *represented* as being. Starting from this classical (Platonic/Scholastic) understanding of reality, then, we confront an immediate question: Represented by *whom*?

The natural first response is: Represented by (any of) *us*, of course. And *if* one treats the classical conception of reality in this fashion, then Berkeley *is* a "realist". For Berkeley, quite as much as for Locke, the truth of *our* ideas (conceptions, representations) consists in their correspondence to things whose being and character do *not* depend upon whether or how *we* represent them as being — in their correspondence to what Peirce termed an "external permanence". To be sure, Locke *calls* his "external permanences" "matter" and Berkeley *calls* his "external permanences" "God's ideas" or "archetypes in the Divine Mind" (Peirce, parenthetically, calls *his* "reals"), but, one might well ask, what difference can it possibly make what such "external permanences" are *called*? Since God is posited as being eternal, omniscient, omnipresent, and unchanging, "God's ideas", just as much as Locke's "matter" (or, for that matter, as Plato's "Forms") will be permanent and inactive (inert), and will transcend any and all *mundane* experience (encounter). Any difference between Lockean "matter" and Berkelean "archetypes in the Divine Mind" must consequently remain, insofar as *we* are concerned, absolutely incognizable. Why not, then, simply follow Peirce in insisting that "we have no concept of the absolutely incognizable" and declare the self-proclaimed "idealist" Berkeley to be a realist root and branch?

Berkeley, of course, has a reply prepared. While we may, indeed, (speaking "with the vulgar") refer to things whose being and character is independent of *our* experiences as "real things", *genuine* reality (i.e., formal being) requires an *"absolute* existence without the mind", that is, a being and character independent of *all* representings. While the difference between Locke's "matter" and the "archetypes in the Divine Mind" makes no difference *to us*, it makes every difference *to God*. It is not from *our* point of view but rather from *God's* that the ontological status of all things can be *immediately apprehended* as objective being, and, in this way, *ultimately* understood as being in actuality no different from the ontological status which *we* (now) understand, for example, pains and afterimages to possess.

This reply brings us to the heart of the issue. What it reveals is that our ability to *make sense* of "idealism", our ability to render Berkeley's putative distinction between "matter" and "archetypes in the Divine Mind" *intelligible*, depends crucially upon — indeed, extends no further than — our ability to make sense of, to render intelligible, the notion of "God's point of view". We need to be able to form a coherent conception of a consciousness *for whom* the *esse* of *all* things is, as the *esse* of, e.g., pains is *for us, concipi*. That is , we need to be able to form a coherent conception of a consciousness which *represents* the being of all things *as* (consisting in) their being experienced (represented) by *it*. But that would be precisely a consciousness which is idealist "from within", the consciousness of a being which possesses and uses exclusively an "idealist conceptual scheme" in *my* sense of that phrase.

Now Berkeley, I think, would be likely to grant this point, but he might well also go on to caution that we should not suppose that this notion of an idealist consciousness must be the notion of an idealist consciousness *otherwise like our own*. The Divine Mind, Berkeley might remind us, is posited as very unlike our own. *We* are temporally discursive and receptive intelligences, but *God*, in contrast, is neither. God is not, as we are, *passive* in experience, but rather possesses a *creative* sensibility — what Kant was later to call an "intuitive *understanding*" or, equivalently, an "intellectual (i.e., *non*-sensible) intuition". And God's eternality, omnipresence, and omniscience conjointly imply that God's experiences are not, as are ours, *successive*, but rather are an "all-at-once knowing" of all there is. Showing, as I propose to show, that a consciousness *otherwise like our own* cannot possess and use exclusively an "idealist conceptual scheme", Berkeley would then conclude, is not sufficient to render nugatory the genuine distinction between his idealism and Locke's realism nor, therefore, to dispose of idealism *überhaupt*.

The last point which needs to be made, however, is that, even by Berkeley's own lights, this line of thought will not do. For what is at stake in this discussion is not the *truth* of "idealism" but the *sense* of "idealism". The question, in other words, is not "Could there *be* an "internally idealist" consciousness?" but rather "Can *we* form *any coherent concept* of such a consciousness?" To the extent that Berkeley, by stressing putative incognizable (infinite) *differences* between the Divine mind and our own, concedes that we cannot, to that extent his ostensible notion of "God's point of view" becomes, like Locke's ostensible notion of "matter", the mere notion of a "something, I know not what" — "which being interpreted proves *nothing*". For Berkeley's criticism of Locke, we recall, was not that there could *be* no "matter" but that we have, and can have, no coherent *concept* of "matter". Insisting upon the infinite difference between the Divine mind and our own, then, simply drives us — even according to Berkeley's standards — to the earlier position of declaring the ostensible distinction between Locke's "realism" and Berkeley's "idealism", between Locke's "matter" and Berkeley's "archetypes in the Divine Mind", to be utterly chimerical. We should then have to say to Berkeley what his Philonous says to his Hylas: "that you mean nothing at all, that you employ words to no manner of purpose, without any design or signification whatsoever. And I leave it to you to consider how mere jargon should be treated" (*TD*: 67–8).

If there is *anything* intelligible to be made of the dispute between "realism" and "idealism", then, the question at issue can *only* be what I am taking it to be, namely: Can we form any intelligible notion, any coherent conception, of an "internally idealist" consciousness *otherwise like our own*? Can we, in other words, coherently represent the representings of a being who possesses and uses exclusively an "idealist conceptual scheme", who represents, that is, the being of *all* things *as* (consisting in) their being represented *by him*? Following Kant, I propose to argue that we cannot. But I submit that it is not *obvious* that we cannot, and that it needs to *be* shown. The first step in showing it must be to discover in what the representing of a thing's *esse* as *concipi* "internally" *consists*, to discover, in other words, how the "ideality" of an "object of experience" — e.g., a pain — manifests itself (is represented) *within* a conceptual scheme or representational system. And this is precisely the step which I had completed immediately prior to embarking upon this long historical-exegetical excursus. The "ideality of objects of experience", I argued, is manifested within a representational system by the *absence* of any distinction between being and seeming for those objects or, positively put, by the *univocity* of (its counterpart of) the copula. The suspicion that I am stalking a horse already long dead having now been, I hope, laid comfortably to rest, it is high time that we took the second step.

Let us, therefore, return from our historical George once again to our hypothetical one.

I will need a notational device to signal this idealist, univocal (functional counterpart of) 'to be'. I shall mark it by an exclamation point. The basic form of an apprehending of a ϕK thing will thus be noted as:

$$a\ \phi K\ !is$$

'ϕ' and 'K' here signal, respectively, George's concepts of forms and contents which, I have already argued, he must have if he is to be able to represent things (in an environment) at all, for to represent a thing in an environment *is* to represent so much thus-bounded (form) such-and-such stuff (content). I shall suppose George equipped with a family of form-concepts (ϕ, ψ, etc.) and a family of content-concepts (K, F, G, etc.). In a moment, I shall say more about just what this supposition amounts to.

First, however, we must note that, since George is a *temporally* discursive intelligence, he will "think in tenses". Some of his representings will be ostensible awarenesses or apprehendings, representing their "targets" as something that !is. But some will be ostensible memories or recollections. Their "targets" will be represented as something that !was. These "targets" themselves (I use the term to avoid the difficulties of both 'content' and 'object' here) are structured in terms of the conceptual resources of what I have called a Minimal Core. The representing of a thing as a thing that !is, I call an N-representing (for "now"); the representing of a thing as a thing that !was, a T-representing (for "then"). George's world-picture, then, is to be built up out of a collection of N- and T-representings of things-in-an-environment. And that is part of what is at stake in imputing to George families of form-concepts and content-concepts.

What more is at stake may be brought out by noting that, in line with the fundamental posit that concepts have instances, forms and contents are represented as *synchronic and diachronic repeatables*. Two *things* may !be "equiform" or "equistuff" (to coin a convenient barbarism) or both equiform and equistuff, that is, exactly similar. Both synchronically and diachronically, however, this observation has consequences, and it is to these consequences which I now wish to turn. Let us hold diachronic questions in abeyance, for the moment, and consider the synchronic situation.

Two compresent things — that is, two things which simultaneously !are — may agree in form or they may agree in content or they may agree in both form and content (or, of course, in neither). To suppose that George is an intelligence is to suppose him to be equipped with a representational system which contains the resources for reflecting each of these possibilities. Thus George's representation of a synchronic manifold must, at least, contain elements of similarity and difference varying systematically with these potential differences in arithmetic, these potential differences in the *counts* of forms *vs* contents *vs* things.

In order to focus upon what is essential, I shall be rather heavy-handed and attribute to George a representational scheme in which things are given "proper names" in the form of numerals. The implications of this supposition, and the principles according to which George does his "proper naming" will come out gradually as we proceed.

If a thing, 1, is both equiform and equistuff with a thing, 2 — that is, if they are both, for example, ϕK's — while being, as *we* would put it, numerically distinct but compresent, then, since George is a *discursive* intelligence, there will be some synchronic relation in which he represents 1 and 2 as standing. Intuitively, 1 and 2 will be in different "places" and each will have a "position" *relative* to the other. The cautionary quotation remarks remind us, however, that these relations need not be spatial in any but a functional sense. But there will, in any case, be some family of relations — $R_1, R_2, \ldots$ — defined over the elements (things) of a synchronic manifold adequate to allow George to represent those elements as occupants of a *synchronic arena*. I shall call these R_i "relations of location".

The reason there must be such relations of location is that synchronic counts are to be *determinate*. Let me recur to the example of pains which, as the clearest example of an idealism, will be our paradigm for the things of George's conceptual scheme. The relations R_i in the case of pains constitute collectively an arena which we might call "the sensible body". The "phantom limb" phenomenon stands in the way of straightforwardly identifying this with the physical body, although, for normal folk in normal circumstances — no amputations, no psycho-active drugs, etc. — the two will coincide and, indeed, our whole vocabulary for assigning locations in the sensible body is a strict analogical derivative of this normal coincidence.[3] A pain, we say, is "in my right foot (lower back, left hand, etc.)".

Our vocabulary for the forms and contents of pains is crude, but we can at least note that, even synchronically pains have an *extent* ("all up and down the whole length of my right arm"), an *intensity* ("mild", "excruciating"), and a *character* ("sharp twinge", "dull ache"). The question of whether two of George's things could !be simultaneously compresent "in the same place" — that is, with *no* relation of location obtaining between them — is strictly analogous to the question of whether there could be simultaneously two pains of the same extent, intensity, and character having the same location in the sensible body. Once we put the question this way, however, it is obvious that, *if synchronic counts are determinate*, the answer must be that there could not.

Suppose that what is at issue is a sharp twinge in (the whole of) my left thumb. Let an *ouch* be a unit of pain-intensity. At a certain time, then, I feel, say, 12 ouches worth of sharp twinge in my left thumb. If exactly similar pains *could* have the same synchronic location, it would follow that there would be no determinate, non-arbitrary count of *how many* pains I felt at that time. For that 12 ouches worth might be *one* 12-ouch twinge, or *two* coincident 6-ouch twinges, or *three* coincident 4-ouch twinges, or five coincident 2.4-ouch twinges, and so on *ad infinitum*. It follows, then, conversely, that if synchronic counts *are* determinate, two simultaneous exactly similar pains must have different locations.[4]

What is true of our pains is true of George's things. Two compresent equiform, equistuff things must stand in *some* relation of location to one another. George, in other words, operates under the normative constraint of what we might call the Principle of Non-Coincident Indistinguishables (Pri-NCI): Two indistinguishable things cannot be "in the same place" at the same time.

What about two *distinguishable* things? Well, here the situation is more complicated. Consider again the case of pains. *We* count a sharp twinge and a dull ache of the same extent in the same location at the same time as *two pains*. But the categorization of pains according to their characters is not somehow given *a priori*. Considered strictly synchronically, without implicit appeal to independent variabilities across time, nothing bars our categorization of this experience as involving only *one* pain of a unique ("mixed") character — say, a "Twache". If we limit ourselves to a strictly synchronic perspective, in other words, nothing militates against our operating with a conceptual scheme which recognizes twinges and aches *and* twaches — and, if we did so, the *whole* burden of synchronic numerical individuation would be carried by forms (extents) or, what comes to the same thing, by relations of location.[5]

I confine myself to a synchronic perspective here because our different synchronic options yield different diachronic consequences. Suppose, for example, that we limit ourselves to pains localized in (the whole of) my left thumb, and that my experience during the interval $t_1 - t_4$ is given, according to our customary description, by:

+——ache——+——ache and twinge——+——ache——+
t_1 t_2 t_3 t_4

To thus classify the experience during the sub-interval t_2-t_3 as the feeling of two coincident pains is to *identify* the ache felt from t_3 to t_4 as a *continuation* of the ache felt from t_1 to t_2. It is to represent the ache as persisting uninterrupted through time from t_1 to t_4 and as having a twinge "superimposed" upon it during the sub-interval t_2-t_3. Diachronically, then, we would count one ache, for there would be no temporal discontinuity upon which to found a non-arbitrary judgment of numerical distinctness.

The alternative description of characters, however,

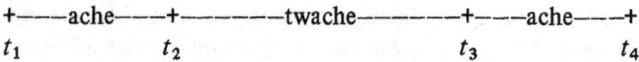

leaves *open* the question of whether the t_3-t_4 ache is a resumption or recurrence of the t_1-t_2 ache or another ache, exactly like the t_1-t_2 ache. And any determinate, non-arbitrary answer to this question of diachronic reidentification would need to rest on something other than merely my experience during the interval t_1-t_4. The adoption for a certain scheme for synchronically classifying the characters of pains, in other words, can have consequences concerning the diachronic reidentification of pains.

As with pains, so again with George's things. We face a choice here. Shall we commit George to a Principle of Non-Overlapping Contents (PriNOC) and require him to proliferate content concepts on the twinge, ache, and twache model? Or shall we let him proceed as he will — perhaps sometimes judging two things of differing contents to !be simultaneously in the same place and sometimes that there !is only one thing of a new, unique ("mixed") content in that place? Our general project is to investigate the limits of a wholly idealist consciousness. Our best course, then, should be to prejudge as little as possible. Let us, therefore, allow George to represent such situations as he wishes. But let us also make a note to return to the question later in our discussion for, as we have seen, what George does here synchronically may not be without its diachronic consequences.

It is time, indeed, to turn to diachronic considerations. George is not merely a discursive intelligence, but an intelligence discursive *in time*. He "thinks in tenses", of things that !were as well as of things that !are. His manifold is thus a diachronic manifold, and, again, the plurality of its elements can be represented by him only as standing in relations. To the relations of location, then, we must add a second family — relations of temporal order. Things which !were are represented as having !preceded things which !are. Indeed, such relations of precedence and succession will be represented as obtaining even among things all of which !were. George's representation of this diachronic manifold is always a here-and-now representation. As things may be *N*-represented as !being compresent or successive, so too things may be remembered (*T*-represented) as !having-been compresent or successive. At any single time, in other words, George's *N*- and *T*-representings combine to yield the representation of a diachronic manifold as a *unitary history*, a history of things !being and !having-been in determinate relations of location and in a determinate temporal order of before and after.

We are now able, in fact, to allow George's "proper names" to assume their full-fledged role as representing *in absentia* things which !were but !are not. Since George is to be an idealist, we must deny him, even implicit, judgments of diachronic identity (unless, of course, they become *unavoidable*. That, of course, is the point at stake). We will suppose him, then, to "name" (that is, to numerate) things in the order of his experiencing them (in the order, so to speak, in which they !occur), and to *repeat* no numerations. George is thus implicitly counting things *diachronically* according to the only determinate principle possible for an idealist: Temporal discontinuity implies numerical diversity.

This will not, of course, be the only sort of constraint on George's evolving world-picture. Judgments of temporal order, for example, must be subject to the constraints of a "chronologic", a Material Logic of Time. The judgment that two things, m and n, !were related as predecessor and successor — that is, the *T*-representing

(T1) m !preceded n

(where the exclamation point again reminds us of the univocity of the verb, the absence of a contrast between actual and ostensible precedence) — for example, is incompatible with the judgment that they !were-compresent or related as successor and predecessor — that is, with

(T2) n !was-compresent-with m

and with

(T3) n !preceded m.

Such a family of judgments as (T1), (T2), and (T3), in fact, must, if they incorporate the same pair of numeral-names in the same orders, form an exclusive set for every pair of numeral-names. One pain of surrendering its *determinate* (linear) temporal order of things' !being, George's world-picture can contain at most one member of every such family.

There will be more to "chrono-logic" than this, of course. '!Precedes' will be transitive as well as irreflexive and asymmetric, and '!is-compresent-with' will be a temporal equivalence relation — reflexive, symmetric, and transitive. These constraints will receive implicit reflection in the contents of George's world-picture — the *non-occurrence* of pairs of representings drawn from the same (T1)–(T3) family in that world-picture and, for example, the regular *co-occurrence* of pairs of representings of the forms

(T4) r !is-(or: !was)-compresent-with s

and

(T5) s !is-(or: !was)-compresent-with r.

It would be nice, however, if we could make these normative constraints of determinateness *explicit* in the internal machinery of George's representational system as well. And there is a way to do so. Let us equip George with the apparatus of *first-order logic*. Each such contraint can then be reflected in a *general* representing — one which will have an interesting epistemological status.

For example, corresponding to (part of) the commentary on the family (T1)–(T3) will be the occurrence in George's world-picture of the generalization:

(T^+) $(x)(y)(x \text{ !preceded } y \rightarrow \sim y \text{ !preceded } x)$

and, corresponding to the regular co-occurrence of representings of the forms (T4) and (T5) in that world-picture will be the occurrence of the generalization:

(T^{++}) $(x)(y)(x \text{ !be-compresent-with } y \equiv y \text{ !be-compresent-with } x)$

(T^+) and (T^{++}) are principles of chrono-logic. They formulate constraints on George's world-picture which are imposed by the bare condition that things be represented as !being in a *determinate* temporal order. Indeed, for '!precedes' to be a relation of temporal *order* just is for its occurrences in George's representings to be subject to these (or analogous) constraints.

There are two important morals to be drawn from this observation. The first concerns the business of *formal* logic. Formal logic is concerned with the constraints on the combination of a plurality of (minimal) representings into a representing of a plurality. Its business is to articulate and to explicitly reflect the relationships which *necessarily* obtain between compound and simple representings (that is, between the representation of a manifold and the manifold of individual representations of its elements, pairs of its elements, etc.). The necessity at issue here is the necessity of *determinateness*. The price of contravening such constraints is that any representation of temporal order becomes wholly arbitrary. The demand for logical *consistency* is founded on this more basic requirement of determinateness or non-arbitrariness. The reason that "a contradiction implies anything" is that it signals a mode of combination of discrete representings which is *in*determinate. But formal logic is dependent upon an underlying "material logic" — in the present instance, upon what I have been calling chronologic — for the constraints of determinateness from which formal logic derives its "force", the constraints which confer upon the demand for consistency *its* necessity, are constraints which are necessarily operative *even* in the case of a discursive intelligence which lacks the *explicit* machinery of logical operators and connectives. They apply, for example, to George, even if we restrict his world-picture to the bare accumulation of uncompound (primary) N- and T-representings.

The second moral concerns the epistemological status which George must assign to such principles of his chrono-logic as those expressed by (T^+) and (T^{++}). Each will have the status of an "analytic truth". The world-story of *any* temporally discursive intelligence will necessarily contain such "analytic truths" (or their equivalents) if it is constructed within a representational system which contains the resources of formal logic required explicitly to formulate them. Here, too, the necessity at issue is the necessity of determinateness. As before, it is the ongoing activity of N- and T-representing which is primary. To achieve a world-picture of things as !being in a determinate temporal order, a temporally discursive intelligence must represent things as !standing in relations of before and after and, thus, there must be *something* in his system of representations which is *functionally isomorphic* to George's !precedes' in the precise sense of occurring in representings only subject to the same constraints, something, in other words, which *functionally is* the "term" '!precedes'.

If this discursive intelligence is also equipped with the apparatus of logical operators and connectives, he will be able to formulate explicit representations which mirror these necessary constraints on his activities — and these representations will themselves inherit the necessity of determinateness which appertains to those constraints. Such representations will thus be *indefeasible*. Abandoning them would be strictly equivalent to abandoning those constraints which are functionally *constitutive* of the "term" '!precedes', for example, as a means of representing things as !being in a *determinate* temporal order. (The scare-quotes around "term" remind us that we are speaking functionally here. The specific representational embodiment of these temporal ordering functions may not look or sound very much like a written or spoken term of *our* language.)

Since the constraints are thus constitutive of the "term", the "analytic" representations — e.g., (T^+) and (T^{++}) — which reflect those constraints on primary representational activity may be said to be true *"ex vi terminorum"* or to be "meaning postulates". And corresponding to each such representation, we may project a "material rule of inference" or "conformation rule" authorizing the concluding of (any instantiation of) its consequent from (any instantiation of) its antecedent, a rule to which — since it is necessarily subject to the constraints of determinateness — the representational activity of such a discursive intelligence necessarily conforms.

As with temporal order, so, we may now add, with synchronic location. Members of the family of relations R_i will have their own transitivities and intransitivities, reflexivities and irreflexivities, and the like. They will, in other words, be genuinely a *family* rather than a mere collection. Like relations of temporal order, in order to give rise to a *determinate* (synchronic) world-picture, relations of location will have converses and consequences and will fall into jointly-exhaustive exclusive sets, reflecting the constraints on their employment which are necessary conditions of a determinate, non-arbitrary representing of a synchronic manifold of !compresent things. These constraints, too, will be implicit in the patterning of George's primary N- and T-representings, and these constraints, too may be made explicit by forming representations with the aid of logical connectives and operators.

Since the business of formal logic is to articulate and to explicitly reflect the relationships which necessarily obtain between simple and compound representings, *the same logical constants will do*. Nothing turns on the fact that the manifold here is synchronic and locational rather than diachronic and temporal. Logic concerns the relationships of the unitary representation of *any* plurality to the plurality of separate representings of its elements, both individually and as standing pairwise (etc.) in relations. Its business is to manifest the constraints of determinateness imposed on a discursive intelligence *as such* — whatever the mode of its discursiveness and the specific contents of its representings. That is what makes such logic *formal* logic, and what sets it apart from the "material logics" embodied in the constraints themselves upon which, I have argued, it necessarily rests.[6]

We have now equipped George with a fairly elaborate conceptual scheme. He operates with a complicated, continually-evolving diachronic world-picture consisting in the representation of a unitary (temporal) manifold of diverse things !being (synchronically) in successive (locational) arena manifolds. While he has, as yet, no use for diachronic reidentifications of things, both forms and contents are synchronic and diachronic repeatables and we could, if we wished, employ the machinery of logic to enable him to make explicit judgments of sameness and difference with respect to them. Finally, the two modes of synthesis to which, as a temporally discursive intelligence, George is necessarily committed (that is, in which he necessarily engages) — synchronic locational and diachronic temporal — are subject to constraints of determinateness which give rise to a "Material Logic of Time" (a "chronologic") and a "Material Logic of Location" (what we might call an "arena-geometry"). And we have equipped George with the appartaus of *formal* logic required to reflect these constraints in representations of explicit "principles of necessitation" or "analytic truths" which are, in the manner I have described, epistemologically privileged. (If we took George's things to be color patches and the locational arena to be the visual field, in fact, it would turn out that George is a familiar character. He would then be a visual *sense-datist* of a reasonably sophisticated sort.) What we must now ask, however, is whether the idealism which we have built into George's conceptual scheme can, in fact, be coherently sustained — that is, whether George ever gets into any *trouble* trying to build the sort of world-picture which we have imputed to him. (What kind of trouble? Some inescapable dimension of arbitrariness or indeterminateness — a region where, representationally, "anything goes".)

The answer is that he does not. Since we have equipped George with the apparatus of first-order logic, of course, he is in a position to represent and express all sorts of *generalizations* about his experiences to date, all sorts of regularities of co-occurrence and succession. And it is possible that some new experience will conflict with one of these generalizations, will be an ostensible counter-example to one of the regularities which George in this way projects. But George has an unassailable fall-back position should this occur. He can always resolve any such potential incoherence in his world-picture by adhering to a Principle of the Dominance of Primary Representations (PriDoPri). Let me explain.

The representation of such a regularity of succession or co-occurrence will make use of a *temporal* quantifier. It will look something like this:

(S) $(t) (a\ \phi K\ !\text{be in}\ p\ \text{at}\ t \rightarrow a\ \psi G\ !\text{be in}\ p'\ \text{at}\ t')$

or like this:

(C) $(t) (a\ \phi K\ !\text{be in}\ p\ \text{at}\ t \equiv a\ \psi G\ !\text{be in}\ p'\ \text{at}\ t).$

(S) would be a regularity of succession; (C), a regularity of co-occurrence. But this use of the apparatus of formal logic is an extended or derivative use from its employment in connection with the "analytic" principles of George's chrono-logic and arena-geometry. While the basic requirement that George's world-story be *determinate* imposes constraints on his representational activity which give rise to a "Material Logic of Time" and a "Material Logic of Location", there is nothing in our account yet which demands an analogous "Material Logic of Contents", Neither (S) nor (C), in other words, will have the epistemological status of an *indefeasible* representing, an "analytic truth". Representings of the forms (S) and (C) will only be *summative*, reflecting a *de facto* regularity of succession or co-occurrence which has *so far* been characteristic of George's experience. Unlike the principles of necessitation of chrono-logic and arena-geometry — e.g., (T^+) and (T^{++}) — they will not, however, be *normative*.

To put the point differently, the only temporal quantifier which George is so far required to employ is the *bounded* quantifier "For any t !preceding now. . . ". Representings of the forms (S) and (C) express *mere* past regularities and not *laws*. And so George is free to abandon them. He can, instead, always assign his *primary* representings (that is, those representings which employ no logical apparatus) an epistemic priority. He can, in other words, treat *them* as indefeasible, and any representations of regularities of succession or co-occurrence will then be abandoned, if necessary, to bring what compound representings remain into a coherent harmony with the totality of such primary representings. This is the Principle of the Dominance of Primary Representings. In the absence of any "Material Logic of Contents", two such primary representings cannot themselves conflict. It will always be possible, then, for George to secure a determinate world-picture by adhering to this principle.[7]

Viewed thus "from the outside", then, a consistent idealist temporally discursive intelligence is a possibility. This completes the first phase of my argument. But is should be noted how thin an "intelligence" this really is. For all we have so far imputed to him, George could almost be a kind of "recording robot" with the constraints of chrono-logic and arena-geometry embodied in the hard-wiring of a continuous "inner clock" and "input grid". George could *almost* be such a robot — but something important has been left out of the picture.

I have twice said that George "thinks in tenses". Our hypothetical George-robot, however, has *time*, but he does not yet have *tense*. The difference is a crucial one, and it cannot be remedied by any simple therapy. An obvious

TIME AND THE SELF

suggestion, for example, is that we equip George-robot's "inner clock" with an "index", having it "print out", not just "$t_1, t_2, t_3, \ldots$" but, successively,

t_1 ! is now
t_2 ! is now
t_3 ! is now
.
.
.

But this will not do. If 'now' is to be a genuine temporal index, the '!is' here must contrast with '!was'. If t_2 !is now, then t_1 no longer !is now. t_1 !*was* now.

The problem is that, while George-robot can locate *things* in time well enough, he cannot locate *himself* in time. But that is what we need for *tense*. A being who genuinely "thinks in tenses" represents his world-history from a (continuously changing) *temporal point-of-view*, and that is just to say that he represents *himself* as in (continuously changing) temporal relations to the things of that world. What we need to add to our sketch of George-robot's conceptual scheme to capture this dimension of a full-fledged consciousness, then, is some form of *self*-consciousness. We need, in other words, to add *apperception*. And that, it turns out, will make a difference. Apperception is the missing "secret ingredient" in the recipe for who *we* are. We are, indeed, temporally discursive intelligences. But that is not *all* we are. We are *apperceptive* discursive intelligences. Kant's key insight is that, once this missing piece of the story has been supplied, it follows that *our* representational system *cannot* be, as was George-robot's, idealist. *Our* representational system must be a (Kantian) Realist Core. The object of the second phase of my argument in this chapter is to secure this dramatic conclusion.

But how are we to add the requisite apperception to George's conceptual scheme? How will it manifest itself in the inner-workings of his representational system? It is obvious that we cannot simply insert George's self as a thing among things. The self which is at issue here is the self-as-subject. It is the elusive Humean self, which is not encountered *as* a self:

For my part, when I enter most intimately into what I call *myself*, I always stumble on some particular perception or other, of heat or cold, light or shade, love or hatred, pain or pleasure. I never can catch *myself* at any time without a perception, and never can observe anything but the perception. (*THN*: I, iv, 6)

The self at issue here is rather more usefully viewed as having the status of a *principle of unity* for such a Humean collection of representings (ideas and impressions). My self is that in virtue of which all my representations are *mine* or, to put it Kantianly, it is that in virtue of which 'I think' can accompany any and all of my representations, severally and collectively.

The natural next suggestion, then, is that we equip George with the explicit form 'I think' as a potential accompaniment of each of *his* representings. But there are a number of good reasons to avoid this course. The form

I think that-*p*

has the look of a relational claim — *xRy*. In particular, the indexical 'I' appears to behave in logic as if it were a proper name (numeral-name). But taking the form at face value precipitates immediate tactical crises. If 'I' here is a genuine substantive, we — and George — are entitled to ask after the corresponding substance. In our present terminology, it will become appropriate to request a form and a content for this I-thing, for the only sort of proper-naming with which George has been equipped is the numeral-naming of things in an environment. But, confronted with the undeniable cogency of Humean non-encounter, we — and George — will lack the requisite field of ϕ's and K's to complete the thing schematism:

I !be a ϕK.

The fallback position, of course, is Descartes' *res cogitans*,

I !be a thinking thing.

But this is only a pseudo-instantiation of the form-content schematism. 'Thing' is not itself a way of bounding contents in an environment but instead adverts to contents *as* bounded in an environment. And 'thinking' is no proper content but, at best, a way of gesturing at the availability of representings *as* contents, that is, of linking the faculty of apperception to the ability to represent representings *as* representings.

If all this sounds terribly familiar, it is only because Kant did it first. What I have just been canvasing is precisely his First Paralogism, of Substantiality:

That, the representation of which is the *absolute subject* of our judgments and cannot therefore be employed as determination of another thing, is *substance*.

I, as a thinking being, am the absolute subject of all my possible judgments, and this representation of myself cannot be employed as predicate of any other thing.

Therefore I, as thinking being (soul), am *substance*. (A348)[8]

The inference which Kant condemns as paralogistic is just the inference against which I have been arguing: From the premiss that of 'I' of 'I think' is necessarily a *substantive* to the conclusion that the I (self) is necessarily a *substance*. Thinking is no more "given" as a mode of activity of a represented substance than it is "given" as a relation between two represented things. Introduced into George's representational system in the manner we have just supposed, the form 'I think' is so far merely an arbitrary accompaniment of representings. It lacks any relevant contrast-class, either pronomial ("He thinks") or temporal ("I thought") and so is no more a representation of a self *qua* active substance than is the 'It' of 'It is raining' the representation of a substantive "rainer".

The moral of Hume's *Gedankenexperiment* and Kant's Paralogisms is that what is represented in apperceptive encounter is not *oneself in relation to one's representings* but merely *one's representings* (*as* representings). The point of Kant's Paralogisms is that the Cartesian form

>I think that-*p*

lacks the putative implications of its surface grammar. Properly understood, 'I' here is a dummy substantive and 'think' a dummy verb. What we should rather say is that 'I think that-' functions here *logically* as a *unit*, to bracket the representing which follows it and thereby represents it *as* a representing. It is, in other words, to put it rather bluntly, nothing more than a form of *quoting* – and this gives us the requisite clue as to how to proceed.

The *minimal* form of apperception with which we can equip George is the ability to represent himself, not as a paralogistic 'I', but as a *Humean continuant*, that is, as a "continuant" in the thin sense of a *temporal sequence* of *N*- and *T*-representings (impressions and ideas, in Hume's terms) represented *as* representings. The least apperceptive competence we must supply George then is some representational apparatus for representing his *past* representings *as* representings which have !occurred. And this, we are delighted to notice, is – as our earlier remarks led us to expect it would be – precisely equivalent to supplying George with *tense* as well as time. For it enforces the missing *contrast* between '!is' and '!was'. It allows the one to fall within the *scope* of the other, by allowing George to represent, so to speak, the !was of an !is. We supply George, in other words, with the ability not only to *T*-represent a past *N*-represent*ed*:

(1) n, a ϕK, !was at p at t

but also to *T*-represent a past *N*-represent*ing*:

(2)   :n, a ϕK, !is at p now: !was at t.

Here the colons bracket what is between them and represent it *as* a representing. *Functionally*, they are quotation marks. They are a way of "mentioning" a representing. But, since George's representings might *structurally* be rather unlike our customary sentences, I have selected a notation which embodies a difference along with its similarities to our customary quoting conventions. (1) schematizes George's remembering (T-representing) a ϕK (of which he was aware at t). (2), however, schematizes George's remembering (T-representing) *being aware of* (N-representing) a ϕK at t. The "target" of (1) is a *thing*, but the "target" of (2) is a *representing* (the N-representing at t of that thing).

As my use of '*at t*' in (2) signals, these apperceived representings are represented by George as !occurring (i.e., as !being) in time − in the same time, indeed, in which things !are. They are not themselves assigned to arena-locations, however. George is sophisticated enough not to suppose that the representing of, say, a green square is itself green and square. Things, not re-presentings of things, are what have shapes. But these apperceived (represented) representings *are* represented by George as !being in an order of before and after − an order which needs to be intercalated with George's determinate diachronic world-picture. (This, by the way, is the substance of the claim that time is the form of both *inner* and outer sense.) The project of a determinate diachronic synthesis thereby takes on an added complexity. Our next task is to determine whether, having supplied George with such a faculty of apperception, we may still conclude that the constraints of determinacy are satisfiable here consistently under the supposition that George is an *idealist* apperceptive consciousness.

The question must be asked anew because something very interesting now happens. The posit of idealism which we have so far imposed on George's conceptual scheme "from the outside" now receives an explicit manifestation "on the inside". To remain *idealist*, George's representational activity must be subjected to a *new constraint*. I have several times characterized idealism as the equating of the being of a thing with its being represented. So far this idealist commitment has been expressed only through our consistent and continued refusal to equip George with realist principles of counting and diachronic reidentification of things. But since George is now able himself to *represent* those representings in which the being of his things idealistically consists *as* representings, he is able to articulate the principle of his own idealism. He must, in other words, build his world-picture in such a way that, to each thing which he represents as !being (in the world) there corresponds (at least potentially) a representing of the *representing* in which the !being of that thing consists. To put this constraint in the form of an "analytic truth", George must endorse

(I^+) $(t)(x)(x$!be at p at $t \equiv :x$!is at p now: !be at t)

as a *non-defeasible* judgment, that is, as a compound representation having the same epistemological status as his (T^+) and (T^{++}). As they were principles of chrono-logic, (I^+) is a principle — in fact, *the* principle — of the "Material Logic of Idealism". And the temporal quantifier here is not summative but normative. It mirrors a constraint on George's representational activity to which he must adhere if he is to remain a thoroughgoing idealist. George, in other words, has just won his first *unbounded* t-quantifier. What we must now see is whether George *can* build a determinate diachronic world-picture while adhering to *all* of the constraints to which he must submit, a diachronic world-picture which is now to include his own apperceived history (his representational autobiography).

Consider the two representings

(3)   A ϕK !was at p at t_1

and

(4)   :A ψK !is at p now: !was at t_1

If none of the constraints on George's representational activity militates against it, we must consider what George is to do in the face of the simultaneous occurrence of (3) and (4) among his representings — that is, we ask what their co-occurrence at some time demands of him in the way of synthesis. Both (3) and (4) interact logically with the principle of George's idealism mirrored in (I^+). (3) and (I^+) together imply

(5)   :A ϕK !is at p now: !was at t_1

while (4) and (I^+) together imply

(6)   A ψK !was at p at t_1

Earlier (in our discussion of aches and twinges and twaches) we asked whether we should or could commit George to a Principle of Non-Overlapping Contents (PriNOC). There we left the issue open, but now, since we have (I^+), we are in a position to say that *if* (3) and (4) can consistently co-occur among George's representings at some time, then we *cannot* have PriNOC as a constraint, for (3) and (6) together precisely ascribe overlapping contents to the K-region p at t_1.

Now it is tempting to say here that we can still have PriNOC as a constraint on George's activity if we wish. For, the argument may continue, if (3) and (4) *do* co-occur among George's representings and he wishes *also* to adhere to PriNOC, he need only invoke the Principle of the Dominance of Primary Representings (PriDoPri), for that principle warrants his disposing of (4) and, hence, of (6). It is absolutely crucial to see that this argument is *not* a sound one.

The point is that PriDoPri is wholly impotent here. *Both* (3) *and* (4) are *primary* representings. An apperceptive representing such as (4) is *complex*, but it is not *compound*. Like (3), (4) simply represents the !being of its "target". The difference between (3) and (4) lies wholly in their respective "targets", not in their mode of composition. The "target" of (3) is a thing; that of (4), a representing. That is the difference. But that is not a difference between a primary representing and a compound representing. It is the difference between *two kinds* of primary representings. What apperception adds is a second kind of *primary* representing. And so PriDoPri is impotent here. Nothing stands in the way of the co-occurrence of (3) and (4) among George's representings, then, and so PriNOC − as a proposed *normative* principle − must go. It is incompatible with the normative constraint of idealism, (I^+). (Of course, George could adopt PriNOC and abandon idealism. But the object of the present exercise is to see how far we can go with our story *without* abandoning idealism.)

Should (3) and (4) co-occur among George's representings, then, he must construct a diachronic synthesis in which *both* a ϕK *and* a ψK are represented as !being simultaneously at p at t_1. What we need to see next is what this move amounts to.

Incorporating (4) into his evolving diachronic world-picture *cum* representational autobiography (or, as I shall put it for brevity: *endorsing* (4)), George attributes to himself at t_1 a representing of the form

(7)   A ψK !is at p now

Endorsing (3) under the constraint of idealism reflected in (the non-defeasibility of) (I^+), George endorses (5) as well, and so attributes to himself at t_1 a representing of the form

(8)   A ϕK !is at p now

But let us now imaginatively relocate George in time at t_1. The arena-location p is a single K-bounded region. The classificatory options then open to George with respect to p at t_1 *apparently* were either to represent p as containing a pair of overlapping contents ϕ and ψ (e.g., twinge and ache)

or

to represent p as containing a single ("mixed") content, say, Ω (e.g., twache).

The important thing to see here — the absolutely crucial observation — is that the choice between these two options is *synchronically indeterminate*. What contents there !are, and how many, cannot be "read off" of a single experience. Contents are not, in that sense, *given*. Rather, *any* representing by George with respect to p at t_1 is a *taking* — and how the experience is to be taken, we now see, depends on diachronic as well as synchronic considerations.

Suppose, for example, that George *in fact* chose at t_1 the second (twache) course. That is, suppose that George's N-representing of the contents of the region p at t_1 was *in fact*

(9)   An ΩK !is at p now

And now let us return to t_2, the time of the co-occurrence of (3) and (4) among George's representings. As nothing stood in the way of that co-occurrence, so nothing now stands in the way of George's apperceptive recall of his actual N-representing at t_1 as well. That is, in addition to (3) and (4), there may *also* occur among George's representings at t_2

(10)   :An ΩK !is at p now: !was at t_1

Like (3) and (4), (10) is also a primary representing, and so PriDoPri again fails to exclude this possibility. The fact of the matter is that primary representings are *almost* entirely independent of one another. There is only one constraint that interrelates them: the Principle of Idealism, (I$^+$). And that is what is going to cause George's trouble.

The attentive reader will have noticed that I have now supplied George with a "conflict of memory". According to (4), he ostensibly remembers having been aware of a ψK at p at t_1, while, according to (10), he also ostensibly remembers having been aware of an ΩK at p at t_1. As I have told the story — although nothing crucial hinges on this fact — the latter ostensible memory is correct, the former incorrect. The attentive reader is essentially correct as well, but there are a number of points which should be made.

First, it is important to stress that such "conflicts of memory" *can occur*

— that is, that they are compatible with all the constraints which I have so far placed on George's representational activities. Nothing, such as PriDoPri, rules them out *ab initio*. Second, however, we should be clear that this "conflict of memory" is not yet a *conflict* — for George. There is nothing *yet* in our story to require him to view (4) and (10) as somehow "incompatible" with each other, although there is about to be. For, third, George *is* committed to the program of attempting to achieve a unitary diachronic synthesis of *all* of his representations, and this he must, in the present instance, do *at* t_2. He cannot "travel back in time to t_1" and "see what really happened". Rather, he must achieve such a synthesis, if he can, at t_2 in the face of the co-occurrence of (3), (4), and (10) among his representations at t_2. What I am about to argue is that he cannot do this *and* remain an idealist.

Endorsing (10) under the constraint of idealism, George must also endorse

(11)　　An ΩK !was at p at t_1

In order to achieve a determinate diachronic synthesis of all his representations at t_2, then, George must construct a determinate world-picture which includes (3), (6), *and* (11). And this, I shall now show, he *cannot* do. By ascribing *all three* contents ϕ, ψ, and Ω to the single K-region p at t_1, he succeeds only in trading an indeterminacy with regard to *how many* contents are present there and then for a indeterminacy with regard to *how much* of each is there and then present. But there is no way in which, while remaining an idealist, he can eliminate indeterminateness or arbitrariness from his world-picture *completely*. The point is easier to see in the context of our pain paradigm, so let me first illustrate it in those terms.

Place George again at t_1 and suppose that what he must choose is how to represent a total of *12 ouches* of pain in his left thumb. Consonant with our supposition (9), what George *in fact* takes his experience to be is given by the *N*-representing

(9p)　　A *12 ouch* twache !is in my thumb now.

Later, at t_2, he recalls this taking. That is, he apperceptively *T*-represents

(10p)　　:A *12 ouch* twache !is in my thumb now: !was at t_1

and, under the constraint of idealism, *concludes*

(11p)　　A *12 ouch* twache !was in my thumb at t_1

Ex hypothesi, however, there also occur among George's *T*-representings at t_2 both

(3p) A twinge !was in my thumb at t_1

and

(4p) :An ache !is in my thumb now: !was at t_1

which, by virtue of the principle of idealism, entails

(6p) An ache !was in my thumb at t_1

Nothing prevents (10p), (3p), and (4p) from simultaneously co-occurring among George's representations at t_2. *That* they thus co-occur is a consistent hypothesis. Such "conflicts of memory" can happen.[9] And if and when this one happens to George, he is faced with the task of producing a determinate diachronic synthesis of his representations which accommodates *all* of (3p), (6p) and (11p). But a *determinate* synthesis is just what he cannot have here. For if he endorses the !being of all three contents — twinge, twache, and ache — at t_1, then he must face the question of intensities. For he could represent his thumb at t_1 as having !contained.

	a 3 ouch twinge and a 3 ouch ache and a 6 ouch twache
or	a 2 ouch twinge and a 2 ouch ache and an 8 ouch twache
or	a 1 ouch twinge and a 1 ouch ache and a 10 ouch twache
or	a 4.6 ouch twinge and a 4.6 ouch ache and a 2.8 ouch twache

and so on *ad infinitium*.

To put this point in its most perspicuous form, if George's system of representations allows for twinges *and* aches *and* twaches, then it will need to contain a distinction between *real* and *apparent* twaches. That is, it will need to contain a distinction among the !being of a twache (alone) in a location, the !being simultaneously of a twinge and an ache (but *no* twache) in that location, and the !being simultaneously of a twinge and an ache and a twache (of appropriate intensities) in that location. *Ex hypothesi*, however, these three possibilities are *synchronically* indistinguishable. To remove the indeterminateness among these three alternatives, then, requires a "Material Logic of Contents". George will need to adopt *normative* constraints on the possibilities of co-occurrence for twinges, aches, and twaches in a given location at a given time, constraints which appeal to something more than merely what he T-represents as having !been at p at t_1 — for that is yet not wholly determinate. And once he does this, he is no longer an idealist!

What holds for twinges, aches, and twaches holds, too, for our earlier ϕ, ψ, and Ω, for, *ex hypothesi*, the !being of a (genuine) ΩK at p at t_1 is *synchronically* indistinguishable from the compresent !being of a ϕK and a ψK of suitable intensities at p at t_1. George's representational system will thus *permit* a distinction between real and apparent Ω-things — and it will therefore permit counterinstances to (I^+)! Once *determinate intensities* are *non-arbitrarily* supplied for the contents represented in (3), (6) and (11), at least one of George's *primary* representings must be excluded from his world-story synthesis at t_2.

What can demand George's excluding one of the primary representings occurring among his representings at a particular time from his world-story at that time are the synchronic constraints arising from the attempt to secure, at that time, a determinate *diachronic* world-picture which includes the apperceptive representings constituting his representational autobiography (or Humean self). An idealist apperceptive, temporally discursive intelligence can satisfy the demands of determinateness then — and, in particular, the requirement that the world (diachronic manifold) be represented as having at any time a determinate synchronic mathematics of how many *and* how much and where (for things and contents) and as containing its elements in a determinate diachronic order of before and after — only by becoming a coherentist *de fond en comble*, exempting not even primary N-representings from retrospective revision in service of a larger synthesis. He must, in other words, abandon PriDoPri, the principle which assigned primary representings the epistemic status of *non-defeasibility*.

But to do this is to abandon idealism as well! To put it paradoxically, a "coherentist idealist" is not an idealist but a realist. For the exclusion of a primary representing from the evolving determinate synthesis (its rejection as "non-veridical") is exactly equivalent to representing its "target" as a mere *appearance*. It is to drive a representational wedge between the !being of that "target" and its !being represented *as* !being. And this puts George squarely into a Realist Core.

That is the point in the terminology of reality and appearance. But the co-implications among the features (R1) through (R8) allow us to make the same point in a variety of different ways. Recall the role of PriDoPri in George's representational activity. It was to afford him an unassailable fallback position in the face of an ostensible incoherence between primary representings and regularities of co-occurrence and succession. If, however, he settles the tensions among (3), (6), and (11) by allowing for real ϕ-contents, real ψ-contents *and* real Ω-contents, then he will need a "Material Logic of Contents" to arrive at a determinate, non-arbitrary arithmetic of *intensity*.

PriDoPri is abandoned — and then he must resolve those ostensible incoherences which emerged *earlier* in the only remaining possible fashion: by assigning at least some regularities of co-occurrence or succession *normative* force, that is, by representing them as necessary. So, once again, George will be operating within a Realist Core.

If, alternatively, he settled the tensions among (3), (6), and (11) by holding that only ϕ-contents and ψ-contents were real, then the inference from (10) to (11) must be rejected and, with it, the *normative* status of (I^+). And George is *still* operating with a Realist Core.

The fact that (R1) through (R8) are co-implicates, in other words, lets us choose *how* George's unitary diachronic synthesis is to fail. He can chase the locus of arbitrariness or indeterminateness in arithmetic about from the *number* of contents to the *intensities* of contents and back again, but to eliminate it entirely, to bring off a wholly *determinate* diachronic world picture at t_2, George must ultimately have recourse to some aspect of a Realist Core.[10] And, as we saw in the last chapter, to operate under *one* of the constraints of such a Core is to operate under *all* of them. An apperceptive temporally discursive intelligence *must* be a realist "from within". He must, that is, structure his evolving world-picture *cum* representational autobiography (representation of a unitary diachronic manifold) according to the constraints of a Realist Core. These necessities are, of course, conditional necessities. They are conditional on the *determinateness* and *non-arbitrariness* of the synthesis achieved. But if we recall the Kantian characterization of "experience" as "an empirical *cognition*", and if we — plausibly — take it to be necessary ("analytic") of anything properly termed a "cognition" — and as thus at least a candidate for endorsement as empirical *knowledge* — that is exclude any element of arbitrariness or indeterminateness, then we might fairly represent our conclusion here in a Kantian formula: Experience is *possible* — for us — only under the Categories, that is, only if our representational activity is subject to the constraints of a Kantian Realist Core. The addendum "for us" is crucial here. For what we have shown is only that for the kinds of beings that *we* are — for apperceptive and temporally discursive intelligences — idealism ("from within") is not a *possible* metaphysics.

There are three corollaries: The first two concern PriDoPri. That abandoning the indefeasibility of primary representings is equivalent to abandoning the ideality of what is represent*ed* in those representings captures what truth there is to the thesis that "incorrigibility is the mark of the mental". If pains are "things", for example, then they are things the *esse* of which is *percipi*, for the existence of a pain consists in its being felt. This ideality will be their "mentality". And if first person, present-tensed pain-*avowals* are correlatively held to be *reports* of the !occurrence (or !being) of pains, then their "incorrigibility" is their indefeasibility. What we now understand is that this "mentality" and this "incorrigibility" are indeed correlatives, that ideality and indefeasibility are as much co-implicates (of, as it were, an Idealist Core) as any pair of elements from our Realist package (R1) through (R8). And that is the first corollary.[11]

A coherentist idealist must be a realist. The abandonment of a throughgoing idealism is a direct consequence of the abandonment of PriDoPri, of the indefeasibility of primary representings. The thesis that even primary (N-) representings are defeasible, however, has another, more familiar formulation within epistemology: There is no *given*. That the *rejection* of an empirical given and the adoption of a *coherentist* epistemology is equivalent to ontological *realism* is the second corollary. And, as any Hegelian (original or neo-) will tell you, it is a shocking bit of news! The exploration of its consequences, however, must be deferred until still more of an epistemological groundwork has been laid.

There is another way of formulating the conclusion of this chapter as well. If we take 'space' to mean, generally, a "form of outer sense", that is, a nontemporal arena in which things are represented as having determinate synchronic location, and if we take "the existence of objects in space outside me" to mean the !being of things in such an arena independently of their !being represented, then what we have shown is that

The mere, but empirically determined, consciousness of my own existence proves the existence of objects in space outside me. (B275)

For it was precisely the addition of an *empirically determined* consciousness of self – that is, of the minimal apperceptive consciousness of self as a Humean continuant by means of representings represented *as* representings – which rendered a continued thoroughgoing idealism ("from within") impossible and a full-fledged realism inescapable. What we had, then, was just Kant's Refutation of Idealism. And that is the third corollary. Since we have two hundred years more of puzzlements and complications to worry about, it took us, alas, a little longer to set it out than it took Kant. But that is the price one pays for progress in philosophy.

CHAPTER IV

CORRECTNESS AND COMMUNITY: FROM THE INDIVIDUAL TO THE SOCIAL

We now have half of our answer to the Cartesian skeptic. What we wanted, recall, were considerations which implied that our representations, our ways of thinking about the world, are not arbitrary but determinate, and, indeed, are so determined as to ensure some connection between our having a particular world-picture and its being a *correct* world-picture. Determinateness we now have. *Our* way of thinking about the world must be the realist's way. *Our* representations must be subject to the constraints of a Realist Core. *We* must represent (at least some) things as existing independently of our encountering them, as having a being which does not consist in their being represented. That is, *we* must be, as I shall put it, Constitutive Realists.

But we still lack any basis for projecting the sought connection between this mode of determinateness and the correctness of our representations. And, as any Cartesian skeptic worth his salt will be prepared to remind us, that is surely the more important part of our project. Indeed, isn't the problem just that all our representations could be radically false? Although we necessarily represent things as existing independently of our representing them, mightn't it be the case that there really aren't any such things? That nothing corresponds to any of our representations?

In fact, this line of thought can be adapted to yield a critique of the entire picture of representations-and-the-world with which both I and the Cartesian skeptic have been operating. According to that picture, speech and thought are systems of representations. The world is what is correlative to such representations. It is what is represented. Now what is represented can be well- or ill-represented; it can be represented more or less adequately. It can, in fact, be represented correctly or incorrectly. If one is a realist, however, the argument continues, it will make sense to contrast what and how the world *is* with what and how the world is said or thought to be. The skeptic's challenge — that the way the world *is* may be radically unlike what and how it is said or thought to be — will thus also always make sense. And this, the argument concludes, constitutes a *reductio* of realism itself. It shows that there can be no *use* for a distinction between what and how the world *is* and what and how it is said or thought to be. And so, the picture of realism, and with it the talk of representations-and-the-world upon which it rests, must be abandoned *in toto*.

The problem, to put it in its shortest form, is that there is no place to stand. We lack a means of *comparing* our putative representations with that which they putatively represent. We cannot hold up our representations alongside the world and thereby assess their adequacy *to* it, their correctness or incorrectness, for *all* our ostensible commerce with that world is mediated by representations. At best, we could compare our representations only with one another. We cannot compare them with the world. And, if this is so, the challenge runs, we cannot compare them in point of adequacy *to* that world. Our basis of comparison must be something else, something *internal* to the systems of representations themselves. But nothing internal to such a system of representations can bear upon its adequacy to something external to it — and the world which realism posits is just such an external something.

Were there *privileged* representations, of course, one could turn to them to seek a touchstone for representational correctness. But realism itself precludes the possibility of privileged representations. In what could such privilege consist? A unique correspondence — a fit or match — between representation and what is represented would convey sufficient privilege, to be sure, but the necessary absence of any standpoint from which such a correspondence could be established is what engendered the search for privileged representations in the first place. If privilege there is to be, then, it must be *epistemic* privilege. But, according to the picture proposed by the realist, it will always make sense to hypothesize that the way the world *is* differs radically from what and how it is represented as being. Since all our ostensible commerce with the world is mediated by representations, this hypothesis will remain available independently of the content and character of any particular representational system. Of *every* system of representations, it will make sense to propose that, perhaps, the world is not *really* at all like *that*. But the continued viability of this hypothesis is sufficient to defeat any claim to epistemic privilege. Any system of representations may be inadequate or incorrect and, hence, every system of representations is a candidate for eventual abandonment. There are no indefeasible representations. But it follows that realism allows for no privileged representations at all, for beyond (ontological) correspondence and (epistemic) indefeasibility, there is nothing in which such privilege could consist.

By now we have assembled enough of the critical picture to begin to have some suspicions. The critic argues that any representational realism has as a consequence the absence of epistemic privilege and, in particular, the lack of any indefeasible representations — and that this result shows realism itself to be untenable. But, in the last chapter, I argued that the thesis that there is no epistemic given, that all representings are defeasible, itself is *equivalent* to Constitutive Realism, and that such Constitutive Realism is an unavoidable feature of any representational system which can be *ours*. It seems, then, that *the very same considerations* which imply that we must be realists also imply that we cannot be. Surely something has gone wrong.

What has gone wrong is that there are *two* "realisms". Constitutive Realism is a thesis about the *contents* of any conceptual scheme or representational system which can be ours. It is the thesis that any such system must answer to the constraints of a Kantian Realist Core. But our current (neo-Hegelian) critic is not arguing against this thesis of Constitutive Realism. His point is that the world — that is, that which is correlative to thought and to speech, to representations — cannot be the *locus of correctness* for our representations. The correctness of our representings cannot *consist* in their correspondence with, in their fit or match with, or — compactly — in their adequacy to that world. That our representations are or are not adequate to the world cannot be the *criterion of correctness* for those representations. Our current critic, in other words, is not making a point about the *contents* of our conceptual scheme. He is making a point about *correctness*. The realism against which he brings his case, then, is not the Constitutive Realism for which I argued in the last chapter, but rather what I shall call Criteriological Realism. Criteriological Realism is the thesis that the correctness of a representing or system of representings consists in its *adequacy to* a world (i.e., to that which it represents).

It is important to be clear that the critical argument does not turn on the notion of representation but rather wholly on that of correctness. Suppose, for example, that we posited for each of us a *direct* and *unmediated* access to the world — an access not impeded by a "screen" of intervening representations. (Let it be, for instance, that we all "grok essences" or whatever.) We may *still* argue that the correctness of our claims and beliefs cannot consist in their adequacy (or correspondence) to this world which now, *ex hypothesi*, we *non*-representationally ("directly") encounter.

Let a claim be set forth for adjudication. Its correctness or incorrectness is to be assessed. Accordingly we, you and I, carry that claim to the world which, to be correct, it must fit. I measure the claim against the world which, we are supposing, I directly encounter, and you do the same. And then we agree — or we do not. But what is the point of our ostensible appeals to the world in this story?

If we agree, then the claim is not in dispute between us. But this is so for *whatever* reason we agree — or believe ourselves to agree. Any talk of the world in this connection is simply idle. The Criteriological Realist would have it said that we agree *because* each of us has discovered the claim to correspond to the world. But this mislocates what you and I have in common. What we share is not the world but the words. I judge the words to fit what I encounter, and you do the same. But our agreement is in judgment, not in encounter. There is no sense to be made of what Criteriological Realism would have us take as a further question: Whether what you encounter in coming to your judgment is or is not the same as what I encounter in coming to mine.

And suppose we disagree. Then, again, any talk of the world must be idle. For, even positing a direct and unmediated non-representational access to the world, our disagreement is one which emerges after our business with the world is finished. The world cannot adjudicate our disagreement concerning the correctness of the claim. We have, each of us, already consulted the world. It is over whether the claim accurately represents what we *ex hypothesi* non-representationally encounter that we ostensibly disagree. That is the ostensible locus of our disagreement, but it cannot be its actual locus. For we have already done all that this newly-supplemented "direct" Criteriological Realism allows us to settle a disagreement thus located — and yet the disagreement remains.

The problem, then, is not one about representations. It is a problem about correctness. Criteriological Realism is through-and-through untenable. The correctness of a judgment or claim, a thought or belief, a representation, an identification or a classification cannot *consist* in its adequacy to (correspondence, match, fit, picturing, mirroring, reflection, or isomorphism with) a world. In what, then, does the correctness of a representing consist? That is the topic of this chapter.[1]

We necessarily think of ourselves as inhabiting a world of enduring things which can appear to us in various ways, but whose existence is independent of their appearing to us in this way or that, or, indeed, of their appearing to us at all. We necessarily think of this world as having a determinate history, and thus of the things within that world as falling within the scope of principles of objective consequence ("causal laws") which represent their modes of appearing and of interaction under the aspects of modality. And, since we also necessarily represent ourselves as having location within this world, some of these "causal laws" represent precisely the modes of appearing of things *to us* as a function of their positions and ours (and, perhaps, many other parameters as well). All this I have argued in the preceding two chapters. What I want to consider now is what we must add to *this* picture in order that we also have a determinate notion of *correctness*.

Since *our* representational system is necessarily thus subject to the constraints of a Kantian Realist Core, I can conduct the argument in this chapter at a less abstract level that what has gone before. I can — and I shall — in fact begin within our *customary* conceptual scheme of material objects in space and time. Some of these things sometimes act on me — reflect light to which my retinas are sensitive, for example — and sometimes, as we ordinarily put it, I recognize them. I judge that what appears before me is, for example, a cat. I identify it *as* a cat. I *call* it a cat. Now such judgments, such recognitions or identifications, may themselves be correct or incorrect. I want to discover in what their correctness consists. To this end, I shall suppose that I am equipped with as much of a representational system as, in the end, we ascribed to George: an "object language" for representing things, their states, and their interactions; and a "metalanguage" for representing my *representings* of such things, states, and interactions. I can, in other words, both judge that something is a cat and judge that I so judge, identify something as a cat and recognize that I so identify it.

What we did *not* supply George was any vocabulary, any representational resources, for *appraising* his own representings. Operating under the constraints of a Realist Core, George, from time to time, was led to include or exclude specific representings from his evolving diachronic world-picture, but he lacked any resources for representing the fact that some representing *was to be* thus included or excluded. He lacked, to put it compactly, any *semantic* vocabulary. He could not *say* or *think* (represent) of one of his own representings that it *was to be* included or excluded in his evolving world-picture, that it was "veridical" or "non-veridical", that it was "correct" or "incorrect".

As George lacked any resources for representing the semantic appraisal of his representings, so I shall suppose, too, that I lack any semantic vocabulary. Ultimately, then, I wish to *add* to my representational scheme a *concept of correctness*, the resources to sort my judgments, recognitions, and identifications into those which are correct and those which are incorrect, and to be able to *represent* the outcome of such a sorting in a family of explicit (meta-)judgments. In other words, in addition to being able to make the judgment

(1)   This *is* a cat

I want to equip myself with the ability to make, as well, the judgment

(2)   This is *correctly called* 'a cat'.

(Or: "My judgment 'This *is* a cat' *is correct*.")

CHAPTER IV

The *minimal* concept of correctness is bipolar. It imposes a dichotomy on the judgments which fall within its scope. To have a concept of correctness, then, is to have a *determinate and non-arbitrary* way of sorting judgments (recognitions, identifications) according to the correct/incorrect dichotomy. As with any concept, what we must avoid here, is a situation in which, representationally, "anything goes". Whether one of my judgments *is* correct or incorrect cannot depend wholly on whether I *judge* it to be correct or incorrect. This meta-judgment too must be subject to determinate, non-arbitrary constraints. One way of putting this point is epistemologically. The epistemology of my new vocabulary of semantic appraisal, of 'correct' and 'incorrect', must be an epistemology of *discovery*, not of decision. But there is another, purely representational, way of putting the same point: The terminology of semantic appraisal admits of reflexive application. Judgments of correctness or incorrectness are *themselves* correct or incorrect. To add a *determinate* "semantic meta-language" to a representational system is thus to add a "meta-meta-language", and a "meta-meta-meta-language" and so onward through the open-ended heirarchy of reflexive applications of the machinery of semantic appraisal as well.

I will need to add my new representational machinery, my vocabulary of semantic appraisal, then, in such a way that there are determinate, non-arbitrary constraints on my using of it in application to both object-language judgments (that is, representings of things – recognitions or identifications) and meta-language judgments (that is, representings of object-level representings as themselves correct or incorrect). There must, to frame the point a little differently, be determinate, non-arbitrary *conditions of correctness*, conditions which will constrain my usings of the new term 'correct' and 'incorrect'. Criteriological Realism is a thesis about the locus of such conditions. It is the thesis that such conditions are to be found *in* the world or in the relations of my judgments (recognitions, identifications) *to* the world. I want to begin with a re-examination of this thesis of Criteriological Realism. I want to argue, carefully and in detail, that such conditions of correctness *cannot* lie in the world or in the relations of my judgments to the world (which I represent). This will be the first step of my larger project of discovering in what the semantic correctness of my judgments *does* consist, discovering, that is, the *actual* locus of semantic correctness. First, then, Criteriological Realism. Does semantic correctness lie *in* the world?

The world does not come labeled. It couldn't. What I *took* to be a label would be, at best, only another among a thing's encountered characteristics. I know cats, for example, when I see them. I know them by their pointy ears, their whiskers, their slitted pupils. Were they to come *ostensibly* labeled, I might know them, too, by their ostensible labels – by the design 'CAT' emblazoned, let us suppose, on their furry flanks. It would be another characteristic feature of cats, a regularity of their markings, as blackness is a regularity of corvine plumage. What it wouldn't be is a label.

The point is that labels are semantic beings. Things can be labeled – or they can be *mis*-labeled. They can be labeled correctly or incorrectly. Cats might come ostensibly labeled. But could they come *mis*-labeled? Would an otherwise feline beast emblazoned with 'DOG' be a mislabeled cat, or would it be an abberant dog? And what of an otherwise canine beast emblazoned with 'CAT'? The correctness or incorrectness of a label is not a feature of the label as an ostensible label *could* be a feature of the thing ostensibly labeled. Such ostensible labels, then, are not *labels*. Correctness does not await discovery in the world like pointy ears and whiskers. Correctness must be located somewhere else.

Can the correctness of my judgment then consist in its *relation to* the world? This, surely, is the classical form which a Criteriological Realism takes. Confronted with something, I say – or think, but let us, for the time being, suppose that I do all my thinking, judging, and identifying "out loud" – what it is. "This is a cat", I say. What I say is correct or it is incorrect. It is correct if what confronts me *is* a cat; incorrect if what confronts me *is not* a cat. And the thing surely either is or is not a cat. There is no third possibility (the "Law of Excluded Middle"). That, in a nutshell, is both the thesis and the intuitive appeal of classical Criteriological Realism.

I want to argue that this line of reasoning is a mistake. In particular, I want to argue that it mistakes something to be a relation between words and the world which is, in actuality, a relation between words and words, a relation between representations. Let me begin with an analogy.

Confronted with something, I say "This is a kloop". Is what I say correct or incorrect? Criteriological Realism would perhaps have it so. What I say is correct if what confronts me *is* a kloop; incorrect if it *is not* a kloop. And the thing surely either is or is not a kloop. There is no third possibility.

But the world does not come divided into kloops and not-kloops. It does not – it could not – come labeled. What we know so far is *only* this: Confronted with something, I say "This is a kloop". That is all the story we have here, for it is all the story which I have so far told. But it is consistent with this much of a story that my utterance "This is a kloop" not be the making of a *judgment* or an *identification* at all. It is consistent with this much of a story that my utterance be a mere ejaculation, something strictly analogous to a shriek or a sigh or a sob, a response which is *wrung* from me like a cry of pain or anguish. We do not yet have sufficient information to conclude that my utterance "This is a kloop" is the making of a judgment at all, or, equivalently, that the *noise* 'a kloop' is a *term* and my uttering that noise the *using* of a term, the *applying* of a term *to* a thing.

Terms (labels, names, common nouns) are semantic beings. They can be applied — or *mis*-applied; used — or *mis*-used. They can be used or applied correctly or incorrectly. They, too, fall within the scope of a concept of correctness. Indeed, the two conditions are equivalent. For a noise to *be* a term, for the uttering of a sentence to *be* the making (expressing) of a judgment, is just for there to *be* conditions of correctness for its use or utterance. It is this equivalence which the Criteriological Realist mistakes for a relation between words and the world.

> My utterance "This is a kloop" is correct
> if and only if
> what confronts me *is* a kloop.

That is the Criteriological Realist's formula. The biconditional is indisputable. But it does not represent a relation between words and the world. It represents the *agreement* of two conditions of correctness, if there *be* such conditions.

Wittgenstein is making precisely this point in §350–1 of his *Philosophical Investigations*. Given that it is five o'clock here now, it will be five o'clock on the surface of the sun if and only if it's the same time on the surface of the sun as it is here now. Two judgments, in other words, will be correct or incorrect together:

(3)   It's five o'clock here and now and *five o'clock* on the surface of the sun, and

(4)   It's five o'clock here now and *the same time* on the surface of the sun.

More generally, one may correctly judge that it is t at place P_1 and t at place P_2 if and only if one may correctly judge that it is the same time at places P_1 and P_2, *viz* t. That is how time-indicators and the phrase 'the same time' fit together. (3) and (4) necessarily *agree* in their conditions of correctness, in their "truth conditions". That is what the biconditional tells us. But that does not tell us in what the correctness of either judgment *consists*. The agreement in correctness or incorrectness of the judgments (3) and (4) provides no information about the conditions of correctness (if any) for the second conjunct of each judgment. Indeed, it does not even provide the information that there *are* such conditions of correctness. All it tells us is that those conditions, if there *be* such conditions, track together.

The Criteriological Realist's biconditional

> My utterance "This is a kloop" is correct if and only if what confronts me *is* a kloop

is exactly analogous to the biconditional linking (3) and (4). What it tells us is that the two "judgments"

(5)   My utterance "This is a kloop" is correct

and

(6)   What confronts me *is* a kloop

are correct or incorrect, *if* at all, together. They have the same conditions of correctness, if there *be* such conditions of correctness. But it does not tell us in what such conditions of correctness consist and, indeed, it does not tell us whether there *are* conditions of correctness for either "judgment". Two things, however, complicate this case. The first is the fact that one of our "judgments", (5), is at the meta-level and the other (6), at the object-level. The second is the fact that there *being* conditions of correctness for *either* "judgment" is equivalent to (5) and (6) *being* (authentic) *judgments* at all, that is, equivalent to 'kloop' being a term rather than a mere noise. The two complications have compensatory advantages and disadvantages. The disadvantage of the first complication — that the "judgments" are respectively on meta- and object-levels — is that it seduces us into the belief that what the Criteriological Realist's biconditional addresses is a relation between words and the world. The advantage of the second — since there are *in fact* no conditions of correctness for "identifying" things as kloops or not-kloops — is that it reminds us that, *at best*, the biconditional reports the parallelism of two sets of such word-world relations ("at best", that is, if Criteriological Realism is right *at all*) but in itself secures neither set. It reminds us, in other words, that we must first locate semantic correctness elsewhere if we are to have (authentic) judgments here at all.

In (1) and (2), we have the disadvantages, but not the compensatory advantage.

(1)   This *is* a cat

and

CHAPTER IV

(2)   This is *correctly called* 'a cat'

are on different levels of language. But the Criteriological Realist's biconditional:

> What confronts me is correctly called 'a cat' if and only if what confronts me *is* a cat

does not, on that account, tell us in what the correctness of (2) consists. It tells us only that the *two* judgments (1) and (2) are correct or incorrect together. More generally, one may correctly judge that something *is* an X (at the "object-level") if and only if one may correctly judge (at the "meta-level") that it is *correctly called* 'an X'. That is how the object-level copula 'is' fits together with the meta-level phrase 'is correctly called'. But this agreement in correctness of the judgments (1) and (2) does not tell us in what the conditions of correctness for either judgments consist. It tells us only that such conditions, if there *be* such conditions, are necessarily the same. But that is not a relation between words and the world. Seduced by a difference in level, the Criteriological Realist has mistaken for such a relation what is, in actuality, a relation between words and words, a relation between representations.

There *are* conditions of correctness for my utterance "This is a cat". My uttering "This is a cat" *is* the making of a (genuine) judgment. That is how this case differs from the case of "This is a kloop". But that is not a difference which secures Criteriological Realism. For the *synchronic relations* between my utterings of "This is a cat" and "This is a kloop" and the world are, in fact, the same. In each case I encounter something – I am confronted with something – which acts on me. And, in each case, in (causal) consequence of this interaction, I utter what I utter. The utterance causally eventuates from the action of the thing on me. That is all the story of *synchronic relations* which there is to be told here. But my uttering "This is a cat" is the making of a judgment which can be correct or incorrect and my uttering "This is a kloop" is not – and so the correctness or incorrectness of my judgment "This is a cat" *cannot* consist in the synchronic relations between my utterance and the world.

The Criteriological Realist is not yet, however, without further resources. The correctness or incorrectness of my judgments (representations) lies neither in the world nor in the synchronic relations of my representings to the world which I represent. That is what I have so far established. But the Criteriological Realist has another proposal. If not synchronic relations then perhaps *diachronic* relations. The correctness or incorrectness of my individual representings, he now suggests, consists in their being instances of a certain *practice*, a practice by which certain of my representings come to be *regularly correlated* with things of a given kind. Our error was to look at a single utterance in its relation to the world in isolation. What we need to do is to see it as an instance of a pattern, as a member of a *family* of utterances which become the making of correct or incorrect judgments by virtue of their *collective* (diachronic) relation to the world. Our next task, therefore, is to assess the adequacy of this variant of Criteriological Realism.

If the Criteriological Realist is right, then, although the world does not *come* divided into kloops and not-kloops, there is nothing to prevent me from *dividing* the world into kloops and not-kloops. I should, in other words, by means of my conduct with respect to *various* utterings of "This is a kloop", be able to introduce a *term* 'kloop' which will then admit of correct and incorrect usings or applications. The way to test this suggestion is to let me try.

I begin, one might think, in an enviable position. I cannot make a mistake. I cannot incorrectly classify a kloop as a not-kloop nor incorrectly classify a not-kloop as a kloop. Until I've finished introducing the *term* 'kloop', nothing is *either* a kloop *or* a not-kloop. So I can't misclassify things or mis-divide the world. I can't do it wrong. But, alas, I can't do it right either. I can't incorrectly classify something as a kloop − but I also can't correctly classify something as a kloop. Nothing either is or is not a kloop *yet*. So all I can do is *decide*, from time to time, to call something a kloop. Suppose, then, that I do this.

In fact, suppose that I go public with my decisions. I propose to *label* all the kloops. I paint 'KLOOP' on them. Does 'kloop' thereby become a term which admits of correct and incorrect use or application? Have I thereby succeeded in introducing a new term?

Well, what exactly has happened? I have wandered through the world. From time to time, confronted with something, I have said "This is a kloop". And then I painted it. Now this might be an odd and provocative behavioral syndrome, but, so far, it does not seem to have anything to do with semantic correctness. So far, it is simply an enigmatic ritual or ceremony. But it is a ritual or ceremony in service of nothing.

For there is nothing that anyone can do with the outcomes of this behavioral syndrome. For compactness, let me say that I have gone around the world *trinting* things. To *trint* something is to say "This is a kloop" upon being confronted with it, and then to paint the design 'KLOOP' on it. Now I have already argued that nothing which *I* do here can be correct or incorrect. I can't trint correctly, nor can I trint incorrectly. But I do leave behind me dichotomy. When I die, there will be two new classes of things in the world: the things which I have trinted and the things which I have not trinted. And perhaps that is enough to allow someone else to use or apply a *term* 'kloop' correctly or incorrectly. Perhaps in this way my diachronic conduct can introduce a term.

Alas, this detritus of a bizarre life has, by itself, no more implications regarding correctness than does any of the indefinitely-many other dichotomies which my life may have engendered: the things I tripped over and the things I did not; the books I read and those I did not; the chairs I sat in, the pussycats I petted, the people I met, the eggshells I discarded, . . . and those I did not.

Of course, someone familiar with my peculiar behavior may indeed inquire of a thing whether it is among those things which I have trinted, as someone may inquire of a pussycat whether it is among those which I petted. And *that* question will presumably have a correct answer. Either I trinted the thing or I did not. But this fact does not imply that 'kloop' is a term. It does not imply that the question "Is it a kloop?" has a correct answer.

Now the expression "This thing is a kloop" *could* be introduced by *someone else* to serve as an abbreviation for "Rosenberg trinted this thing". It would be a natural sort of abbreviation for her to employ, given that the things which I trinted all bear the design 'KLOOP' painted on them. But the design 'KLOOP' which I painted and the vocable 'kloop' which I uttered were not usings of *this* term 'kloop'. *This* term 'kloop' was introduced by someone else, but what was wanted was that *I*, by my diachronic conduct, introduce a term 'kloop' – and this we have not yet achieved.

The question "Is it a kloop" asked by my successors will be strictly analogous to our present question "Is it a Rembrandt?" In his lifetime, Rembrandt executed many paintings, each with a characteristic style, pigmentation, and brushwork. Our question "Is it a Rembrandt?" asks of a painting whether it is among those painted by him. And this question will have, in each instance, a correct answer. 'A Rembrandt', then, is a term which *we* may use correctly or incorrectly to classify works of art. It abbreviates 'painted by Rembrandt'. But it is not a term which Rembrandt, by his conduct, introduced. He did not introduce terms at all; he painted canvases. The canvases which he painted bear the characteristic marks of their origins – style and brushwork and pigmentation. But these characteristic marks are not terms of our, or any other, language. They are neither correct nor incorrect. And a person who now undertakes to mimic Rembrandt's activities, to execute a painting with the same style and brushwork and pigmentation, is not making a mistake but producing a copy — an imitation or a forgery.

On the envisioned scenario, the *term* 'a kloop' introduced by someone else is like 'a Rembrandt'. It is a term which she may use correctly or incorrectly to classify things. It abbreviates 'trinted by Rosenberg'. But it is not a term which I, by my conduct, introduced. I did not introduce terms at all; I trinted things. The things which I trinted bear the characteristic mark of my actions — the design 'KLOOP' painted upon them. But that characteristic mark is not a term of our, or any other, language. *It* is neither correct nor incorrect. Its resemblance to the *term* 'kloop' from time to time inscribed by my successors is purely epiphenomenal. A person who now undertakes to do what I did — to trint something — is neither making a mistake nor using a term correctly. She, too, is producing a copy — an imitation or a forgery.

But we have still not heard the last from our Criteriological Realist. He now objects that I have not fairly set out his diachronic case here. What I have said is true enough, he admits, if I go about the world trinting *capriciously*. That is not the way for me to introduce a new term. But I can nevertheless, by my conduct, introduce such a term. All that is necessary is that I trint *consistently*. I must initially decide what kind of thing I am going to call a kloop and then hold firmly to that resolve, applying the appellation 'kloop' only to things of the *same* kind. If I do this, he continues, then 'kloop' will be a genuine term which is correctly applicable to *more* than the things which I actually encounter and trint. If my practice is not capricious but consistent, then there will also be things which I did not encounter but which I *would have trinted* had I but encountered them. My trinting practice thus brings my usings of 'kloop' into a *regular correlation* with things of a given kind in the world — and that is the sort of diachronic relationship in which the correctness of a representing consists.

Now this line of reasoning will secure the Criteriological Realist's conclusion only if there *is* a distinction between my trinting capriciously and my trinting consistently. More precisely, it is necessary that *I* have such a distinction. Some outside observers of my trinting behavior may judge my practice to be consistent or capricious, but, so far, any such judgment is completely irrelevant. 'Kloop' is to be a term which I, by my conduct, introduce. If you, then, judge my trinting to be wholly capricious, I can always protest that you do not yet properly understand my new term 'kloop'. If you did, why then you would see quite clearly that I consistently apply it always and only to the same kind of thing. And if I do register this protest, there is nothing to which you can appeal to correct me. It does not avail you to ask "What kind of thing?" My answer, of course, is "To kloops". If we already had a term for that kind of thing, there would be no need for me to introduce one. The point is that we are looking for an answer to the question "In what does the correctness of a representing consist?". Now, if I could give a *descriptive equivalent* to the expression "That is a kloop" what I would have told you is that the conditions of correctness for my judgment "This is a kloop" are the same as the conditions of correctness for its descriptive equivalent. While that is sometimes the case, such information does not tell us in what the conditions of correctness for any judgment consist. It is merely another of those biconditionals which earlier proved impotent to elucidate the concept of correctness. What we are looking for then is an *original* correctness, a correctness which — according to the Criteriological Realist — is to consist in the diachronic relations between my trinting conduct and the world. But by supplying a descriptive equivalent, I refer you, not to the world, but from representing to representing. And then we should need to look at the diachronic relations between my usings of the putative descriptive equivalent and the world.[2]

By allowing you to arbitrate between the consistency and capriciousness of my trinting practice, I make 'kloop' a term whose correctness or incorrectness depends not on my practices but on yours — on your judgments of consistency or capriciousness. But that is not what we are trying to achieve. If Criteriological Realism, in its current (diachronic) variant, is to be secured, then, the distinction between my trinting consistently and my trinting capriciously must be one which *I* can make, one with respect to which *I* have final authority.

But can I have a determinate, non-arbitrary distinction between my trinting capriciously and my trinting consistently? My practice is this: From time to time, upon encountering something, I say "This is a kloop" and then paint 'KLOOP' on it. With *what* is this practice to be consistent? I would like to say that it is consistent with the world — but that, alas, is something which I will say *whatever* my practice is. All the things which I trint have this in common, of course: that, upon being confronted with them, I trint. And so I say of them that they all have something else in common: they are all kloops. But what does this amount to? Suppose I change my mind about one of them. Does this imply that I originally *mis*-classified it as a kloop? It could imply this, but only if my new *re*-classification of it as a not-kloop is *itself* correct. Unfortunately, what I cannot do is distinguish between mistakenly trinting and then correctly changing my mind on the one hand and correctly trinting and then mistakenly changing my mind on the other. For what could I do beyond taking yet another look at the thing? This might, indeed give me a verdict — but it would only be my *latest* verdict. It would not, on that account alone, be a *correct* verdict. I can, after all, make the same mistake twice. I could ask you what you thought, of course, but I have already argued that your opinions about my trinting practice are completely beside the point. In order to know whether to accept *your* verdict, I would need to know whether you understood how to trint correctly. But I couldn't know that unless I could already distinguish correct from mistaken trinting — and that is exactly the distinction I'm trying to equip myself with. I cannot do that by consulting you, because whatever you said would be something which I couldn't use unless I already had the distinction.

My sequence of trintings cannot be consistent or inconsistent with the world, in brief, simply because any sequence of trintings which I produced would bear the *same* relation to the world as any other. My relationship with the world lacks the requisite bipolarity to fund a distinction between consistent and capricious trinting practices. *Any* sequence of trintings (and mind-changings) is a sequence of responses evoked in me by the action of the world on me, so any such sequence bears the same relation to that world as any other. The world is not an object of comparison for me. I cannot measure my trinting practice against it for consistency. I can always take another look at it, of course, but, as I have just argued, that yields only another instance of the practice. It does not resolve the question of whether earlier instances of the practice were or were not consistent with the world, for I cannot even tell whether this new instance of my practice is or is not consistent with the earlier instances.

Here, of course, the Criteriological Realist will object. You are forgetting *memory*, he says. The way to discover whether your later trintings are consistent extensions of your practice (that is, are consistent with the world) is by determining whether that are consistent with your *initial decision or resolve*. And that, surely, is something which you *can* determine. But is it?

Suppose that, confronted with something, I suspect that it may be a kloop — that is, I find myself with a tentative inclination to trint. So I recall my initial resolve. I remember what I decided to call a kloop, and I ask myself whether this thing which I have just now encountered is in fact the same kind of thing.

Now there are indeed two ways in which this experiment can turn out. I may judge that what I encounter *is* the same kind of thing as what I remember, in which case I succumb to my inclination. I trint it. Or I may judge that what I encounter is *not* the same kind of thing as what I remember, in which case it goes without trinting. But both of these outcomes guarantee the continued consistency of my practice only if we suppose *both* that I have not *mis*-remembered that "original kloop" *and* that my present judgment of semaness-of-kind is itself correct.

For, *a priori*, there are four possibilities here:

(a) I correctly remember the original item and correctly judge this new item to be of the same or of a different kind;

(b) I correctly remember the original item but mistakenly judge this new item to be of the same or of a different kind;

(c) I mis-remember the original item but correctly judge this new item to be of the same or of a different kind as that which I ostensibly remember;

and

(d) I mis-remember the original item and mistakenly judge this new item to be of the same or of a different kind as that which I ostensibly remember.

I may judge, in other words, that my present ostensible memory and my current impressions cohere, or I may judge that they conflict. In the former case, I trint; in the latter, I do not. But even supposing that my *judgment* in such a case cannot be incorrect — thereby disposing of cases (b) and (d) — I still cannot fund a distinction between a practice which *is* consistent with my initial resolve and one which merely *seems to me to be* consistent with that resolve. For the most that this experiment in recall can tell me is whether my current impression is or is not consistent with my *present* ostensible memory. It cannot tell me whether that ostensible memory is itself correct, however, and so it cannot tell whether my present inclination to trint is or is not consistent with my *past* practice or initial resolve.

By restricting my actual trintings to those occasions on which my current impression coheres with my ostensible memory, I again lose the bipolarity needed to distinguish consistent from capricious trinting practices. Any actual trinting will bear the *same* relation to my compresent ostensible memory as any other, and so any sequence of trintings will bear the same relation to the decision or resolve which initiates it as any other. It will be a sequence of trintings each of which is consistent with the contemporaneous ostensible memory of that decision or resolve. The only locus of consistency, however, is in this repeated *synchronic* consistency of impression and ostensible memory, and this does not yield a *diachronic* distinction between consistent and capricious *practices*. All of my trintings will, necessarily, *seem* to me equally consistent with my past practice whenever I raise the question of such consistency.

The upshot of these reflections is that a determinate, non-arbitrary distinction between a consistent and a capricious practice is one which I, operating alone, cannot have. I cannot fund the notion of correctness by appeal to an individual consistency of this sort because consistency of this sort in fact *presupposes* correctness. Consulting the world gives me a latest verdict, but it cannot guarantee the consistency of my practice unless it yields a correct verdict — and so correctness is presupposed. And consulting memory can yield a synchronic consistency between two representings — current impression and ostensible memory — but this, too, does not guarantee a diachronic consistency — the consistency of a practice, consistency with my actual initial resolve — unless my ostensible memory is itself correct. And so correctness is again presupposed. The Criteriological Realist's very notion of the diachronic consistency of my trinting practice thus necessarily presupposes the notion of the correctness of an individual representing — and so it cannot be used to elucidate that notion. Diachronic consistency cannot be in what the correctness of a representing consists. And so, at last, we must bid farewell — finally and forever — to Criteriological Realism.

For I began by positing a world and allowing myself full access to it. (That is, I can address myself to the world — allow it to act on me — and then examine the representations with which, in consequence, I *find* myself. For the world does not, and could not, come labeled.) But this posited world turns out to be *irrelevant* to the question of semantic correctness. It is not an object of comparison and, therefore, it can serve no adjudicatory function. It imposes no bipolarity on my conduct. Like the beetle in Wittgenstein's box (*PI*: §293), it cancels out. We can "divide through by it".

Limited to my own resources, I can only *decide* that any given thought or utterance is a consistent extension of my earlier practice. But the epistemology of correctness is an epistemology of discovery, not decision. It must be possible for it to *turn out* that my current conduct is or is not consistent with my past practices. But the only discovery permitted me by my own resources is the synchronic consistency or inconsistency of my contemporaneous impression and ostensible memory. If they cohere, I proceed without dissonance; if they conflict, however, I must legislate in favor of one or the other. But any legislation here is wholly arbitrary. In either case, insofar as the question of *diachronic* consistency is concerned, "Whatever is going to seem right to me is right" (*PI*: §258). Once again we have lost the determinate and non-arbitrary bipolarity requisite for a concept of semantic correctness.

These Wittgensteinian echoes are not accidental. The setting in which I ventured to search for semantic correctness is precisely that of Wittgenstein's "Diarist" (*PI*: §258). Like the Diarist, I undertook to go it alone. And the outcome of the two experiments is also the same. Neither I nor the Diarist could successfully introduce a *term*, a name or a label that stands for or represents a kind of thing.

So what I have just offered you is the "Private Language Argument" — but with a difference. Contrary to the usual interpretations of that argument, it has nothing to do with private *objects*. It has to do with correctness. My posited world is as public as one could wish. I have allowed you as much and as good access to its objects as I have allowed myself. And I have allowed you to form, and even to express, any number of judgments concerning the consistency and appropriateness of my utterances. What I have *not* allowed, however, is that your judgments *bear* on questions of correctness. Correctness, not the world, is what I have try to reserve to myself. But having so reserved it, I lost it — for I cannot fund a distinction between correct and incorrect judgments wholly from my own resources. It follows that *the locus of semantic correctness must be found in the community*. This is the sense in which a language cannot be private. The using of a language is, at least, a system of conducts which admit of correctness and incorrectness — and correctness is a *public* matter.

If the objects of a putative discourse are private — a family of "inner states," for example — it will of course also follow that there must be epistemic access to them which is public if they are to be spoken of (or thought of) at all, correctly or incorrectly. They will, in other words, stand in need of "outer criteria". But that is not the theorem; it is a corollary. For what the argument shows is that thoughts or utterances can only *be* correct or incorrect if there exist public "criteria of correctness", quite independently of what sort of thing ("inner" or "outer") the thoughts or utterances are ostensibly "about".

In what, then, does the correctness or incorrectness of a thought or an utterance (of a representing) consist? What is the locus of semantic correctness? A representing is produced by an individual at a time. What is correct or incorrect is, so to speak, punctiform. The (meta-) judgment of its correctness or incorrectness is a synchronic ascription of a semantic status to a dateable occurrence. *That* a given representing is correct or incorrect, we should recall, is supposed to be a fact. (The meta-judgment is itself correct or incorrect.) Its epistemology is to be the epistemology of a discovery, not a decision. But what fact could it be? What is left here to discover? It is not the fact that the representing stands in a particular relation to the world. We have seen that each of an individual's representings stands in the same *causal* relation to the world, and that such further putative relations as "correspondence" or "matching" or "mirroring" or "fitting" or "isomorphism" all presuppose the concept of correctness. Nor is it the fact that the representing is a consistent or inconsistent extension of the individual's diachronic practice. The only consistency available to the individual here is the synchronic consistency of present impression and simultaneous ostensible memory, but this becomes the sought diachronic (semantic) consistency only if impression and ostensible memory are themselves correct. The only place which remains to seek the *fact* of correctness, then, is in the one place we have not been allowed to look — in the community. The correctness of an individual's representing can only consist in this: *that others agree*.

More precisely, we must say that correctness consists in the fact that others *would* agree. They would agree synchronically because they *do* agree diachronically. They agree in their practices. One individual's practice cannot sensibly be supposed to be found consistent or inconsistent either with itself or with the world (in the absence of an independent, antecedent fact of correctness). But it can be sensibly supposed to be found consistent or inconsistent with the practices of others. The mutual consilience of individual practices among members of a community can be a fact and its epistemology can be the epistemology of a discovery. Each of us can (individually) discover that we (collectively) agree in some practice. It is facts of this sort that semantic correctness consists.

There is a reasonably tidy analogy between the notions of the correctness of an individual representing and the mathematical concept of the direction of a line, when the latter notion is given a Fregean parsing. For Frege, the concept of *direction* rests on the relation of *parallelism*. To say that a line has a particular direction (e.g., is horizontal), on Frege's account, is to say that it belongs to a specific family of mutually parallel lines. An individual singular ascription of direction amounts to positing a line as a member of an equivalence class of lines generated by the *relation* of mutual parallelism. Similarly, to say that an individual's use of a word is correct is to say that this synchronic using of the word is a manifestation of a diachronic practice which belongs to a family of mutually consistent (consilient) diachronic practices. It is to subsume the synchronic representing under a diachronic practice which, in turn, is posited as an element of an equivalence class of representing practices (e.g., trinting practices) generated by the *relation* of consilience. Where the analogy breaks down, of course, is that through any given spatial point, lines of *all* directions may be drawn, and the selection of a particular family of parallel lines is dictated by factors extrinsic to the analogy. It is the mutually consistent diachronic practices of members of the community themselves, however, which single out *the* "direction" through an individual representing event which constitutes its being a manifestation of the representer's mastery of the correct use of a specific term.

The diachronic notion of mastery of a practice is thus prior to the synchronic notion of correctness. To judge of a single representing that it is correct or incorrect is to assign it a location in a two-dimensional conceptual space, one axis of which is time and the other community. It is to judge the representing *as being* the manifestation at a given time of such a persisting diachronic mastery.

The concept of correctness, therefore, is properly addressed precisely where Wittgenstein addresses it — at the point of "knowing how to go on". His examples of a mathematical novice, trained to agreement with our common practice in developing the number series '+2' (= 2, 4, 6, 8, ...) through 1000 who then unexpectedly continues by producing '1004', '1008', '1012', ... and so on, throws the point into sharp relief. (*PI*: §185–90) The novice's protestation "But I *am* going on in the same way" can be defeated only by recourse to our shared mathematical practices, for the concept of "the same way", like that of correctness, derives its whole content from the fact of communal agreement. Nothing is served by recapitulating the novice's previous training — it is what has brought him to this point — and there is no sense to be made of the suggestion that we direct his attention to "the numbers themselves" (i.e., to the world). His going on *in the same way* is nothing more than his going on *as we do*. He goes on in the same way if and only if he goes on *correctly*, however, and so there is also nothing for this correctness to consist in beyond the consilience of his practice with ours.

Every synchronic ascription of semantic correctness, then, embodies, so to speak, a double hypothesis. It hypothesizes a synchronic agreement within the community, and it projects this hypothetical present agreement across time. Like any hypothesis, however, these hypotheses are defeasible. Correctness itself may be ascribed incorrectly. The presumed consilience of practices may not obtain. Thus there is scope, too, for a person *inadvertently* to use a term correctly only once, as a drunk at the chessboard may, inadvertently and only once, produce a brilliant move. And, as with the mathematical novice in Wittgenstein's example, the representing practice of any individual could at any time suddenly diverge wildly from those of the balance of the community. In such a case, we must say of him what we say of the mathematical novice: what he said and did up to that time was correct, but only, it has turned out, *per accidens*. He didn't *understand* the correct use of the term, however, (he didn't understand how to count by twos) – he didn't *know how* to use it correctly.

It is important to note, however, that the community as a *whole* stands collectively to the correctness of its representations as did the individual in semantic isolation. The world is still not an object of comparison here. There is no way that a community can measure *its* collective practices against the world. There is no fact of the matter here beyond the attainable consilience of individual practices within the community. There is no way to confront the world with the putative question of a correspondence between it and our collective practices. This ostensible question could only arise when our business with the world was finished. Turning to the world here could, again, yield only a latest verdict – fresh instances of our practices, a new agreement or disagreement among us. But the world is impotent to serve as an *arbiter* of any such disagreement. The locus of correctness, then, remains within the community itself. The notion of the world as something external to our collective representing practices against which those practices may be measured turns out to be vacuous and idle. We can divide through by it, and it cancels out.

What I will need to add to my conceptual scheme in order to *have* a concept of correctness, then, is the ability to represent myself as a member of a community of representers and to represent my representings as in agreement or disagreement with the collective practices of that community. I will need, in other words, a *non-vacuous* 'I' – an 'I think' which contrasts not only with 'I thought' but with 'He thinks' and 'She thinks' and 'They think' as well. I will need, in fact, tó add the resources to represent *my* practice as an instance of *our* practice.

The effect of these additions epistemologically, of course, can only be to add another layer to the cake of coherence. The conditions of defeasibility for any of my representings must remain through and through coherentist. But my world-picture will now expand to include representings of other representers and their representings, all of us co-inhabitants of a single world of things in relation and interaction, and my selection of individual representings to include in or exclude from this evolving world-picture will be governed now not only by my need to find a place for my own representational autobiography within that world-picture but also by my need to find a place for the representational biographies of others, as they are represented by me as standing in relations of agreement or disagreement (consilience or conflict) with my own. The second half of my Realist dichotomy of being and seeming thus will split again, now into seeming *to me* and seeming *to him* (her, them), and the states and positions of other perceivers will come to join my own state and position among the explanatory appeals available to me to account for divergences in our perceptions and judgments.

What the addition of a concept of correctness will recover, then, is our *full* customary conceptual scheme, a non-solipsistic scheme in which my own representings are defeasible in light of the representings of others. I can determinately and non-arbitrarily think of my own representings as correct or incorrect only by thinking of them as thus consilient with or in conflict with the representings of others, for it is only in this, I have argued, that the correctness or incorrectness of an individual representing can consist.

CHAPTER V

REALISM AND IDEALISM:
EVOLUTIONARY EPISTEMOLOGY

The conclusion of the preceding chapter is likely to produce a variety of reactions. In particular, it is likely to reopen the question of realism and idealism. The idealist has been patiently biding his time since the conclusion of Chapter III. There, you will recall, I completed the argument, begun with the exploration of Realist Cores in Chapter II, that, for the kinds of beings which *we* are — for apperceptive, temporally discursive intelligences — idealism ("from within") is not a possible metaphysics. Now, however, since I have divorced the concept of correctness entirely from the correspondences posited by the Criteriological Realist, since I have, in this way, "divided through by the world", our idealist comes to life again. He begins by reminding us of another Kantian distinction. In establishing that idealism is not a possible metaphysics for us "from within", he claims, what I have shown is that we must be *Empirical Realists*. But now I have gone on, as he suspected, to secure the balance of the Kantian picture. Kant, he reminds us, was an Empirical Realist — but he was also a *Transcendental* Idealist. Idealism may not be a possible metaphysics "from within" — but it is the *only* possible metaphysics "from outside"!

According to Transcendental Idealism, objects of experience are empirically real but transcendentally ideal. From the transcendental point of view, their *esse* is *concipi*. Our idealist critic is now prepared to accept my Constitutive Realism. But this, he hastens to add, is only a thesis concerning the *contents* of our conceptual scheme. We necessarily *represent* things as existing independently of our representing them. That is what we discover when we look at our conceptual scheme "from inside". But looked at "from outside", the *esse* of all things — *both* those which we represent as ontological reals (existing independently) *and* those which we represent as mere appearances — is *to be represented*. The distinction between being and seeming with which an apperceptive, temporally discursive intelligence necessarily operates is a distinction drawn wholly *within* a collection of entities all of which are, however, *in themselves*, simply represented*s*.

The difficulty with this fully Kantian line of reasoning is that it relies on an "outside" perspective which is wholly chimerical. From what standpoint does the Transcendental Idealist propose to speak of what represented entities are "*in themselves*"? The line of idealistic reasoning which I have just sketched is intended by our critic to apply to any apperceptive, temporally discursive intelligence or, as I shall put it for brevity, to any *experiencer*. But *we* are experiencers. To suppose, then, as does the Transcendental Idealist, that we could think of experiences "from outside" is to suppose that we could think of *ourselves* "from outside". It is, in other words, to suppose that we can make sense of a distinction between how objects are *for us* (how we – necessarily – represent them) and how objects are "in themselves".

But this is just what the argument of the preceding chapter has shown us that we cannot do. The Transcendental Idealist's putative question of whether "objects for us" are "in themselves" as we represent them as being can only be the question of whether objects as they are represented by us are represented *correctly*. It is surely a necessary truth that an object is represented correctly *if and only if* it is (in itself) as it is represented as being. The biconditional is, indeed, indisputable. But, as it gave no aid and comfort to the Criteriological Realist, so it will give none to the Transcendental Idealist. As we have recently seen, the correctness of any representing *consists* in its consilience with our collective representational practices. These collective practices themselves, however, cannot be called into question in point of correctness or incorrectness. There is no way that a community can measure its collective practices against the world, no fact of the matter beyond the attainable consilience of individual practices within the community.[1] The Transcendental Idealist's putative question of whether objects as they are represented by us are represented *correctly* thus fails of sense. And so the supposed distinction between how objects are for us and how objects are "in themselves" which gave rise to that question evaporates. It is not itself an intelligible distinction. It is empty of any content.

These results secure the *correctness* of Constitutive Realism! We are experiencers. Hence we are *necessarily* Constitutive Realists. We *necessarily* represent at least some things as existing independently of our representing them. That is the conclusion of Chapters II and III. What and how things *are* (in themselves) is (analytically) what and how they are *correctly* represented as being. But what and how things are correctly represented as being is just what and how *we* (collectively) represent them as being. It is in the communal consilience of our individual representings that the correctness of those representings consists. This was our conclusion in the preceding chapter. But if what things are is what we represent things as being, and if we *necessarily* represent at least some things as ontological reals – that is, as existing independently of our representing them – then it follows that at least some things (necessarily) *are* ontological reals — that is, *do* exist independently of our representing them. It follows, in other words, that Constitutive Realism is not only inevitable (for us) but also *correct* — and, indeed, correct *because* it is inevitable for us.

And now it may well seem that I have pulled off the ultimate in ontological sleight of hand. If at least some of what are objects for us *do* exist independently of our representings, won't it then make sense to ask *which ones*? And doesn't this once again simply amount to the drawing of a distinction between what we represent objects as being and what those objects are in themselves — the very distinction prohibited by the argument of the present chapter? What has gone wrong here?

At this point the Criteriological Realist is likely to add a scholium. You have argued, he says, that semantic correctness *überhaupt* consists merely in communal agreements. But this makes a mockery of any talk of "truth" or "knowledge". If what we (collectively) say must be correct, may we not, then, say whatever we choose? And will this not make truth merely a "higher orthodoxy", falling on a continuum with shared faith? Have you not, in other words, reduced science to the epistemological status of just another religion — a religion which happens to be suited to the temperament of our times?

The answer to both of these objections requires that we bring some observations from a recent footnote into the main text. Our collective representation of the world is, indeed, a dynamic creature. It evolves and changes across time — and our communal consensus at a time thus gives way to another at some later time. We replace Ptolemaic cosmology by the Copernican scheme, Newtonian dynamics and kinematics by special and general relativity, representations of homogeneous stuffs by representations of swarms of atoms and congeries of quantum-theoretical sub-atomic entities. There is, then, an undeniable locus of *variability* within our conceptual scheme. The question which we must confront, however, is whether this locus of variability is also a locus of *indeterminateness* or *arbitrariness*. For only if this is so will it be the case that "we may say whatever we choose".

But while there is this indisputable locus of variability in our representational systems, there is also something which does not vary. It does not, because it cannot. Any representational system which can be *ours* must be subject to the constraints of a Realist Core. It is this in which the correctness of Constitutive Realism consists. The reply to both idealists, the Transcendental Idealist of the present chapter and what we might call the "Empirical Idealist" typified by George in the preceding chapter, focuses on this invariable core. The question "*Which* among what are objects for us do exist independently of our representings?" is a question which can arise only *within* a representational system which *is* a Realist Core — and *within* any such conceptual system this question *will have* a determinate answer. Diachronically, one representational system comes to be (collectively) replaced by another. But the replacement, *necessarily*, always contains a Realist Core — for, like the conceptual scheme which it displaces, the new conceptual scheme is *ours*, and any conceptual scheme which is ours *must* be subject to the constraints of a Realist Core.

Our first objector wished to parse his question "Which among what are objects for us do exist independently of our representings?" as a question asked "from outside". But this he cannot do. It is always, and necessarily, a question asked "from inside" some conceptual scheme which is ours and, as we have seen, asked "from inside" any *such* conceptual scheme, the question will always, and necessarily, have a determinate answer. If there remains a question here, then, it can only be a question which arises on account of the diachronic plurality of such representational systems. The first objection, in other words, collapses into the second. Given that our collective representational system *as a whole* is diachronically variable, while at *each* time there will (necessarily) be a determinate answer to the question of which objects exist independently of our representing them, must we not conclude that there is nothing non-arbitrary which can be said from the *diachronic* point of view about which objects are ontological reals? After all, the objection continues, you have just mentioned that there are *many* representational systems which are (successively) ours — but surely any realism worthy of the name must be committed to the thesis that there is only *one* world. It cannot be that *all* of our (successive) world-pictures are correct, if for no other reason than for the simple one that they are (logically) incompatible with one another.

What our objector insists upon, then, is that a realism properly so-called posit but one world, a world to which our representings may then *collectively* be more or less adequate. While this way of putting the objection, of course, substantially presupposes Criteriological Realism, we cannot rely entirely on our earlier criticisms of that view here, for the position of the Criteriological Realist can now be revived with a subtle twist. The fact that we are necessarily Constitutive Realists, it may be pointed out, implies that we necessarily *represent* our own representings *as* more or less adequate to (corresponding to, isomorphic with) a *single* world. To be a Constitutive Realist then is necessarily to be a Criteriological Realist as well, for it is to endorse as necessary (analytic) the biconditional that a representing is correct if and only if it *is* adequate to the world.

Ingenious and insightful as this objection is, it does not secure Criteriological Realism. The proper response to it is to point out that, while the Criteriological Realist does indeed endorse the stipulated biconditional as a necessary truth, there is more to his thesis than is captured by the biconditional alone. The Criteriological Realist holds as well that it is in their adequacy to the world that the correctness of our representings *consists* (that their adequacy to the world is the *criterion* of correctness for our representings). It is this further thesis which, I have argued, we must reject — but we can reject it *without* rejecting as well the associated biconditional claim which erroneously gives rise to it. We remain free, in other words, to hold *both* that the correctness of our representings does not consist in their adequacy to the world *and* that, nevertheless, our representings are correct if and only if they are adequate to the world. All that we need to do is to complete the syllogism: The correctness of our representings is the criterion of their adequacy to the world. It is in correctness that adequacy to the world consists!

This is nothing but Kant's "Copernican revolution" in contemporary dress. Epistemology is prior to ontology. That is the moral. But epistemology is prior to ontology not only in the straightforward sense that the answerability of ontological questions presupposes the existence of epistemic procedures for answering them, but in the deeper sense that the *content* of ontological questions is epistemological. Questions of existence (of what are ontological reals) just *are* questions of correctness.

Now, however, it will appear that we have leaped from the frying pan to the fire, for to make sense of the realist view that there is only one world, it will immediately be pointed out, we need something more than all those time-bound, "internal", synchronic "correctnesses" which appertain to representings successively as they are elements of successive conceptual schemes. We need also an *absolute* sense of "correctness" — a sense in which an entire *system* of representations can, *as a whole*, be said to be correct or incorrect. And nothing of this sort is provided for by the line of argument which I have so far sketched.

This objection puts us once again squarely in the center of the general problematic of Empiricism with which I opened this book. For the question which is now being posed concerns the conditions of defeasibility for a representational system or a conceptual scheme taken as a whole. Within any conceptual scheme, considerations of maximal diachronic and apperceptive coherence yield a determinate answer to the question "Which things are ontological reals?" But now we have noted that a conceptual scheme can be, as a whole, up for replacement, and a replacement of this sort, the objection runs, stands itself in need of justification. But such a justification cannot be forthcoming. It cannot proceed by demonstrating that the successor system is more nearly adequate to the world than was its predecessor, for I have argued that questions of ontological adequacy are questions of correctness, that epistemology is prior to ontology. But surely the only justification which one *could* have for replacing one representational system by another must at least entail that the successor is *more nearly correct* than the predecessor which is supplants — and, having eschewed Criteriological Realism, I have cut myself off from any way of making sense of the *absolute* (diachronic and holistic) concept of correctness which I need here to make any such notion even intelligible.

To put the point in Kantian terms, we may say that Kant has ingeniously secured for us a *partial* description of any representational system which can be ours, but we have now reached the limit of what is arguable in the Kantian way from our natures as experiencers. And, what is worse, that limit — as I admitted at the close of Chapter II — stops with the constraints of a determinate *mathematical form*. It cannot, however, yield a determinate *descriptive content* for a world-picture, and so the adoption of any conceptual scheme — which necessarily embodies some such descriptive content — remains wholly arbitrary. To *justify* the replacement of one representational system by another would again seem to require an appeal to a form of epistemic warrant which is neither logical nor evidential, to a "third way". But Kant's "third way" — an argument from our natures as experiencers, which *is* compatible with empiricist epistemology — has reached the limit of its applicability. It appears, then, that I can purchase my *diachronic* Realism, my "one world", only at a price which I have repeatedly indicated I am unwilling to pay — the price of abandoning Empiricism.

Now this objection indeed focuses our attention on central matters. But its conclusion would follow from our current reasonings only if the process of replacing some synchronic representational system by its diachronic successor were not *itself* subject to determinate and non-arbitrary constraints. And this crucial premiss, while it has been asserted, has not yet been established.

In this connection, it is important to notice that questions of justification may arise prospectively or retrospectively. The prospective stance is appropriate to contexts of *decision*, occasions on which one is deliberating about what to do, while the retrospective stance applies in contexts of *evaluation*, when one is assessing what has been done. It is crucial to keep these two perspectives separated in our thinking. If we do not, we are in danger of mistaking the correct conclusion that, for example, the employment of some conceptual scheme cannot be justified *in prospect* for the stronger, but erroneous, conclusion that it cannot on that account be justified *at all*.

Once sensitized to this distinction it becomes open to us to approach the current objection from another direction. Even if successive passages from one system of representations to another are genuine "scientific revolutions", incapable of being anticipated in a "logic of discovery" and not amenable to justification in prospect (as were the categorial features of a Kantian Realist Core), we are not precluded from seeking, and even finding, an invariant pattern of *retrospective* justifiabilities characterizing the epistemic *process* of succession of conceptual schemes at all of its stages. To invoke once again my evolutionary analogy, we can see ourselves retrospectively as evolved apes even through our evolutionary ancestors could not similarly envision themselves prospectively as potential rational hominids.

While this retrospective epistemic determinancy would not, by itself, answer the current objection, it does give us a clue to a possible strategy, for it shows us how we can effect a reconciliation between determinateness and defeasibility. It introduces the *possibility* that the desired absolute sense of correctness might be funded diachronically by appeal to a sequence of comparatively better *approximations*. *If*, from a pattern of retrospective justifiabilities, we could extract a set of invariant constraints on the process of succession of conceptual schemes which would arguably guarantee something like a commonality of focus or direction for that sequence of systems in their determinate diachronic succession, then it would become open to us to think of them as aimed at and converging upon the (absolutely) correct conceptual system. The final answer to the Cartesian demonaic skeptic would then consist in this: that the connection between our (collective) espousal of a representational system and its (absolute) correctness is a connection *in prospect* and, for us — embedded as we are in these diachronic epistemic processes — no more than a regulative ideal. But that the notion of absolute correctness is in this way a regulative ideal or limit-concept would *not* imply, on that account alone, that it is a fiction or an illusion.

By thus relocating the absolute correctness of a conceptual scheme in the limit, we could make sense of the notion of correspondence or adequacy of our representations to *one* world without a commitment to any form of givenness or foundationalism. For, to recur once again to the evolutionary model, just as organisms with hearts can evolve from ancestors universally lacking them, so a world could *bring* our representations into increasing conformity with it without producing in us *any* representations which conformed to that world *ab initio*. The world can act on us not only productively but also *selectively*. As an environment selects from among random genetic mutations those traits conducive to the survival of the organism and the perpetuation of the species, so our representings might be brought into increasing conformity with the world by a process of successive selection, from among the representations continuously — and even randomly — produced in us, of those representings which more nearly conform to it than their predecessors. And if we note that, as with biological evolution, the *survivors* of one phase of the process would become elements of the *environment* into which the mutations driving the next phase emerge, we may begin to get a glimpse of where the constraints which could render such process determinate, non-arbitrary, and convergent might be located.

I have been speaking of a diachronic sequence of conceptual schemes each of which is *retrospectively justified* as a replacement for its predecessor(s). But what sort of justifiabilities could there be which would imply a set of constraints on the process of succession of conceptual schemes which was adequate to ground the desired notion of diachronic convergence? Earlier, in recalling the general problematic of Empiricism, I wrote that "the only justification which one *could* have for replacing one representational system by another must at least entail that the successor is *more nearly correct* than the predecessor which it supplants".

There is nothing wrong with this observation. *But* — and it is a crucial 'but' — we must take care to see it for what it is. It is the schema of another *biconditional*. The Criteriological Realist insisted, correctly, that a representing was correct if and only if it was adequate to the world. But he went on to conclude, erroneously, that the correctness of a representing therefore *consists* in its adequacy to the world. We, however, argued that the correctness of a representing could not thus consist in any form of "correspondence" and so we went on to drawn the opposite conclusion: that the adequacy of a representing to the world consists in the correctness of that representing, that is, that epistemology is prior to ontology.

Our present situation is exactly parallel. The current objector observes, correctly, that replacement of one conceptual scheme by another can be justified *if and only if* the successor is more nearly correct than the predecessor. But, like the Criteriological Realist, he inverts his priorities. He goes on to conclude, erroneously, that the justification for such a replacement would consist in an argument to the effect *that* the successor was more nearly (absolutely) correct than the predecessor. As we have just seen, however, the only way in which we *could* make sense of the notion of (absolute) correctness which is mobilized in this objection is in terms of a diachronic convergence of representational systems *in the limit* which emerges from an invariant pattern of retrospective justifiabilities. It follows, then, that what we must do here is not to reject the biconditional, but again to complete the syllogism in the opposite way. That a successor conceptual scheme is more nearly (absolutely) correct than its predecessor(s) *consists* in its adoption or espousal *as* a successor being warranted or justified. The notion of justification is *prior* to the notion of correctness as the notion of correctness was itself prior to that of adequacy to the world. Absolute correctness is nothing but the diachronic limit of justification. (The truth is, analytically, what in the last analysis, we *ought to believe* – another biconditional.)

But now it may look as though I have discarded the results of the preceding chapter. Did I not argue that the correctness of a representing *consists* in its being the manifestation of a diachronic practice which is consilient with the diachronic representing practices of others? Now, however, I have said that the notion of justification is prior to that of correctness. How are these *two* accounts of correctness themselves to be reconciled?

I think that they can be reconciled. In order to do this, however, we shall need to take a closer look at just *how* the notion of justification is prior to that of correctness. And to do this, I must begin to take much more seriously an observation made in passing at the outset of this study and remaining more or less tacit thereafter – that a conceptual scheme is properly understood not as a structure of representations (things, entities, or items) but as a system of conducts or practices. I must take a few minutes, in other words, to spell out in greater detail the relations between our customary vocabulary of semantic or epistemic appraisal ('correct', 'incorrect', 'valid', 'invalid', 'justified', 'warranted', and the like) and the language of conduct as such.

In the last chapter, I devised the verb 'to trint' to designate the initially bizarre behavior of uttering the *noise* 'kloop' in the presence of a thing and painting the *design* 'KLOOP' on that thing. Trinting was, thus, a complex kind of behavior, in particular, of auditory and inscriptional *tokening behavior*. But the verb was hardly a transparent one. That is, one could not readily diagnose from the verb itself what sort of behavior it was designed to pick out for our attention. I might instead have designed a verb which *did* suggest its own interpretation, thus: 'kloop'ing. In doing so, I would have been trading on many things we share, primary among them a family of consilient practices of associating noises with designs. That we do share such practices is the pragmatic content of the fact that we possess a phonetic alphabet – that language is, for us, something which may be expressed in writing or in speech, and that our writing is a "picture" of our speech. Our customary quotation marks presuppose – and then gloss over – this family of mutually consilient practices. Instead, we customarily make reference to using the *word* 'kloop', and we think of this as a *generic* conduct of which both our acoustical productions containing the noise 'kloop' and our inscribings containing the design 'KLOOP' are instances.[2]

There is no reason, however, why we might not allow ourselves even a greater catholicity with quotation marks. Given that there is a consilience of 'kloop'ing behavior within our community, we might discover within the tokening behavior of *another* community certain utterings and inscribings which play the same role in their overall behavioral economy as do 'kloop'ings in ours. Where we 'kloop', perhaps, they 'gret'. If this should happen, it would be nice to have a vocabulary in which we could signal this parallelism of consilient behaviors. One way would be by becoming even more catholic with our quotation marks, allowing them to sort tokening conducts within *any* community by their place in the *overall* behavioral economy of that community without regard to the specific structures of acoustical or inscriptional tokens produced in those behaviors. Thus, for example, we might say that when those folks over there use the word 'gret', they *are* 'kloop'ing. This would be a little awkward, however, for our quotation marks would thereby have become ambiguous. The first set ('gret') would be tied to specific inscriptional or acoustical structures; the second ('kloop'ing) would not. At this point we might introduce two styles of quotation marks, one to pick out conducts as incorporating tokens of specific structures and another to pick out conducts as having a certain place in the overall behavioral economy of individuals within a community. (Sellars' star-quotes and dot-quotes. See e.g., *AE*) But there is another way in which we might proceed here as well. We might drop the quotation marks from 'kloop'ing and signal the second way of picking out conducts – according to their place in the overall behavioral economy – by a *special form of the copula*. Instead of saying:

(1)   their 'gret'ings *are* 'kloop'ings,

using the first form of quotes on the left and the second on the right, we might, in other words, say

(2)   'gret'ing (by them) *means* klooping.

The job of *means* here would be to advert to the role of 'kloop'ing *behaviors* (where I here use the structural style of quoting) in *our own* behavioral economy, and to *classify* 'gret'ing behaviors as having a role in *their* behavioral economy paralleling the role of 'kloop'ings in ours.

At this point, however, we might be tempted to introduce still a further economy. Since *all* the behaviors we are talking about are tokening behaviors, it may occur to us that we can dispense with the 'ing's. All we need do is to transpose our talk about tokenings into talk about *tokens*. While the sorting or classification *principle* used on the right hand side of our classificatory statements (sorting by place within an overall behavioral economy) would remain one *literally* applicable only to conducts, our new idiom would *ostensibly* classify not tokening conducts but the tokens themselves. We would then put in place of (2):

(2′) 'gret' (used by one of them) means *kloop*.

And this is beginning to look familiar.

This notational convention need not be applied only to "one-word" tokenings, of course. We might have "whole sentence" tokenings as well, and put, for example:

(3) 'Dir binen gret' (used by one of them) means this is a kloop.

There is a small problem about (3) which might well lead us to introduce one more slight modification into our practices here. (3), as it is written, is syntactically ambiguous. It has two principal verbs. It might be parsed

(3a) / 'Dir binen gret' / means / this is a kloop/

as we would ordinarily parse it, but it might also be parsed

(3b) / 'Dir binen gret' means this / is a kloop,

with the copula 'is' as the main verb. To avoid such ambiguity, we could introduce a scope indicator to show which part of (3) would go into the second (behavioral economy) kind of quotation marks were we using a more transparent notation. Instead of (3), then, we might put

(3⁺) 'Der binen gret' means *that* this is a kloop

where 'that'ing a sentence would be a form of quoting it in the second (behavioral economy) way.

There is no need to go on in this fanciful style. The conducts and practices at stake in our having a conceptual scheme are just *tokenings* on the model of 'kloop'ings thus broadly construed — for example, 'cat'ings and 'red'ings and 'This is red'ings and 'Snow is white'ings. And one job of semantic discourse is to classify such behaviors across community lines as having parallel places in the overall behavioral economies of communities other than our own — thus, for example, German speakers' '*Katze*'ings and '*rot*'ings and '*Dies ist rot*'ings and '*Schnee ist weiss*'ings. More precisely, that is *almost* the job of semantic discourse. But we must first allow ourselves even one more degree of catholicity in the notation.

"The word 'kloop' suddenly popped into his mind", we may say, while remaining *wholly non-committal* about in what that word's "popping into his mind" consists – auditory or visual imagery, or no imagery at all; modifications of "mental substance" or changes in the electro-chemical state of some neural structures; or perhaps something else entirely. We can, in other words, think of a stratum of *covert* conduct or behavior on the model of *overt* conduct or behavior, and extend our second (behavioral economy) style of quotation to embrace *occurrent thinkings* (whatever they might consist in structurally) as well as utterings and inscribings as specific instances of the generic behavior of 'kloop'ing. We can, that is, adopt a level of catholicity where what one can write or say is also something which one can *think* – and we can introduce our cross-community semantic devices at this level of catholicity. The job of semantic discourse, then, would be to classify tokening behaviors or *covert analogues* to tokening behaviors according to their parallel places in the overall (overt and covert) behavioral economies of members of various communities. Our *having* a conceptual scheme will then consist simply in our *being* suitably disposed to engage in such tokening conducts – or in whatever covert conducts which, by virtue of their places in our internal behavioral economies, are functional analogues of such tokening conducts.[3]

The semantic idiom is thus a transposed mode of speech. Fundamentally, it classifies *behaviors* – in the first instance, *tokening* behaviors – in terms of their places in our overall behavioral economy, but it does this not by talking about the behaviors as behaviors but by talking about the *tokens* which are in fact characteristically produced in the course of those behaviors, when overt – and then by analogically extending this way of talking to behaviors which are not literally tokening behaviors at all.

Now the terms of semantic and epistemic *appraisal* take the form of ostensibly referring to semantic *properties and relations*. We say, for example,

(4) that snow is white is true

or

(5) that Sidney is triangular entails that Sidney is trilateral.

Here *being true* has the look of a *property* and entailment has the look of a *relation*, and we are tempted to cast about for some kinds of *things* to exemplify this property or to stand in this relation. The surface grammar of the semantic idiom leads us to take its that-clauses as singular referring expressions (names), and then to invent a genus to which these named things belong — "propositions" or "statements" or the like. But if, as I have suggested, 'that'ing gestures at a form of quoting (of a certain maximal catholicity and functional style) and the semantic idiom is a transposed mode of speech, then we can better see (4) and (5) as themselves unperspicuous, transposed, ways of talking about *behaviors* which are *for us*, in fact, characteristically tokening behaviors (or covert analogues to tokening behaviors), but which need not be.

Had we instead chosen to introduce a second style of quotation marks to sort tokening behaviors according to their places in the overall behavioral economy of members of a community — say, following Sellars, dot-quotes — and had we eschewed the convenience of dropping from talk of conduct to talk of tokens, we would, in other words, recognize (4) and (5) as saying something about

•snow is white•ings

and

•Sidney is triangular•ings

and

•Sidney is trilateral•ings

in general, where these behaviors *may* be utterings or inscribings, but where they may also be occurrent thinkings, in English or in French or in German or . . . or, indeed, even some wholly unanticipated conducts of alien non-human intelligences, provided only that those conducts had certain parallel places in the *overall* behavioral economies of the entities in question.

But if the job of terms of semantic appraisal is thus, essentially to say *something* about behavior just *what* is it designed to say? And if those behaviors are to be sorted and classified in terms of their places in the overall behavioral economy of an individual within a community, what principles of sorting and what kind of *places* are at issue? At this point it will pay us to recall what I shall call the *fundamental project* of any apperceptive, temporally discursive intelligence. What engaged George, for example, was the building up through time of a comprehensive and coherent *unitary* determinate world-picture which included his own representational autobiography. What I argued in a previous chapter was that any apperceptive, temporally discursive intelligence — any experiencer — is *necessarily* committed to this project as a condition of his own existence *as* an experiencer. George couldn't *be* an experiencer unless he engaged in this fundamental project and, in fact, unless he engaged in it according to certain *constraints*.

We can think of those conducts of George's which I earlier called *endorsings* of representings — the adding of those representings to his evolving world-picture — *on the model* of the tokening-behaviors which I have just been discussing. When George adds to his world-picture a representing to the effect that

$$a \, \phi K \, !\text{is in } p \text{ at } t$$

for example, in terms of our maximally-catholic functional quoting convention for describing behaviors, we can say that what George is doing is

$$^{\bullet} a \, \phi K \, !\text{is in } p \text{ at } t \, ^{\bullet}\text{ing}.$$

Our semantic vocabulary, in other words, has reached a level of abstraction which allows us to use *it* in describing the necessary activities of *any* experiencer. The overall behavioral economy in question in our functional classifyings of conducts for semantic or epistemic appraisal, then, will just *be* the fundamental project of any apperceptive, temporally discursive intelligence, and the *place* of a specific behavior within that overall behavioral economy will be given by an accounting of its relation to other behaviors in the project, and its relation to the constraints which necessarily govern the project as a whole.

Let us look further at this matter of constraints. What I argued in Chapter III was that the fundamental project of any experiencer was necessarily subject to the constraints of (at least) three "material logics" — of time ("chrono-logic"), of forms ("arena geometry"), and of contents ("causal laws"). If our experiencer is also equipped with the apparatus of first-order logic, he can himself represent each of these families of constraints by "analytic truths", non-defeasible compound representings. That is how the constraints are reflected at the object-level. But might not our experiencer, who can represent his own representings as representings, also undertake to represent these constraints at the meta-level — to represent them *as constraints*? What sort of apparatus would this take?

Consider, first, an example of a principle of chrono-logic, reflected in the "analytic truth"

(T^{++}) $(x)(y)(x \, !\text{be-compresent-with } y \equiv y \, !\text{be-compresent-with } x)$.

(T^{++}) reflects the symmetry of '!be-compresent-with'. Operating under the constraint which (T^{++}) codifies, George has a certain representational *license*. Whenever he is authorized to endorse a representing of the form

x !be-compresent-with y

he is also authorized to endorse a representing of the form

y !be-compresent-with x.

His endorsing a representation of the first sort is, on the view of representational conducts which we have just been taking, his ˙x !be-compresent-with y˙ing; his endorsing a representation of the second sort, his ˙y !be-compresent-with x˙ing. What (T^{++}) reflects, I propose, is a *conditional permission*, George's being *entitled* to ˙y !be-compresent-with x˙ on the condition that he has ˙x !be-compresent-with y˙ed (and conversely). If Geroge were to represent his own representings as conducts, rather than as (tokenish) things, he might articulate this principle of permission *as such a principle*, by endorsing the meta-representing:

Whenever I :x !be-compresent-with y:, I may :y !be-compresent-with x:

If, on the other hand, he were to retain the thingish-style of representing for his own representings, he would need a term transposing such a principle of permission, and its deontic 'may', into the grammar of thing-talk. Instead of endorsing something of the form "Whenever I do such-and-such I may do so-and-so", then, George would instead employ an idiom which represents this principle of permission as a *relation* between the *targets* of the two representings (between the tokens):

:x !be-compresent-with y: *implies* :y !be-compresent-with x:

The thesis which I am now advancing, in other words, is this: Just as semantic talk ostensibly "about statements or propositions" is a transposed mode of speech, a way of talking about *conducts* or *behaviors* which are *paradigmatically* tokening behaviors — but which may, in fact, be any behaviors which have a parallel place in the overall behavioral economy of an individual — so the terms of semantic and epistemic appraisal which ostensibly predicate properties and relations of such "statements" or "propositions" are properly to be understood as transpositions into a nominal idiom of principles of permission, prescription, and prohibition governing the correlative conducts — that is, as having a fundamentally *deontic* content. The *sense* of a claim to the effect that

> that-*p implies* that-*q*.

on this view, is an authorization that something *may be done*. To say that

> that-*p implies* that-*q*

is to say that

> that-*q may be inferred from* that-*p*.

And an inference is a performance. Adapting our behavioral-economy style of quoting, what inferring that-*q* from that-*p consists in* is a performance of `*q*`-ing on the condition that (and because) one has just •*p*•ed.

What allows the deontic character of semantic relations to be safely suppressed in the transposed, nominal mode of speech is the *impersonal* character of the conduct normatives at issue. A moment ago, I allowed George to represent the principle of permission reflecting the constraint on his activities which underlies (T^{++}) by a license expressed in the first person. But such 'may's (and the analogous 'must's and 'must not's) are properly addressed to experiencers *as such*, for the constraints which they reflect are constraints which are necessarily binding on the representing activities of experiencers as such. In our customary manner of speaking, this fact is embodied in an *impersonal pronoun*, 'one'. '*One* may. . . ', '*One* must . . . ', and so on is how the formulas go. If the principles of permission, prescription, and prohibition which I am offering as the senses of terms of semantic and epistemic appraisal were addressed now to one experiencer, now to another, then we could not safely suppress their deontic character by a transposition into the semantic idiom. We would need an explicit means of indicating *which* experiencers' activities were to be constrained by the principles expressed in such conduct normatives. But since the constraints at issue are those which necessarily apply to the representing activities of experiencers *as such*, the subjects to whom the explicit conduct normatives are addressed are always the same — and so a transposition into a semantic idiom which eliminates explicit mention of any such subjects remains unproblematic.

But what does all this have to do with correctness? Well, earlier we noted that the fundamental constraint on the meta-level concept of correctness could itself be expressed in the form of a family of biconditional "analytic truths" represented by the schema:

> that-*p* is correct (true) if and only if *p*.

According to the present proposal, the *sense* of the ostensible semantic *predicate* 'is correct' will be given by some explicit conduct normative — a principle of permission, prescription, or prohibition. In order for these analytic biconditionals themselves to be validated, however, the performance authorized by such a conduct normative will need to be a performance which is authorized *whenever*, for example, a ·*p*·ing performance is authorized. And this tells us straightaway what we should make of "that-*p* is correct". As a deontic principle, it simply expresses a license to endorse the representing that-*p*, that is, a license to ·*p*·. The sense of George's meta-level representing

:*n* is a ϕK: is correct (true),

for example, will be given (in the first person) by

I may endorse :*n* is a ϕK:

or, in pure conduct talk,

I may :*n* is a ϕK:

(where for George *to* :*n* is a ϕK; is for him to do *whatever* it is which in fact constitutes his adding an "*n* is a ϕK" representing to his world picture). A claim of correctness for a representing stands to that representing itself, then, as authorization to performance. To *say* of a "statement" or "proposition" that it is correct (true) is to authorize the tokening-behavior (in our most-catholic sense of such behavior) to which talk ostensibly "about statements or propositions" adverts.

And now we can see how the putatively-two accounts of correctness which I have offered can be reconciled. In the last chapter, I argued that the correctness of a representing consists in its being the manifestation of a diachronic practice which is consilient with the diachronic representing practices of others. Earlier in this chapter, however, I argued that the notion of justification was prior to that of correctness. We can now appreciate in what sense the latter claim is itself true. The notion of justification is prior to that of correctness in that the sense of a *claim* of correctness is given by a principle of permission, a conduct-normative which *says* of a representing performance *that* it is justified, that is, that it *may be done*.

But this is compatible with my original account of correctness. For I did *not* earlier propose to give an account of the sense of a *claim* of correctness. What I earlier argued was that it is in a diachronic communal consilience of representing practices that correctness *consists*. Let me give an analogy. Winning a game of chess consists in checkmating the opponent's king. Winning a game of checkers consists in capturing all of the opponent's pieces. But the sense of the *claim* "I won" in

> I played chess with Sidney and I won

is the same as the sense of the *claim* "I won" in

> I played checkers with Margaret and I won.

To *say* that I won a game is to say that I did *whatever* it is the doing of which constitutes winning. But it is *not* to say *what* it is which constitutes winning.

Correctness is like that. To *say* of a representing that it is correct is to *say* that a certain performance is authorized. It is to articulate a principle of permission. But it is *not* to say *in virtue of what* that performance is authorized. It is the latter, however, which answers the question "In what does the correctness of a representing *consist*?" To say what constitutes correctness is to say in virtue of what the performance authorized by a claim of correctness *is* authorized.

But if all this is so far right — if the *sense* of terms of semantic and epistemic appraisal is indeed given by deontic principles addressed to certain species of cognitive conduct — then I must immediately repair what turns out to have been a half-truth at the conclusion of the last chapter. I said there that what I would need to add to my conceptual scheme in order to have a concept of correctness was the ability to represent myself as a member of a community of representers and to represent my representings as in agreement or disagreement with the collective practices of those others. I said, in other words, that I would require a non-vacuous 'I'. Now, however, we can see that, while this is indeed true, it is not the *whole* truth. For there is something else which I will need as well. I will need some apparatus to represent both my representings and those of others *as* subject to conduct normatives of the sort which I have been sketching in this chapter. I will need, in short, an apparatus of *practical* rationality. The surprising result is that, in a deep sense, the bestowing of this "something else" will turn out to be, at base, *the same* as the supplying of a non-vacuous 'I'. But before this thesis can be secured, there is considerable groundwork to be laid. Let me begin, then, by setting the stage for the next phase of the argument.

If to say that a representation is correct or warranted or justified is to say (in a transposed mode of speech) of a represent*ing* that it may be done, then an argument which has as its conclusion that a representation is correct or justified or warranted will be a transposition of a more fundamental argument which has as its conclusion *an authorization for certain conducts*. A piece of justificatory *reasoning*, then, will be a piece of practical reasoning. To be in the "logical space" of semantic or epistemic appraisal, therefore, I must be a being capable of *practical* rationality, a being which can engage in the requisite forms of practical reasoning. The fundamental form of an argument which has as its conclusion that a representation is correct will be an argument which mobilizes this capacity for practical rationality. It will be an argument which has as its proximate conclusion that something may be done.

Addressed to a conceptual scheme or representational system as a whole, such an argument would emerge as a blanket authorization subsuming a *family* of cognitive performances. To say of a representational system that it is warranted is to say that its *use* is warranted — that is, it is to address its adoption or espousal as a system of conducts, responses to the ongoing flux of sensation in terms of its concepts and categories, and drawings of conclusions in accordance with the inferential principles (the "material logics") which are collectively constitutive of its descriptive content. But to say that the *use* of a conceptual scheme is warranted or justified is to say, simply, that *caeteris paribus* it *may* or *ought to be* used. And such an ought-to-*be* predicated of a *using* is nothing but an ought-to-*do* addressed to the relevant *users*.

The concept of warrantedness in application to conceptualizing conducts parallels in these ways the notion of the (moral) rightness of an act. To say of an act (type) — e.g., promise-keeping or aiding those in need — that it is (morally) *right* is to say (allowing certain *caeteris paribus* hedges to remain tacit) that it ought to be done. And this ought-to-be predicated of an act-type similarly reflects an ought-to-*do* addressed to the relevant agents. To say that promises ought to *be* kept is just to say that one ought to *keep* them. The concepts of right and wrong are thus embedded in an ethics proper, presupposing the notion of a moral agent and a family of moral conduct normatives governing the activities of such an agent.

Analogously, the concepts of semantic and epistemic appraisal — of correctness and incorrectness, warrantedness and unwarrantedness — are embedded in an "ethics of belief". They presuppose the notion of a cognitive agent and a family of what we might call *rational* conduct normatives (permissions, prohibitions, and prescriptions) governing the activities of such an agent.

A cognitive agent as such is just an experiencer — an apperceptive, temporally-discursive intelligence engaged in what is necessarily the fundamental project of any such being, the building up through time of a comprehensive, coherent, unitary, and determinate world-picture which includes his own representational autobiography *and the representational biographies of other experiencers* as they are manifested in their interactions with him.

The business of any 'ought' is to advert to the obtaining of *reasons*. Without putting too fine an edge on it, the sense of a claim to the effect that A ought to do X, where A is an agent and X a type of act, is given, roughly, by: There are adequate reasons for A to do X. The notion of *a* reason, however, is in turn bound up with that of reason*ing*, and with the practices of giving and having reasons and acting for or because of reasons.

To say of something, R, that it is *a* reason for A to do X is to assert its suitability to play a particular role in A's reason*ing*, if A *were* to reason about what to do. Reasoning about what to do, of course, is practical reasoning. Thus the claim that R is a reason for A to do X specifically amounts (in first approximation) to a claim to the effect that R could function as a premiss in a *sound practical reasoning* for A, the conclusion of which is that X is to be done. To say of conducts that they are what an agent ought to do, then, is to presuppose that the agent is capable of the requisite forms of practical rationality, or, to put it pleonastically, that the agent is genuinely an *agent*.

What we need to do to *complete* our understanding of the notions of correctness, justification, warrant, and the like is, therefore, to come to grips with the details of such practical rationality. We need to understand in what a bit of practical reasoning consists, to understand how something enters such reasoning as a premiss, and, in particular, to understand in what the *soundness* of a bit of practical reasoning for an agent consists, before we can have a full grasp of what *could* be a reason for the replacement of one conceptual scheme or representational system by another and of how that reason would function *as* a reason in a piece of (retrospective) justificatory reason*ing*. We require, in short, nothing less than a full-fledged theory of practical rationality, a theory of action, of the reasons for action, and of the appraisal or assessment of such reasons. Only when at least the rudiments of such a theory are in hand can we once again address – and perhaps resolve – the residual tensions between the diachronic variabilities of our conceptual schemes and our fundamental inescapable collective commitment to an ontology which posits but *one* world. It is to these matters, then, which I shall turn in the next chapter.

CHAPTER VI

ATTRIBUTION AND APPRAISAL: ELEMENTS OF A THEORY OF CONDUCT

Our project has developed some unexpected directions. We are now called upon to give an account of the actions of a being capable of practical rationality — of the conduct of an *agent*. But I shall not begin by straightaway embarking on such an account, by attempting to develop *ab initio* a theory of action. Instead, I shall first lay some extensive groundwork. I want to approach the topic of practical rationality circuitously, through a development of what I will call "attribution theory".

By attribution theory, I intend a general theory of the *explanations* of behavior. Since not all behaviors are actions, attribution theory is not equivalent to — although it will subsume — a theory of actions proper. But such rational agency is located within a complex hierarchy of "teleological behaviors", and a preliminary consideration of less elaborate and complex members of the genus will allow us to isolate certain generic patterns of explanation at a level of simplicity which, with any luck, will cast light on the issues which emerge with the force of acute puzzles when it is *our* behavior which is to be explained. In particular, I hope that by looking at the sorts of explanatory accounts which we can and do properly give of the behaviors of primitive organisms, we can come to grips with the classical problematic dichotomy of the theory of actions proper — the distinction between reasons and causes.

Attribution theory, in this sense, is prior to what I shall call "appraisal theory". Behavior can be appraised along a variety of dimensions — as adaptive or maladaptive, appropriate or inappropriate, reasonable or unreasonable, justified or unjustified, rational or irrational. What these assessments amount to, and what — in the way of explanatory attributions — they presuppose, are the topics of appraisal theory. It is with the semantic and epistemic appraisal of cognitive (representing) conducts which we are ultimately concerned, of course, but from our present perspective, there is a long road to be traveled before we can begin even to raise the appropriate questions.

Before embarking on this journey, it will be well to reflect on what we might like by way of an outcome. What we require, if we are to be able to complete our case for a Realism compatible with Empiricism, is a theory of action and of the appraisals of action which posits no *special mechanism*.

This desideratum can be interpreted in both an "internal" and an "external" sense.

Viewing the representational activities of an experiencer "from within", we have systematically equipped such a being with a representational system evolving under the constraints of determinateness — of formal logic, and of the underlying material logics of time, forms, and contents. We have found that such an experiencer necessarily represents himself as having location within his world's arena and encounters himself apperceptively as a representer through ("meta-level") representings of his own representings *as* representings. These, in turn, are assigned determinate positions within his world's time, thereby giving rise to the perspectival phenomenon of tense. Our rejection of special mechanism in this "internal" setting, then, amounts to the demand that our account of such an experiencer's *practical* rationality be constructable in terms of *these* materials. Our account of intentional action should, in other words, allow that the self which acts is *this* self which apperceptively encounters itself as a representer and as *in* the world, and not require us to posit some incognizable "transcendental" or "noumenal" self. And we should, if possible, construct our picture of an experiencer's practical or deliberative *reasoning* from the forms of representing which we have heretofore attributed to him, avoiding — to the extent that we can — the introduction of new and special representational "targets" and, in particular, any new and *special logic*, over and above the material logics of determinateness already provided for and the formal logic to which they give rise.

In the preceding chapter, however, we found occasion to introduce an "external" viewpoint, which sees the representational activities of experiencers as (causally) evoked responses to the actions of a world on those experiencers, as a first step toward locating the connection between epistemic correctness and ontological adequacy in a limit toward which successive representational systems converge. The corresponding "external" rejection of special mechanism amounts to the requirement that our theory of rational agency should be compatible with an Empiricist epistemology *thus "naturalized"*. And this, in turn, requires that we be able to give an explanatory account of such agency without invoking 'entelechies' or 'final causation' or 'agent causality'. And it requires as well that we show how an appraisal of the conduct of an intentional agent which proceeds by attributing and then assessing *reasons* for that conduct can be compatible with a world-picture in which all *material* "necessary connections" are *causal* in that sense of causality which we located originally in application to the represented changes in and interactions of (represented) *things*.

These are demanding constraints. The surprising and pleasant fact is that they are satisfiable ones. To show this, however, one must proceed slowly and carefully. I shall begin, then, as I have indicated, by adopting the "outside" perspective and considering the modes of explanation of simple and rudimentary "teleological behaviors", approaching a discussion of the actions of a full fledged rational agent only gradually through a systematic deepening and enrichment of the schematic picture which emerges from such elementary studies.

The most fundamental sort of behaviors which allow something like the dichotomy of reasons and causes to get a foothold are *simple tropisms* — for example, the phototropistic behavior of a plant whose leaves vary in orientation systematically according to the position of the sun in the sky. I say that "something like the dichotomy of reasons and causes" is possible here because this primitive behavior already allows explanation in the teleological idiom. "The leaves turn", we may say, "*in order to* present the maximum surface area to the sun". I have already (in Chapter I) suggested how we are to understand this style of explanatory remark. Teleological appeals, I argued, encode complex explanatory accounts which ultimately invoke the theory of evolution. In the present case, there is, first, an implicit synchronic causal appeal in which the angle of incident sunlight is singled out as a specific environment stimulus initiating a series of internal biochemical changes in the leaf in consequence of which its orientation to the light undergoes systematic variation. But there is also, second, an implicit diachronic evolutionary appeal, citing the role of photosynthesis vis-à-vis organic well-being and species survival. Organic behaviors which optimize photosynthetic efficiency in plants are, in accordance with the general evolutionary story, *selected for* by the environment. Being so constructed as to enact the phototropistic causal sequence is such an optimizing feature. A randomly mutated plant thus genetically "wired" to enact this tropistic sequence is consequently more likely to survive and to propagate its kind than one not so constructed. It is the availability of this sort of diachronic evolutionary account of how phototropistic plants came to exist and persist in the present environment which, I have argued, both renders appropriate the use of the teleological explanatory vocabulary and captures the sense of such teleological appeals as well.

We can, in this simple example, distinguish two parameters which correspond roughly to the two aspects — synchronic causal and diachronic evolutionary — of the explanatory account embodied in such teleological appeals. On the one hand, there is the internal state of the organism which results from its genetic heritage and in virtue of which it is disposed to enact the tropistic causal sequence in particular circumstances, and, on the other, the specific environmental stimulus which initiates the behavioral patterns for which the organism is thus genetically "pre-wired". In the case of a simple phototropism, the synchronic occasion is an environmental stimulus — the angle of incidence of ambient sunlight — which *triggers* a (possibly extremely complicated) causal sequence eventuating in the behavior to be explained, behavior which may be described in an austere idiom as a variation in the orientation of the leaves. The internal state is some determinate structural condition in virtue of which the plant has the *propensity* to behave thus in appropriate circumstances, a structural condition which is to be understood in terms of an evolutionary history which has selected such behavioral propensities as survival traits. The general pattern of a teleological explanation of simple tropistic behavior can thus be represented by a crude equation which reminds us of these two aspects:

(TRO)   Propensity + Trigger = Behavior.

The equation is explanatory, as we have seen, only against the background of a theory of natural selection. A useful mediating notion for structuring and elaborating such an evolutionary story is that of an organic *need*. For optimal growth and propagation, a plant *needs* maximal photosynthetic efficiency. Maximal photosynthetic efficiency is achieved when the maximum surface area of the leaves is exposed to direct sunlight. The propensity appealed to in a teleological explanation of tropistic behaviors is precisely a propensity conditioned by this need. It is a propensity to so alter the orientation of the leaves as to maximize their surface-area exposure to direct sunlight. The triggering stimulus is a direct satisfaction of the need at issue. The sunlight which is the proximate cause of the leaf movements is precisely the sunlight which is a necessary condition of photosynthetic activity. It is in this way that the notion of a need serves to bring the tropistic behavior of the plant to be explained, its propensities toward such behavior, and the stimulus which synchronically triggers it into connection with the evolutionary story conducted in terms of survival, growth, and reproduction. A full explanatory account of tropistic behavior adverts to both a *need-conditioned* propensity and a *need-satisfying* trigger.

In a brief explanatory sketch, however, either aspect may be left tacit. This possibility gives rise to two kinds of "reasons" or accounts — I shall say '*logoi*' — which can be offered for some observed tropistic behavior. One logos focuses on the need conditioning the behavioral propensity, while disregarding the specific triggering mechanisms by which the need comes to be synchronically satisfied:

> "The leaves turn in order to maximize photosynthetic efficiency".

The second sort of logos focuses on the synchronic occasioning mechanisms, while allowing the need-conditioned propensity part of the story to remain tacit:

> "The leaves turned because, when sunlight strikes them at such-and-such an angle . . . ".

Either of these accounts can, quite properly, be considered as supplying *a* "reason" for the leaves' turning. Given a suitable background understanding, either can correctly be counted as embodying *an* explanation of the behavior. But neither response can lay exclusive claim to being *the* "reason" (*the* explanation) for that behavior. Both of these accounts are incomplete sketches of a single complex explanatory story which, when it is set out in full, has a place for both a synchronic causal appeal and a diachronic evolutionary appeal.

A word about terminology is in order before proceeding further. A "reason", in the sense of a logos, does not, as we have just seen, contrast with a cause. Indeed, the whole complex synchronic and diachronic story accounting for tropistic behavior is, in that sense, *causal* through and through. It requires no special explanatory principles, no special teleological arcana. A logos, as I intend to use the term, is just whatever we correctly offer as an answer to the question "Why?" (e.g., "Why did/do the leaves turn?"). To give a logos is to give an explanatory account — and, like 'explanation', 'logos' is neutral as between the teleological and the non-teleological, and between propensity and trigger. 'Because' has a similar generic use as well. I gave my first (conditioning need) explanatory sketch a moment ago in the teleological vocabulary of "in order to"; for the second, I employed "because". But I could have used "because" in the first instance as well, had I wished to mention the need which evolutionarily conditions the relevant behavioral propensity explicitly *as* a need:

> "The leaves turned because the plant needs all the sunlight it can get".

It is because (or for the reason that) 'because' and 'reason' are thus generic terms of explanatory accounts that I have appropriated the Greek 'logos' to do the generic job here.

In what follows, I shall thus speak generically of logoi. I will reserve 'because' ('in consequence of', 'triggered by', and the like) for the synchronic causal side of the story and 'reason' ('in order to', and the like) for the diachronic evolutionary side. In the former case, I shall speak broadly of what *occasions* behavior; in the latter, of what *conditions* it. The specific pattern of propensity + trigger which I have elicited in the case of simple tropisms, then, will serve as both a model for and a particular instance of a general pattern which, I shall next argue, characterizes all explanations of teleological behavior, even the most complex:

(TEL) Condition + Occasion = Behavior

What I propose to do is to systematically enrich the picture of a simple tropism which I have been belaboring until we arrive at something like the deliberate actions of a rational agent. In the process, I shall produce a series of descriptions of teleological behaviors which fall in various ways between these two extreme cases. For convenience, I will label each of these intervening stages as I describe it, but it is worth saying in advance that both the descriptions and the labels should be taken *cum grano salis*. Attribution theory is a jungle, not an orchard. Nothing is tidy there. My classification scheme will be a family of "ideal types" – simplified and, on occasion, even simplistic – designed as an instrument for mapping a convoluted terrain. Inevitably, then, it will elevate blurs into dichotomies and quantize continua. A general apology is thus doubtless in order, and this is it. Despite this blanket warning, I shall, as the spirit moves me, from time to time insert additional specific *caveat* hedges as well.

The leading idea of what I shall shortly be about is that either or both of the components of the teleological equation (TEL) may be instantiated by a representation – or by something *functionally akin* to a representation (an important hedge). To get the process underway, consider to begin with the component which, in the case of a tropism, I labeled 'trigger'. Let us look in more detail at the way in which such triggers relate to the organic needs which condition tropistic behavioral propensities.

An organism's *needs* are what are necessary *for* its continued existence and well-being (a conditional necessity). It is because it directly satisfies such a need that sunlight comes to serve as a behavior-triggering stimulus in tropistic plants. But we might observe that it would be evolutionarily adaptive for organisms to be so structured that a mere *deficiency* in some need would *itself* function as an *"internal"* stimulus, triggering behaviors which, while not directly need satisfying would increase the probability of the deficient need being met. Were organisms so structured to appear, they would, in consequence, be selected for by their environments over time. We may further note, however, that a *serious* deficiency in some need could easily render an organism incapable of appropriate 'compensatory" behavior. A starving predator, for example – in consequence of prolonged food-deprivation – may be too physically debilitated to capture and subdue its prey. It would thus be further adaptive if compensatory behavior could be initiated in prospect of such serious deficiency. We should expect, then, to find organisms which possess *anticipatory mechanisms*, that is, which are so structured that the mere falling of a need below some critical *threshold* is itself sufficient to occasion suitable compensatory behavior. As a final step in this process, we can envision some specific organic state, initially correlative to such a threshold, ultimately assuming the role of such an internalized stimulus trigger. Such an internal stimulus state could thus be thought of as a sort of *displaced* or *surrogate* need. What I wish now to propose is that a surrogate need of this sort, functioning as an internalized occasion to trigger appropriate behaviors, is the prototype of a *desire* or a *want*.

The root notion of a want is exactly that of a deficiency or a lack – of something *wanting*. But it is not too great a stretching of the notion to apply it instead to the sorts of displaced or surrogate needs which I have just been sketching, that is, to such internal states of an organism which are, with respect to the production of manifest behavior, functional analogues to external stimuli which trigger behavior by virtue of being direct satisfactions of some authentic need-deficiency. If we do so extend the notion, we arrive at what I shall call "want-directed" behavior, schematized according to the equation:

(WAN)   Propensity + Want = Behavior.

Since the behavior here at issue is not directly need-satisfying but is rather behavior likely to increase the probability of a (potential) need-deficiency being met, it is natural to characterize it as "seeking", "searching for", "looking for", or "trying to find" whatever it is which *would* directly satisfy the (potential) need. And this observation, in turn, tells us where to look in nature for some examples of want-directed behavior.

Perhaps the best examples are classic cases of so-called "drive-reduction". The paradigm of a want, in this sense, would be a *felt lack*, typified by such organic states as hunger or thirst. We attribute such states to organisms as occasions for "food-seeking" or "water-seeking" behavior, and this behavior, which we thus appeal to states of hunger and thirst to explain, is terminated by the acquisition of food or water.

Hunger and thirst have given rise to a variety of philosophical puzzlements. On the one hand, there is a distinct temptation to suppose that to attribute hunger or thirst to an organism just *is* to attribute to it a disposition or propensity to exhibit food-seeking or water-seeking behavior. But it is clear that this is a temptation to which we ought not succumb. On the one hand, we know well enough from our own cases that hunger and thirst are genuinely *felt* states. On the other, the having of the appropriate behavioral dispositions is simply not equivalent to the having of hunger or thirst. Amoebae, for example, exhibit a permanent disposition toward food-seeking behavior. Indeed, all of their behavior, such as it is, can be thought of as "food-seeking" in the sense that their "exploratory" motions are terminated by the encounter with and ingestion of a piece of food. But no-one is the least bit tempted to ascribe to an amoeba a felt state of hunger, and rightly so. And, further up the evolutionary scale, many of us overweight humans know all too well that a disposition to seek out and consume food can exist without being accompanied by any felt hunger.

Yet it is equally clear that it would be incorrect to characterize hunger and thirst as *mere* feelings or sensations. There seems to be some sort of essential *connection* between those particular feelings and the disposition to eat or to drink, a connection which would become wholly unintelligible were we to relegate hunger and thirst to the miscellany of random itches, tickles, and twinges which come and go in the course of our day to day lives. Hunger and thirst seem somehow to be *directed toward* food and drink without, however, being either mere dispositions to seek food and drink or full-fledged conceptual representations of food and drink. They are somehow "about" food and drink, but their "aboutness" is not the aboutness of intentionality — the aboutness of thought or speech.

All of this falls tidily into place, however, on the account which I have been giving of such wants. They are the *displaced surrogates* of authentic *needs* for food and drink. It is the diachronic evolutionary story of how it comes to be that there are organisms for whom such felt states come to serve as internal triggers occasioning food-seeking and water-seeking behavior which provides the missing linkages. Their "aboutness" to food and drink consists in their being adaptive mechanisms arising out of authentic needs for such food and drink. It is the diachronic evolutionary story which traces the behavior-occasioning role from external need-satisfying stimuli to internal states of need-deficiency, from such internal states to further internal threshold states anticipatory of them, and from these to still other internal (now *felt*) states which are causal correlates of such need-thresholds, that establishes the *connection* between what is phenomenologically a mere sensation and the sorts of behaviors for which it serves as an occasion.

Yet while the evolutionary perspective in this way supplies a connection between felt lacks and certain behaviors and behavioral propensities, it severs the connection between wants and authentic needs. Such felt lacks are distinct and autonomous organic states, and a feeling of hunger or thirst can, on this account, come to exist and to perform its behavior-occasioning role in the *absence* of any authentic or prospective (threshold) deficiency of food or water. Just as those organic states which are the sensory components of veridical perceptual takings can occur in organisms in consequence of other than standard causes (thus, for example, in drug-induced hallucinations), so a want — which derives its connection to certain specific compensatory behaviors through an original evolutionary history of need-displacement — *logically* can occur in organisms which are well above any critical need-threshold as a result, instead, of particular atypical adventitious causal circumstances.

Such a want, then, while not literally a conceptual representing, is *twice functionally akin* to such a representing. It is like a representing, first, in its "aboutness", in its "standing for" — in the manner which I have sketched — an organic need-deficiency in prospect (by virtue of its original evolutionary role as an anticipatory mechanism). And it is like a representing, secondly, in being "useable *in absentia*", that is, in being *logically* detachable from its "referent" and thus capable of "non-veridical" occurrences.

Like the need-satisfying tropistic triggers of which they are generalizations, such wants may be attributed to organisms as part of an explanatory account of their observed behaviors. We can classify the stealthy movements of a cat through the weeds as *stalking*, for example, and go on to say of it that it *wants* to catch and consume the bird pecking on the lawn. That is a logos for the cat's hunkering down and moving with such exquisite care and silence. Like an account of tropistic behavior, such a want-explanation is teleological. It says more than that the cat's behavior will terminate if and when the bird either is captured or departs. But, as with all teleological explanations, the cash-value of this "more" is unproblematically causal. It lies not in some arcane form of final causation ("The bird moves the cat by attraction") but in the *quasi-representational* role of the attributed want and, thus, ultimately, in the complex diachronic evolutionary account in terms of which that quasi-representational role is to be understood — an account of the way in which *this* attributed state is related, on the one hand, to certain organic survival needs and, on the other, to specific patterns of manifest behavior.

A parallel displacement or surrogation can take place on the condition side of the teleological equation as well. In place of the innate, need-conditioned propensities of the tropistic organism, we can have *acquired* propensities for behavior to be initiated not directly by need-satisfying occasions but, to begin with, by displaced surrogate stimuli which are originally connected with those need-satisfactions as "natural signs". This in fact is nothing but the classical schema of a conditioned response.

A maze-running laboratory rat which has been rewarded with food-pellets whenever it proceeds down the lighted branch, let us say, of a *T*-maze, will acquire a propensity to turn systematically down the lighted branch, even in the absence of such rewards. The lighted-branch-selection behavior persists for a time after food-pellets cease to be supplied, the length of this "extinction period" being a function of, among other things, the rat's specific reward-history or "reinforcement schedule". We sometimes say that the rat has "learned" to select the lighted branch. A lighted branch has become a sort of "displaced stimulus", functionally equivalent to the food pellets in its capacity to evoke "approach behavior" in the hungry organism. By virtue of the rat's acquired propensity, such branch-lighting assumes, in other words, what is again a quasi-representational role. Within the behavioral economy of such a rat, branch-lighting "stands for" food. Like a want, however, such a "displaced stimulus" is *logically* detachable from its "referent", capable of occurring, and of serving its behavior-conditioning role by means of the animal's acquired propensity, in the absence of any food.

Such an acquired propensity to act on the condition of this sort of "displaced" (or, technically, conditioned) stimulus is the prototype of a *belief*. It is, in fact, tempting and natural to employ the full language of intentionality in giving explanatory accounts of the rat's behavior: "The rat turned down the lighted branch because it *believed* (or: had learned) that food (usually or often) lies at the end of that branch". As in the case of wants, however, there are no grounds for imputing this much conceptualizing to the hungry beast. What we have is rather, again, something *functionally akin* to a full-fledged conceptual or representational item in a variety of respects. I shall call it a *"set"*. A set, in this sense, is an acquired internal state of an organism which is functionally equivalent to an innate genetic propensity in its capacity to condition behavior. It is a propensity to act on the condition of a "displaced stimulus", which, however, is — in the way I have described — quasi-representational, that is, logically detachable from any actual correlative need-satisfactions and able to occur in their absence.

That organisms should be so structured as to be capable of acquiring (as to have the meta-propensity to acquire) such sets is itself explainable in evolutionary terms paralleling the explanation of their having wants. The source of that which an organism needs is not always environmentally available to serve as an immediate occasion for behavior. Thus it is evolutionarily adaptive that an organism should come to have propensities to respond to "natural signs" of such a source — that is, to regularly-occuring environmental *correlates* of need-satisfactions — with behavior likely to optimize the ultimate fulfillment of their needs. But, since such "natural signs" are diverse and subject to changes in frequency, intensity, and kind, it is further adaptive that the organisms come to be so structured as to be capable of "learning from experience" what such "natural signs" from time to time *de facto* are — that is, that they come to have the meta-propensity or *plasticity* to acquire and lose such first-order behavioral propensities in a time-dependent fashion as their environmental circumstances change. Organisms possessing such plasticity will, in fact, have their needs satisfied more frequently that those lacking such mechanisms of "displacement" and "association", and so, in the familiar way, will more frequently survive and reproduce. Thus these capacities, too, will be selected for by the environment over time, and in this way organisms possessing sets and the meta-propensity to acquire and lose sets will come to exist and persist in the world.

Behavior structured by wants and sets I shall term "purposive behavior", and I shall represent it by another instantiation of the generic teleological equation (TEL):

(PUR) Want + Set = Behavior.

Purposive behavior, on this understanding, may be — and often is — *non-conceptual*. Despite this, however, there is a sense in which a purposive organism can be spoken of as intelligent or unintelligent and in which the logoi attributed to such an organism in explanatory accounts of its behaviors may be said to be, not merely reasons, but "good" or "bad" reasons. For a set may fit or not fit the actual environmental circumstances. The acquired behavioral propensity may or may not contain associational components which are irrelevant to the actual ultimate satisfaction of the organism's need-deficiencies. Such irrelevant associational components are manifested in what behavioral psychologists term "superstitious behaviors". Random coincidences of lighted-branch-selection and, say, whisker-twitching during the conditioning period may result in a rat's acquiring not the simple propensity to traverse the lighted maze-branch which (by virtue of the experimenter's design) alone is relevant to its ultimate encounter with the food pellets, but instead the complex propensity to select-the-lighted-branch-and-twitch-whiskers. This sort of whisker-twitching would be an example of a "superstitious behavior". A purposive organism acts for a "good reason", we can then say, if the set which one is justified — on whatever grounds — in attributing to that organism (from "outside") as conditioning its behavior is one which, when described in its quasi-representational character as *analogous to* a belief, *in fact* fits the actual environmental circumstances. Thus we ascribe to the tidily-conditioned rat the quasi-representational set *that* food lies down the lighted branch — and since, by reason of the experimental design, that is in fact (most frequently) the case, such a set is a "good reason" for the rat to traverse the lighted branch. But we may also attribute to the "superstitious" rat a quasi-representational set to the effect *that* whisker-twitching is a necessary condition of, or facilitates, food acquisition — and since, according to the experimental design, this is *not* the case, the rat does not have a "good reason" for whisker-twitching.

We can call an organism *intelligent* to the extent that its meta-propensities to acquire and lose sets are such as to allow it to adapt effectively to *changing* environmental circumstances, that is, to the extent that its set-acquiring propensities exhibit a plasticity and selectivity to allow it to rapidly acquire sets appropriate to new environmental circumstances and to "weed out" irrelevant associational components of the "superstituous" sort.

(Of course, both the notion of a "good reason" and that of intelligence, in this sense, are fuzzy-edged. They admit of continuous variation of degree and appropriateness, and grade off smoothly into cases of elaborate tropisms and want-directed behaviors on the one hand and full-fledged intentional action, on the other, where a more complicated system of appraisals come into play).

What is important to notice about this picture of purposive behavior is the two-level structure of innate meta-propensity and acquired propensity. To attribute *intelligence* to a creature is to advert to the evolutionary history of its *species*. It is to ascribe to it a behavioral plasticity and a corresponding meta-propensity to acquire and lose sets, and this attribution is cashed explanatorily in terms of an evolutionary story of how organisms with such behavioral plasticities come to exist and persist in an environment which selects for the capacity to "learn from experience" and how that capacity becomes an adaptive characteristic of a species. To attribute *reasons* to a creature — in the present sense of appealing to an acquired set, a propensity to act conditioned by a "displaced stimulus" in its quasi-representational role vis-a-vis some need- or want-satisfaction — is, in contrast, to advert to the experiential history of the *individual*. Such an attribution presupposes the innate plasticities established evolutionarily through its species-history, and directs our attention instead to the specific history of stimuli and reinforcements or rewards (need-satisfactions) which, as behavioral psychology puts it, "shape" the organism's behavior — that is, in virtue of which it comes to acquire that particular set. The specific conditioning-history ("learning history", "reinforcement schedule") of the individual organism thus assumes a explanatory role which parallels that of the evolutionary history of its species. As the (global) environment selects for organisms possessing a set-acquiring plasticity of behavior, the (local) environment selects for *specific* behavioral sets in an individual organism which possesses such behavioral plasticity. The logical structure of the two explanatory accounts is the same. In each case, we have an initially adventitious occurrence of behavior followed by a "favorable outcome" which selects for a repetition or preservation of the occurrence. It is this (broadly) evolutionary style of explanatory account, I have argued which warrants employment of the *teleological* idiom wherever it occurs. The behavior of a purposive organism can thus be teleological through and through — while nevertheless being such as can be afforded an explanatory account which is, in the ordinary and unproblematic sense, *causal* from the ground up. Synchronic attributions of wants and sets (as quasi-representational "reasons") encode diachronic explanatory appeals to evolutionary histories — of species and of individuals. What we found in the case of simple tropisms holds true here as well.

In this case, however, since the evolutionary story has now recapitulated itself in the specific conditioning-history of the individual organism, we can build on the foundation of such attributions of wants and sets a much more elaborate account of assessments and appraisals. We can now say more than that behavior is adaptive or maladaptive. We can say, in addition, that it is intelligent or unintelligent, and even that it is justified or unjustified (reasonable or unreasonable) in any of a complex variety of ways.

Even a tropism can be appraised as adaptive or maladaptive. What brings the additional dimensions of intelligence and "good reasons" into play in the case of purposive behavior is the fact that we have added something functionally akin to representations (what I have been calling "quasi-representations") to our story in the form of attributions of wants and sets. It is important to emphasize that these wants and sets are *only* functionally akin to representations. They are internal states which *we attribute* to organisms as elements of explanatory accounts of their behavior (hence "attribution theory"), and such an attribution is itself justified from our point of view, then, only to the extent that it is explanatory. It is for this reason that attributions of full-fledged representational conceptualizings would be out of place here. The behavior standing in need of explanation lacks the complexities requisite to give such attributions an explanatory force. They become gratuitous. Nothing a rat could do would warrant our distinguishing between its "believing" that there *aren't* any food pellets down the dark branch of a T-maze and its *not* "believing" that there *are*, not to mention its not "realizing" that there *could* be or its "mistakenly believing" that disaster would ensue *if* it went down the dark branch, and so on. That the rat has an acquired behavioral propensity in virtue of which a lighted-branch has become a "displaced stimulus" "standing for" food in the quasi-representational way is all the explanation that the phenomena of lighted-branch-selection demands and can support here.

Yet, because we have access to the "outside" (experimenter's) point of view — and a command of the forms of appraisal appropriate to our own (intentional) actions — it is possible to construct a quite complicated array of forms of appraisal for the conducts of even a rudimentary purposive creature. We can, for example, find an analogue to the distinction between there *being* a "good reason" for certain behavior, on the one hand, and, on the other, the organism's *acting for* a "good reason" (something's being *its* reason for behaving so, rather than simply *a* reason for so behaving). There is a point to developing just this sort of distinction, for one expression which is commonly mobilized in explanatory accounts of behavior is, in fact, systematically ambiguous between these two possibilities — the expression: "the organism *had* a 'good reason' (or simply a reason) for its behavior".

There *is* (or was) a reason for the behavior, we can say, if for some R (e.g., that food most frequently lies down the lighted branch), it is (or was) a fact that R, and, given that R, the organism's engaging in the behavior at issue — call it 'B' — *will* result (or would have resulted) in its satisfying a want W which it in fact has (or had). In this sense, indeed, there can *be* a reason for a phototropistic plant's turning its leaves toward the light.

An organism *acts for* the reason R, in contrast, (i.e., R is *its* reason for so behaving), if its behavior B is a manifestation of the appropriate *set*, that is, of a propensity to act conditioned by the quasi-representation that R, whether or not it is in fact the case that R. Here our use of the expression "in fact" represents precisely the story which we tell about the environmental circumstances from our "outside" perspective as experimenters and observers of experiments. It is important to note that such an "outside" perspective is operative in reason-attributions of this sort, for just this biperspectival, self- and-other, possibility is *lacking*, as we have seen in our discussions of idealism, in the case of our own collective representational activity, and we shall, in consequence, need to examine carefully whatever, in our own case, in fact stands in its place.

In terms of these distinctions, we can now find a foothold for the claim that some purposive organism is or was *justified* in behaving in a certain way, B, given that it had the want W. This claim, in fact, might mean any one of three things:

(i)   that there is or was a reason R for its engaging in B; or
(ii) that the organism acts *for* the reason R, and, although it is *not* the case that R, if it *were* the case that R, then, given that the organism has the particular want W, R *would be* a reason for its engaging in B; or
(iii) that the organism acts *for* the reason R, and R *is* a reason for its engaging in B.

From our complex appraisal-apparatus for the activities of intentional agents, we can derive some compact idioms for distinguishing among these variants of the notion of justification. We can say

(i)   that the behavior was justified in (or by) the *circumstances*; or
(ii) that the behavior was justified "given what the organism *believed*", that the behavior was *reasonable*; or
(iii) that the behavior was *fully* justified or simply justified (full stop); that the organism "acted for a good and sufficient reason".

All of these distinctions in appraisal will be more or less appropriate and warranted to the extent that the organism's overall behavioral economy is sufficiently complex to demand our attributing to it more or less in the way of quasi-representational wants and sets in giving our explanatory accounts of its behavior.

It is worth noting, too, that each of (i), (ii), and (iii) posits only a *relative* justification. Each presupposes the attribution of a want. But wants, too, may themselves be appraised as reasonable and unreasonable. To do this, we harken back to the organism's evolutionary history. Appraising a *want* as reasonable or unreasonable comments, from the "outside" perspective, on the prospects for an organism's survival and well-being were the want, in fact, to be satisfied in consequence of its behavior. An individual organism which wants to rush lemming-wise over cliffs has, from this perspective, an unreasonable want.

(Although I gather that the emergence of periodic suicidal behavior is adaptive for lemmings *as a species* in that it relieves accumulated Malthusian pressures. In this case, although the individual's suicidal want might still be appraised as unreasonable, we could go on to say that it is reasonable – i.e., that there *are* reasons – *that* individuals of that species periodically have such wants.)

Against this background, we can, at last, turn to the system of concepts in terms of which we offer explanations of the behavior of intentional agents, that is, of our own behavior. What the consideration of the wants and sets of a purposive organism has shown us is how the elements of a teleological explanatory account of behavior – ranging in sophistication and complexity even unto the conducts of Kohler's apes – can be "internalized" in the organism without the importation of any teleological arcana on the order of entelechies or final causation. And we have seen, too, how a system of assessments and appraisals can be built on a foundation of such teleological explanatory attributions. The key move in understanding the conduct of an intentional agent is simply this: that what occasions and conditions the behavior of such a being is not something *quasi*-representational but fullfledged representings as such. The fundamental explanatory scheme remains that of the teleological equation.

(TEL)   Condition + Occasion = Behavior.

What assumes the role of conditioning behavior, however, is no longer a system of quasi-representational sets but rather a system of representings or *beliefs*. And what assumes the role of occasioning behavior is a family of representings which I shall call *motives*. The generic teleological equation is thus to be instantiated, in the case of intentional agency, to a new specific variant.

(INT)   Belief + Motive = Behavior.

What we now need to do is to explore in detail the substance of this instantiation and its implications for the theme of appraisal.[1]

"Motive" I shall use very broadly. It subsumes ends, goals, desires, aims, plans, policies, purposes, and intentions. What sets motives off from what I have called wants is that motives are authentic representations. A motive, indeed, is simply a *representation which occasions behavior*. Like any other representations, motives stand in logical relations to other representations — to other motives and to beliefs — and fall within the scope of the constraints of those material logics and their resultant formal logic which are collectively determinative of the elements of a representational system. What sets motives apart from beliefs is precisely their behavior-occasioning, causal role. This behavior-occasioning role may, in fact, be more or less attenuated, more or less immediate or remote, but for a representation to qualify as a motive, it must be embedded in a network of *causal propensities* at the periphery of which lie representations which are *immediate* occasions ("triggers") of manifest behavior. Such an *immediate* occasion is called a *volition*.

The role and character of these volitions can best be appreciated by comparing them with perceptual takings. A perceptual taking is a *representing occasioned by a sensing*, where a sensing is itself a *non*-conceptual state of an experiencer. A perceptual taking is a representing (a judgment) with which one finds oneself. It is essentially a *response* to something which is not itself a representing. It is a response, in fact, which mobilizes a representational system already fully constituted "internally" by the inferential constraints of a family of formal and material logics. The defeasibility or endorsement as veridical of such a perceptual taking is, as I have argued, a question of coherence, a matter of tracing its inferential connections among the representings which constitute an evolving world-story in accordance with the principles of such logics in an effort to afford its occurrence in the experiencer a determinate accommodation. It is, to speak metaphorically, a rogue star, encroaching on an initially-stable galaxy of representings, and it finds a permanent place in the new and larger whole by a mutual readjustment of the forces between and among the multitudinous parts into a new coherent and determinate equilibrium.

It is here that the fact that it is *our* collective world-picture into which a new perceptual taking must fit or which it fails to fit comes into play. To put it briefly, one learns to perceive. The propensity to find oneself with such representings is an *acquired* propensity. It is in fact acquired during that part of an individual's history which is his *learning a language*. Thought of on the model of behavior-shaping, the process of language learning consists in part of its coming to be the case that an individual's responsive propensities are diachronically consilient with those collectively characterizing the linguistic community to which that individual belongs and by whose own responses to his representings his linguistic behavior is, in fact, shaped. It is because the individual's language-acquisition history thus again recapitulates the evolutionary pattern that the *fact* that he does find himself inclined to a particular perceptual judgment, say that-*p*, can be a *reason* for him to endorse the judgment that-*p*, although, of course, a reason which is merely "prima facie", since the judgment necessarily remains defeasible.

We shall have more to say about this mode of justification once further groundwork has been laid. What we must now be sensitized to is the fact that a perceptual taking that-*p* is a representing which, in virtue of the mode of acquisition of the *propensity* to such representings, comes to be *both* causally *and* logically related to the circumstances that-*p*. The logical tie, however, is roundabout. It is mediated by the specific language-learning history of the individual in the community during which his propensities to find himself with a spontaneous representing that-*p* are gradually and systematically restricted and shaped to those occasions which the community consiliently represents *as* that-*p* occasions (in consequence of which, as we saw in the preceding chapter, they *are* that-*p* occasions). Here again, then, the specific learning history of the individual assumes an explanatory role paralleling that of the evolutionary history of the species.[2]

What I am calling volitions are, in essence, the converse of perceptual takings. As a perceptual taking is a representing which is a response to something not itself a representing, a volition is a representing which is the immediate (causal) occasion ("stimulus" or "trigger") for something not itself a representing — for a bit of manifest behavior. It is a fact about people that such volitions are *future-tensed first-person* representings. They are representings in prospect or hypothetically of *oneself as engaged in conduct* — conduct which, in the case of us humans, is or includes bodily movement. I say that this is a *fact* because there is no logical incoherence in the supposition that, for example, my representing, in prospect or hypothetically, of a cup as moving should be the immediate causal occasion of the cup's moving in the manner represented. (Psychokinesis) It is a fact of the same order, indeed, as the fact that humans can learn to respond with perceptual judgments to peripheral stimulation by light rays but not by X-rays.[3]

I say that a volition is a first-person representing of conduct which is or *includes* bodily movements because, within the limits of the restriction to the first-person, behavior can be conditioned to representings of any degree of complexity. Such complex skills as driving an automobile and typing begin by demanding pluralities of volitions in which individual arm, leg, and finger movements are separately represented, but develop into behavioral gestalts which are represented and can be willed as *units*. Here, too, there is an analogy with perceptual takings. A novice automobile mechanic, for example, may begin by *inferring* loose valves from various knocking and pinging noises. But he becomes the seasoned veteran who listens to an engine and *hears loose valves* — that is, who responds to the ambient peripheral stimulation *directly* with a representing of loose valves. This is a commonsense counterpart to such rarified cases as the particle physicist who *sees electrons* passing through a cloud chamber, and the astronomer who sees the plane of the ecliptic as a true horizontal and the earth as tipped relative to it.[4]

Like a perceptual taking, then, a volition comes to be *both* logically *and* causally tied to the conduct which is its representational content. Again, it is the specific learning history of the organism (representer) which mediates the logical tie. The propensity to engage in represented conducts upon the occasion of their representings, hypothetically or in prospect, is again an acquired propensity. Indeed, it is a propensity acquired in much the same way. Just as our responsive representing behavior is shaped during the course of language learning into consilience with that of the balance of the linguistic community, so too our propensities to respond with the relevant actions to representings in prospect of ourselves *as* acting are selected for and shaped in the course of the same language learning.

It is this evolutionary picture which resolves the perennial, Humean, puzzles about the connection between volition and act. The volition to raise one's arm should be more intimately connected with a raising of one's arm than with, to cite a classical fanciful example, one's nursemaid bursting into flames. It is argued, however, that any connection here can be, at best, a causal one, and hence merely *de facto*. There is no prima facie *logical* reason to suppose that volitions to raise one's arm *should* eventuate in arm-raisings rather than in governess-burnings.

What the evolutionary pattern of explanation has shown us, however, is how a connection can be (broadly) logical without being one of entailment. That one wills to raise one's arm does not *entail* that one raises one's arm or even that one's arm goes up. Nevertheless, it is not simply a matter of *brute* fact that it is representations of *that* sort which, generally and for the most part, eventuate in arm-raisings. What *is* a fact about us is that we can be so conditioned as to respond to representings hypothetically or in prospect of conducts which are or involve our own bodily movements by manifestings of *those same conducts*, just as it is a fact about rats that they can be conditioned to respond to branch-lighting in a *T*-maze by "approach behavior" appropriate to food pellets. It is in virtue of this fact that the community can *bring it about* that, for example, my representation in prospect of myself as raising my arm not only "stands for" (represents) a raising of my arm but also *occasions* (come to serve as an immediate causal stimulus for) my arm's moving upwards. My specific learning history within the community can *select for* this causal propensity.

We can schematize the content of a representing which is a volition, then, by

>I will *now* do X,

where 'doing X' stands surrogate for a description of conduct of the appropriate sort and '*now*' signals the relevant immediacy.

It is important to notice that I have here supplied my representer with a first-person singular pronoun. In the balance of this chapter, I shall be taking this 'I' for granted. It is precisely the non-vacuous 'I' the demand for which emerged earlier. But — and this is a crucial observation — we do not *yet* know how to account for it. That, in fact, will be our main task in the next chapter. What we need to do first, however, is to pursue the current investigation of intentional action to the point of its associated family of appraisals. Only when we have done this, it will emerge, will we be able to supply the missing story of this non-vacuous 'I' — for only then will we command a clear understanding of what, precisely, the 'I' is wanted *for*.

Other members of the family of motives are best understood as related in various ways to volitions. An *intention*, for example, is a volition in prospect. It is a representing of an *executable* conduct (that is, for us, a conduct which is or includes bodily movement) which is *caeteris paribus* a proximate or remote causal occasion, not of the behavior directly, but of the corresponding volition. Intentions thus differ from volitions in immediacy, and may be represented according to the schema

>I will do X *at* t (in n minutes, etc.)

We can, in fact, fruitfully botanize motives by thinking of them as representings of differing contentive and temporal specificity. A motive may be as diffuse as this:

>I will be wealthy (someday),

In such a case, we speak of it as a *desire* — or, depending largely on the likelihood or improbability of its realization, as a *wish* or a *hope* or a *longing*. If we particularize it a bit, however,

>>I will have a net worth of over one million dollars (by the time I am forty years old),

we are more inclined to speak of an *aim* or an *end* or a *goal*.

ATTRIBUTION AND APPRAISAL

Since motives are representings, like any representings they can have an arbitrarily complex internal structure. If we add to the representing of an aim, end, or goal a specification of a *means*, what results is the sort of motive which we call a *plan*:

> I will have a net worth of over one million dollars (by the time I am forty years old) by investing the royalties from my textbooks in high-yield common stocks.

As a plan is a conditional *end*, there is also a variety of conditional *intention* which will prove important in what follows, namely, a *policy*. It has the general form

> I will do X whenever I am in circumstances C and p is the case,

where doing X here is an *executable* conduct — one which, for us, is or involves bodily movement and which one has "learned to do at will", that is, which *caeteris paribus does* occur upon the occasion of one's having the appropriate volition.

What makes representings of such various forms motives is simply their embedding in a causal matrix. The key point is the volition, which, *caeteris paribus*, has as its immediate causal consequence a doing of what it represents the agent *as* doing. The *caeteris paribus* hedge here adverts to the familiar, open textured set of ways in which this normal causal sequence may misfire — unsuspected paralysis, sudden explosions, and the like. A volition is an exit point from representation into manifest behavior. A being is an intentional agent just in case it is — or has come to be — so structured that (*caeteris paribus*) its volitional representings regularly trigger their corresponding behaviors and, working back along the dimension of specificity and time, so structured that its intentions regularly occasion the appropriate volitions (after the lapse of a suitable time interval), its plans and policies give rise to intentions (in the relevant circumstances), its ends or goals eventuate in definite plans, and its realizable desires give rise to the increasingly specific series of ends, plans, policies, intentions and volitions which issue in the actions by which the desires (may) come to be realized. What qualifies a being as an intentional agent is just that a subset of its first-person prospective conduct representings have this behavior-initiating causal force.

I say "a subset" of such representings because any of the representings which we have been canvasing — even those which are standardly volitions — *could*, in specific (more or less abnormal) circumstances, be not a motive but a (*mere*) belief — that is, in particular, a *prediction* about one's own future or immediate states or conducts. What distinguishes a motive from a belief is nothing in point of representational content ("target"). It is simply a difference in the causal embedding of the representing, in its relation to the doings which it represents the agent *as* doing. To classify such a representing as a motive is thus to appeal to it in the context of an explanatory account of manifest behavior. It is to locate it on the occasion side of the teleological equation (TEL) and thus, implicitly, to invoke a complex evolutionary appeal to the specific learning history in virtue of which such representings have acquired their causal relationships to the conducts of the representer. This explanatory role is customarily signaled by a variety of devices – by certain uses of the auxiliary 'shall' and of the infinitive form of verbs (e.g., "A wants, plans, intends, etc. *to X*"), for example – but such devices may tempt us to suppose that a motive differs *qua representation* (i.e., in its content) from the corresponding first-person prospective belief. Rather than adopting such an alternative mode of speech for schematizing an agent's motives "from within", therefore, I shall instead fly a pair of flags in the form of cent-signs ('¢') to remind us of the ¢ausal story which stands behind the attribution of a motive to an agent. Thus, my intention to telephone my stockbroker at 2 o'clock this afternoon I will note by

(M) ¢ I will call my broker at 2 P.M. today. ¢

while the corresponding belief or prediction will be simply

(B) I will call my broker at 2 P.M. today.

My principal thesis here can then be put, somewhat paradoxically, by saying that my motive (intention) (M) just *is* my belief (B) in the event that my specific learning history has brought it about that I have acquired the causal propensity to *respond* to representings of that sort (*caeteris paribus*) by telephonings of my broker at two in the afternoon. To say this is not, of course, to endorse the thesis that motives are *nothing but* beliefs. For to *say* of a representing that it is *nothing but* a belief is precisely to *withhold* ascription of a behavior-occasioning causal force. I want rather to make the point that – *qua representing* – a motive is, in its *intrinsic* character (its "content" or "target"), no different from a (mere) belief of a certain sort.

The most important consequence of this general thesis is that *there is no special logic of motives*. What is implied – formally and materially – by a motive is exactly what is implied – formally and materially – by the corresponding belief (i.e., by the belief which is identical in representational content to that motive). The difference between practical and theoretical reasoning, then, is not a difference in content but simply a difference in the relation of the reasoning to behavior or conduct. A bit of practical reasoning will simply be a bit of reasoning with a motive as its conclusion and one or more motives among its premises.

Any experiencer who possesses a conceptual scheme or representational system will *a fortiori* be a reasoning being. That is, its representings will be subject to the constraints of material logics of time (chrono-logic), form (arena-geometry), and contents (causality) — and these constraints will manifest themselves as "internal" behavioral propensities. A bit of reason*ing*, in other words, (practical or theoretical) will be a *series of representing conducts* — representings occasioned by other representings in accordance with the constraints of such material logics (and formal logic as well, if we suppose our representer equipped with the appropriate apparatus).

It will often be explanatorily fruitful to *attribute* such reasonings to an agent in giving an account of his observed behavior. A standard teleological explanatory account according to the pattern codified in (TEL) — or in its specific instantiation (INT) — turns out, in fact, to embody the schematic attribution of just such a course of reasoning to an agent.

In accordance with the teleological equation (INT), the fundamental form of explanation of an intentional agent's doing X is:

A, believing that R, did X in order to achieve E.

Here, the motive or occasion-logos is cited as an *end*, E, and the condition-logos as a *belief*, that R. In offering such an account as explanatory, however, we necessarily presuppose the availability of a connection between the attributed *end*, E, and the executable *conduct*, X, the occurrence of which is to be explained — a connection which is somehow to be mediated by the agent A's belief that R. Roughly, such a teleological account will do its explanatory job only if A's doing X when it is the case that R can be connected with the end E as a *means* to that end. What the teleological equation explicitly suggests is that we understand A's doing of X *as if* it eventuated from a course of reason*ing* by A of the schematic form:

(R.1)   ¢ I will achieve E. ¢
It is the case that R.
(Ergo) ¢ I will do X. ¢

where the represented *intention* which stands as the conclusion to this reasoning is, in turn, the proximate or immediate causal occasion (I have suppressed the time parameter) of the doing of X by A which is to be explained.

But while this much of an attributed reasoning is *explicitly* given by the teleological equation, the demands for securing a means-end connection between X and E suggest that, in offering such an explanation, we also *implicitly* attribute to the agent, A, a second, mediating, motive and a second, mediating, belief. The mediating motive is one which brings the condition-logos belief that R into connection with the intention to do X by means of a general policy *to* do X whenever it is the case that R. And the mediating belief is a belief to the effect that adopting and acting in accordance with such a behavioral policy *is* a means to A's achieving his given end, E. In offering a standard-brand teleological account of the behavior of our intentional agent A, then, we may conclude that we are *implicitly* attributing to that agent not simply the schematic reasoning (R.1), but a full-dress practical reasoning of the more detailed form

(R^+)   (1)   ¢ I will achieve E. ¢
           (2)   My doing X whenever R is the case will facilitate my achieving E.
           (3)   ¢ I will do X whenever R is the case. ¢
           (4) R is the case.
           (5)   ¢ I will do X. ¢

where (2) is the requisite mediating belief and (3) the requisite mediating policy (motive). (The circumstances C have been absorbed into the general condition expressed by 'R'). As before, the intention, (5), which stands as conclusion to this reasoning is to be understood, in turn, as the proximate or immediate causal occasion of the doing of X by A which is to be explained.

The schema (R^+) is, of course, itself indefinitely complexifiable, but I want to advance it as the fundamental or basic form of a piece of practical reasoning. What I have been arguing is that it is the schema (R^+) which is implicit in the teleological explanation of the behavior of an intentional agent. *Whether it occurs or not*, in offering a teleological explanatory account of A's doing X we attribute (R^+) to the agent A in the sense that we propose to view that conduct *as if* it were the outcome of the actual occurrence of such a course of reasoning in A. And, whether it occurs or not, it is on this implicitly attributed scheme (R^+) that our *appraisals* of the agent's conduct are built and in terms of it that they are to be understood.

As I did earlier in the case of purposive behavior, let me hold the occasioning end, E, as fixed and given. And, as before, let me assume an "outside" perspective. I will suppose, in other words, a perspective from which we can intelligibly *correct* A's beliefs both about particular circumstances (whether, for example, it is actually the case that R) and about general relations of material consequence represented by A as principles of natural necessitation (whether, for example, A's doing X whenever R is the case *will* facilitate his achieving E). The crucial point — which will form the focus of our work in the next chapter — is that *the appraisal of conduct necessarily presupposes such an "outside" perspective.* Only from this "outside" perspective can one distinguish between there *being* a reason for A to do X and A's doing X *for* a reason.

There *is* a reason — let us say, p — for A to do X if (i) it is the case that p and (ii) *that* it is the case that p implies that A's doing X will facilitate A's achieving E. A does X *for* the reason that R, in contrast, if A's doing X is conditioned by the belief that R, that is, if the belief that R figures suitably in the practical reasoning (R^+) which we are justified (on whatever grounds) in attributing to A (if only in the "as if" fashion which I have been adumbrating above).

The mention of the full-dress practical reasoning (R^+) however should remind us that there are in (R^+) *two* beliefs in which its being the case that R is represented — the simple belief *that* R is the case, (4), and the complex belief that doing X when R is the case facilitates the achieving of E, (2). In consequence of this observation, just as A's *having* a reason splits (from our "outside" perspective) into there *being* a reason and A's acting *for* a reason, the latter notion now splits again. We must now distinguish between A's acting for what *is* a reason and A's acting for what A *takes to be* a reason. For A's belief (2) is just such a taking. (2) is A's belief that, given the end E, R's being the case *is* a reason for his doing X.

All of these distinctions give rise to variations in the modes of appraisal of A's conduct — in the ways in which A's doing X may be or fail to be "justified". As before, we can say that A's conduct was justified in (or by) the circumstances just in case there *is* a reason (it need *not* be what A *takes* to be a reason) for A to do X, given his end E. We can also speak of A's conduct as "justified given what he believed" (namely, that R) in the event that R is not the case but *were* R actually the case, it *would* be a reason for A to do X, given his end E. In speaking in this way of A's being "justified given what he believed", in other words, we are ourselves endorsing, from our "outside" perspective, his mediating belief, (2), that doing X does facilitate achieving E whenever R is the case, while withholding a similar endorsement from his belief, (4), that R is indeed the case.

But there is a mode of appraisal which focuses not in this way upon the situational belief (4) but instead directly upon the means-end belief (2). For

A may be correct in his belief, (4), that *R* is the case and nevertheless be incorrect in his belief, (2), that *R*'s being the case *bears* in the appropriate way upon the question of his achieving *E* or doing *X*. And, if this is the way things stand, what we say is not that *A*'s doing *X* was not justified in the circumstances or not justified given what he believed but that, although what *A* believed (namely, that *R*) was true, it was not a *valid* reason for his doing *X*, given that he had the end of achieving *E*.

To speak in this way about the *validity* of reasons tells us something about the particular character of the mediating belief, (2), that doing *X* whenever *R* is the case facilitates achieving *E*. To put the matter briefly, such talk of validity suggests that the means-ends belief (2) is itself essentially the sort of thing which should be viewed as the outcome of a course of reasoning. Fortuitously, we are, indeed, in a position to do just this. For (2) is, at base, a *causal* belief. It is a belief to the effect that doing *X* when *R* is the case *causally necessitates* (an increased likelihood of) achieving *E*.[5] But, as I argued earlier, such "object language" principles of causal necessitation are the reflections of material principles of objective consequence — the constraints of the material logics of time, form, and contents — which necessarily structure an experiencer's conceptual scheme or representational system. In commenting on the *validity* of the reason for which an agent acts, in other words, we are attributing to him a complex world-picture evolving under the constraints of such material logics, and we are commenting, again from our "outside" perspective, on the correctness of that world-picture — a world-picture in which the *agent* can trace an inferential route from the hypothesis that he does *X* whenever *R* (that is, from a representing of himself as doing *X* in circumstances *R*) *via* such principles of objective consequence to a conclusion which represents him as achieving *E* (or as more likely to achieve *E*).

The reasoning to which we implicitly advert in appraisals of *A*'s reasons as *valid* or *invalid* is this theoretical reasoning which moves under the constraints of material logics from a representing of a conduct in circumstances to a representing of (the increased likelihood of) an achieved end. In denying that *A*'s reason for doing *X* is valid, in other words, we are denying that there is a valid *reasoning* of this sort which issues in a representation of the achieving of *E as* an immediate or remote causal consequence of *A*'s doing *X* when *R*.

We are now fairly approaching the terrain over which the last battles between realism and idealism must be fought. By approaching from "outside" and from, so to speak, below, we have arrived at the rudiments of a family of appraisals for the conducts of an intentional agent, and at the schemata of attributions — motives in the forms of ends, policies, intentions, and volitions; beliefs in the form of representings under the constraints of material logics governing the diachronic evolution of a conceptual scheme; and particular reasonings in which such motives and beliefs are mobilized — which are presupposed by such forms of appraisal. We have done this carefully, from "outside" and from "below", to ensure that no special mechanisms are required — to ensure, briefly, that the self who acts and whose actions are appraised need not be some incognizable "noumenal" self, but *can* be the self who encounters himself apperceptively as a representer and who (necessarily) represents himself as having location in the world's arena and his representings as having positions in that world's time.

In this we have been successful. We have seen how the *internal* apparatus of practical rationality — in the sense of conduct being occasioned and conditioned by representation — can be built on the internal apparatus of theoretical rationality — in the sense of an agent's being an apperceptive discursive intelligence — without invoking anything more in the way of representational *content* than machinery for representing *oneself* (a non-vacuous 'I'), prospectively or hypothetically, *as* engaged in conduct subject to causal constraints no different from those applying to the *things* of one's world. And we have seen how the *external* apparatus of practical rationality — in the sense of teleological explanations and appraisals which cite and assess logoi — can be grounded, without appeal to entelechies or "agent causality", by a suitable explanatory recourse to patterns of exosomatic and endosomatic evolution in the species, in the community, and in the learning history of the individual, provided that we have available to us in our *appraisals* something answering to an "outside" perspective from which the validity and goodness of reasons (logoi) can be intelligibly assessed.

But this last remark precisely sets the problematic for our next chapter. The very possibility of rational appraisal of intentional action presupposes a contrast between the agent's own "internal" or "subjective" perspective — *his* world-picture — and an "outside" or "objective" perspective against which that world-picture can be measured for adequacy. But have I not been systematically arguing that no such "outside" perspective *can* be available to *us*? Well, I have ... and I haven't. Thereby hangs a tale. The telling of this tale is my next order of business. It is the story of the non-vacuous 'I'.

CHAPTER VII

COMMUNAL NORMS: STEPS TOWARD A COLLECTIVE PRAGMATICS

It is time to begin pulling together a variety of loose ends. Each of the last three chapters has left one dangling. In Chapter IV, I argued that the correctness of a representing *consists* in its being the manifestation of a practice belonging to a family of consilient practices within a community. I concluded there that, in consequence, in order to have a *concept* of correctness, a representer will need, at least, to be able to think of himself as a self *in contrast to other selves*. He will need, in other words, a non-vacuous 'I'. And there, for the moment, I let the matter rest.

In Chapter V, I argued that the *sense* of a *claim* of correctness was at base deontic. The semantic idiom, I suggested, is a transposed mode of speech. It classifies behaviors which are for us tokening behaviors in terms of their places in the overall behavioral economy of a representer (his fundamental project) not by speaking of them *as* behaviors but by use of an illustrating and analogical mode of discourse in which the tokens characteristically produced in the course of *our* overt representings are used to *indicate* the relevant behavioral moments. On this understanding, a claim of correctness does not predicate a property of a represent*ation* but rather authorizes a performance of a represent*ing*. It is a principle of an "ethics of belief" which says of something that it may be done. The upshot of this chapter was that a representer who is in the "logical space" of correctness will need, at least, to be a being capable of practical rationality – an intentional agent. He will, in other words, be at least a being who can engage in practical reasoning and whose conduct can be an outcome of such reasoning. With this conclusion in mind, I again abandoned the mainstream of my arguments to inquire into the question of what is involved in the concept of such an intentional agent.

This investigation formed the substance of Chapter VI. It had two principal outcomes. The first concerned the ontology of practical rationality, and amounted to the comfortable conclusion that the concept of an intentional agent demands in this respect nothing more than that of a representer who possesses a conceptual scheme embodying the resources to represent himself *as* acting in a world (that is, in particular, a representation of himself as located *in* the space and time of world and thereby as subject to the material constraints of that world's causality). Apart from the possession of a non-vacuous 'I', we have already given this picture of an experiencer a Kantian grounding in the nature of an apperceptive, discursive intelligence *as such*. Our second conclusion, however, was less comfortable. It concerned the rational appraisal of intentional actions, and amounted to the troubling conclusion that the possession of such notions as those of "good" or "valid" reasons presupposed an "outside" perspective against which a world-picture can be measured for adequacy.

To pull all these elements together, I want to advance yet another step beyond the notion of an intentional agent developed in the last chapter. I want to introduce the concept of a *rational* agent. In the last chapter, the practical reasoning characteristic of intentional agency was attributed to organisms and appraised from without. But nothing in my description there, we should now notice, demanded that the organism to which motives and beliefs were attributed and whose reasons and reasonings were appraised *himself* have the concept of an intentional agent. I there attributed to an intentional agent the ability to represent himself *as* acting – but it must now be pointed out that to thus describe the situation runs the risk of radically misleading us. For these attributed apperceptive representings were of a self as "acting" only in the narrow sense of being representings of himself as manifesting particular executable conducts (behaviors) and as being or coming in consequence to be in certain conditions or states (goal- or end-states).

We can, however, form the notion of an intentional agent who can represent himself as acting not merely in this narrow sense but in the richer sense of representing himself *as* an intentional agent. Such a being would not only be one who does act for (what he takes to be) reasons, but one who can represent himself *as* acting for reasons – and who can therefore retrospectively apperceptively attribute such reasons to himself and retrospectively appraise such self-attributed motives and beliefs as good or valid reasons. (he could also, of course, appraise reasons prospectively, *sub specie possibilitatus*: "If it were the case that R, that would be a good reason for me to do X, given that I want to achieve E.") A being who is in this strong sense in the "logical space" of practical rationality is what I call a *rational* agent. What we must now determine is how such a being's rational agency manifests itself "from within" – in terms of the contents and the structure of his representational system or conceptual scheme. The principal thesis which I wish to advance in this connection may be stated very compactly: what needs to be added to the conceptual scheme of an intentional agent to arrive at rational agency is precisely the fundamentum of an authentic non-vacuous 'I' – that is, it is an operative *term of contrast* for the agent's 'I' in virtue of which it becomes a genuine *personal pronoun* signaling something more than the purely formal Kantian "transcendental unity of apperception".

The problem which we confront here is that a rational agent, as I have characterized him, must be *biperspectival*. He must possess a standpoint from which *he* can (retrospectively) assess his own reasonings *as* reasonings, from which *he* can appraise his reasons as good or poor, valid or invalid, and correct those beliefs and reasonings which fail to qualify. He must, in other words, have a *critical stance* from which to assess his own conducts — a critical stance which is determinate, non-arbitrary, and (somehow) *objective*.

At the close of the last chapter, I observed that the very possibility of the rational appraisal of intentional action presupposes such a contrast between the agent's own "internal" perspective and an "outside" perspective against which his world-picture can be measured for adequacy. And I briefly raised the question of whether such an "outside" perspective can be available to us, only to reply with a cryptic remark and move on. The time has come to be less cryptic. *We* do indeed have such an "outside" perspective. It is precisely *our* perspective — our collective (shared) communal world-picture against which the world-picture of an individual agent (attributed *by* us *to* him in our explanatory accounts of his conduct) can be measured for consilience or divergence.

But what of a rational agent? How can he *himself* have two world-pictures — one "internal" and one from "outside"? The answer to this question brings together the results of the last three chapters: He can do this only by being *one of us*. A rational agent can have two world-pictures by having his own and by having *ours* as well.

To put the point less paradoxically, a rational agent must represent himself *as* a member of a *community* (*as* one of us). He must represent his representings as subject to correction by the community collectively (by the rest of us) and must operate under the fundamental overriding constraint of bringing his own world-picture into consilience with the collective world-picture of the community to which he belongs (into consilience with ours). And what I wish to propose is that it is this which locates the *primary* function of the non-vacuous 'I'. It serves to represent the self as a self *in contrast to a community of selves to which it belongs*. The fundamental contrast with 'I' on this understanding is neither 'you', nor 'he' nor 'she', then, but rather 'we'.[1]

If correct, this observation successfully locates as well the place of the "impersonal pronoun" 'one'. To put the point in first approximation, 'one' signals a *communal norm*. What is useful to note in this connection is that, if the community at issue is *our* community, we may, in fact, freely substitute our 'we' for this "impersonal" 'one':

> In our tribe, one never acts (*we* never act) without first consulting the witchdoctor.
>
> Here in Ridgefield, one keeps one's lawn mowed (*we* keep our lawns mowed).

The *unqualified* use of 'one' by an individual does not only signal such a communal norm, however, it also endorses it. It accepts the norm as binding on the individual by virtue of his being a member of the community. To put it crisply, what *one* does is what (every) one of *us* does — and does *because* he is one of us. And this tells us what to make of "communal norms". A communal norm is one of our reasons. It is, in fact, a communal *motive*.

I am proposing, thus, that a rational agent who assumes a "critical stance" with respect to his own (retrospectively represented) conducts undergoes a shift of motive. He undertakes to appraise *his* beliefs and reasonings in light of *ours* — under the constraint of certain overriding *communal ends* which are, however, and importantly, also his by virtue of his representing himself as one of us.

It is crucial to contrast a *communal* end, in the sense which I am now introducing the notion, with a *common* end. The distinction can be brought out in connection with a difference in the order of explanation. A common end is one which is ours by virtue of its being among my ends *and* his *and* hers and so on. If, for example, among my motives is

(a) ¢ I will achieve *E*. ¢

and among *Henry's* motives is

(b) ¢ I will achieve *E*. ¢

then there is a clear sense in which each of us has the same end, namely to achieve *E*, and in which, in consequence, to achieve *E* can be spoken of as *our* (common) end. It is the same sense as that in which, if my head aches and Henry's head aches as well, each of us suffers from the same condition, namely a headache, and in which, in consequence, a headache can be spoken of as *our* (common) condition.

But there is, of course, another — equally clear — sense in which my headache here is *mine* and Henry's *his*, but in which there is no *one* thing which is to be attributed to both of us *collectively*. To speak in this sort of case of "our common condition" is, in fact, to speak only in what one might call a *nominal* plural. It is to speak in an *abbreviatory* or *summative* idiom of two *singular* attributions. The plural claim is explained by citing the plurality of singular claims and it is, in fact, dispensible in favor of a *conjunction* of those singular claims in every context in which it might occur.

In a parallel fashion, in speaking of "our common end" in the case of (a) and (b), the movement of the explanatory reasoning is from the pair of singular attributions to the plural attribution. The latter is, again, a *nominal* plural and, in its logic, again abbreviatory, summative, and conjunctive.

For Henry and me to *have*, in this sense, a common end, it is not requisite that *either* of us should possess a non-vacuous 'I' — that is, that either of us should be capable of *plural representings*, of representings of 'we'. Intentional agents which are not yet rational agents could *have* such common ends (that is, we could conjunctively attribute such ends to them) without however being themselves able to represent, even conjunctively, what they have in common *sub specie* 'we'. (that is, *as* a common end). For to attribute such a common end ("from outside") to a plurality of intentional agents is not to attribute to each of them some one, invariant, univocal representing which is *itself* plural and which can function as an occasion-logos (reason) for many behaviors, but to attribute to each of them as an occasion-logos one *of* a plurality of similar, equivocal representings, functioning as an occasion-logos for one of a plurality of behaviors.

A *communal* end — in contrast to such a common end — will be one which is *collective* without being *conjunctive*. It will be an end which is mine and hers and his by virtue of the fact that it is *ours* and that each of us represents himself/herself *as* one of us. It will, in other words, be a genuinely *plural* end, attributable to all of us collectively and *therefore* univocally to each of us severally and to all of us conjunctively.

A communal end, in other words, requires (attributions of) a *new* form of representing — not a plurality of similar (singular) representings but a *plural* representing which can function as an occasion-logos for us collectively by functioning *univocally* as an occasion-logos for each of us. It will be the representing of an end, say E, which can serve as the proximate practical major premiss of a form of reasoning by which each of us can arrive at an endorsement of his/her corresponding *singular* motive to achieve E and by an appeal to which one could *explain* the fact that to achieve E can be attributed to us conjunctively as our *common* end.

What I propose, in brief, is that a rational agent will differ from a (mere) intentional agent in his capacity for (and propensity to) representings which we can schematize by the form

(C)   *We* will achieve E

which serve as occasion-logoi for his behaviors by means of a mediating condition-logos representing of himself *as* one of *us*. To explain a being's behavior as the manifestation of *rational* agency, in other words, is to attribute to that being practical *reasonings* of a form which includes, but is more elaborate than, the (R^+) of last chapter's intentional agents by virtue of including, as well, a component of the general form:

(CE^+)   (1) ¢ *We* will achieve E. ¢
      (2) *I* am one of us.
      (3) ¢ *I* will achieve E. ¢

If, to recur to a previous example, Henry and I each reason according to the pattern (CE^+), not only will it be the case that we come to have a *common* end in the manner sketched above, but there will also, in addition, be a stronger sense in which each of us has the *same* end. Not only will our respective singular motives − call them (3h) and (3i) − be the "same", but our *plural* motive, (1), will be the same as well. And this *latter* "sameness" is not a matter, as was the former, of intentional similarity and extensional equivocality − (3h) having a place in Henry's behavioral economy parallel to the place of (3i) in *mine* − but of a single, *extensionally univocal* representing having the same place in each of our behavioral economies, serving as a practical major premiss from which our parallel separate singular motives are severally derived by means of our respective mediating representings of ourselves *as* members of the single community adverted to by each of our usings of 'we'.

I have so far proposed that the non-vacuous 'I' the possession of which is requisite to an experiencer's having a concept of correctness (being reflectively in the "logical space" of appraisals) is the 'I' of a rational agent − an 'I' which derives its content from a contrast with a 'we' which makes its fundamental appearance in communal motives functioning as occasion-logoi in (attributed) practical reasonings of the form (CE^+). What I now wish to add to this picture is the recognition that it is, in fact, in the having by its members of communal motives of this sort that the existence of a community *consists*. What makes a collection or group of individuals a *community*, in other words, is just that each of them has the capacity and propensity to act on the occasion of a representing of the form (1) which is represented by each of them *as* having all of them within the scope of its 'we'. A simple example should serve both to clarify and to secure the point.

CHAPTER VII

Suppose that Dick and Jane and I resolve to form a *club* — call it "The Neo-Realists' Club" — which will meet in the Mensa every Monday for lunch. The question I wish to put is this: In virtue of what does our lunching together on Monday in the Mensa constitute a meeting of the Neo-Realists' Club?

When the question is framed in this fashion, the lines along which an answer must lie are not difficult to discern. The key observation is this: To *say that* our thus lunching together is a meeting of the club is to advance (a sketch of) an *explanation*. It is to supply the outline of an account of *how it comes to be* that we are lunching together. By redescribing our luncheon as the meeting of a club, the remark adverts to a single explanatory story which can be appealed to in accounting for my presence *and* for Dick's *and* for Jane's at the same Mensa table at Monday noon. It says, very crudely, that each of us is there *in order to* attend a meeting of the club — that each of us is there *because* the *club* meets there on Mondays and because each of us is a *member* of the club.

Such explanatory accounts, as we have seen, in general are to be understood as attributing (practical) *reasonings* to the agents whose conducts are to be explained. They view such conducts *as* (if they were) the products of (explicit) reasoning. The reasoning here attributed to Dick and to Jane and to me, then, must be a reasoning in which each of us *represents* himself/herself *as* a member of the Neo-Realists' Club and in which the fact of our severally so representing ourselves itself *gives rise* to our several separate *singular* intentions to be in the Mensa on Monday. It must, in other words, be precisely a reasoning of the form (CE^+):

(M^+)   (4)   ¢ *We* (Neo-Realists) will lunch in the Mensa on Mondays. ¢
             (5)   *I* am one of *us* (a Neo-Realist).
             (6)   ¢ *I* will lunch in the Mensa on Monday. ¢

To say that our lunching together in the Mensa on Monday is a meeting of the club, then, is to attribute to each of us a reasoning of the form (M^+) as a (partial) explanation of his/her presence at the same Mensa table on Monday at noon. And correlatively what *makes* our thus lunching together a meeting of the club is just what would render such an explanatory redescription of it correct — namely, the fact *that*, for each of us, his/her Monday lunching conduct *is* occasioned by representations of the form (4) and conditioned by representations of the form (5). It is in our several separate propensities to act on the occasion and condition of such representations as (4) and (5) that the *existence* of the Neo-Realists' Club *consists*. Dick and Jane and I bring the club into existence by severally adopting such *communal* intentions as (4) — by agreeing what *we* (collectively) will do and thus what each of us will do *because* he/she is one of us.

It is important to note in this connection that motives of the form (4) can occasion *diverse* behaviors. In particular, *my* endorsement, for example, of (4) can not only directly occasion my presence at the Mensa table on Monday but also, indirectly, can be a determinant of Dick's and/or Jane's presence as well, by virtue of its influence on *other* of my conducts vis-à-vis them. What I have in mind here is nothing mysterious but simply draws on the fact that I not only represent myself as a member of the club but so represent Dick and Jane as well. Thus, I have available to me not only the reasoning (M^+) but also such reasonings as

(D^+)   (4) ¢ We (Neo-Realists) will lunch in the Mensa on Monday. ¢
      (7) *Dick* is one of *us* (a Neo-Realist).
      (8) ¢ Dick will lunch in the Mensa Monday. ¢
      (9) ¢ I will do what I can to *bring it about* that Dick lunches in the Mensa Monday. ¢

              .
              .
              .

     (10) ¢ I will *remind* Dick to be in the Mensa at noon on Monday. ¢

Here (8) is what we might call my *third-person intention* that Dick be present at our Monday meeting — a representing which, although *not* cast in the first-person, can nevertheless be a motive and be mine — that is, can have an occasioning connection with my volition-triggered executable conducts — by virtue of its regularly giving rise to (causally occasioning) such *first-person* intentions as (9). And the inferential passage from (9) to (10), in turn, is mediated by such of my *beliefs* as concern which among my executable conducts *would*, if done, increase the likelihood of Dick's in fact being present at that meeting.

I shall refer to this phenomenon as the "*double* action-guiding force" of communal motives. The key point is that the causal efficacy of such plural representings bears on the shaping of common communal behaviors not only directly — by occasioning singular first-person motives which, in turn, give rise to the relevant behaviors themselves — but also indirectly — by occasioning singular first-person motives to *other* behaviors which, in turn, may be causally efficacious in shaping the conducts of *others* to the collectively-intended communal norms. What makes this an important observation is that it shows us how a representer who is *not yet* a rational agent can be *brought into* a community of rational agents. It shows us, that is, how the conducts of a representer who is not yet even able to represent himself *as* a member of the communal 'we' can nevertheless be shaped by causal factors (the conducts of full-fledged rational agents) which *are* to be explained in terms of the behavior-occasioning causal role of genuinely collective communal representings. It is this double action-guiding force which thereby allows a community of rational agents to *create* new members from (merely) intentional agents, for *among* those conducts-to-be-shaped can be propensities toward those very communal representings themselves, that is, toward conducts which are *reasonings* on the model of (CE^+). To put it in a somewhat different – and perhaps more traditional terminology – behavior *in obedience to* rules can be part of an *explanation* of how there comes to be behavior which *conforms to* those rules without *itself* being behavior in obedience to them. (For a discussion of this point in connection with language-learning, see Sellars *LTC* and my *LR*, pp. 43–7.)

And now, finally, we have gathered sufficient understandings, I think, to achieve some sort of closure on the epistemological problematic which has been with us since the opening pages of this study. Let me begin by reminding you of how things stood when we went off in search of rational agency.

Our problem, broadly set, was one of epistemic legitimacy. Viewed through the lens of Cartesian skepticism, what it asked of us was "an argument to the effect that – even if defeasible – our ways of thinking about the world are not arbitrary but determinate, and, indeed, are so determined as to ensure some connection between our having a particular world-picture and its being a correct world-picture" (Above 11). By the end of Chapter III, a determinateness of one sort, at least, had been secured on Kantian grounds – the categorial determinateness of Constitutive Realism, embodied in the family of co-implicate features (R1)–(R8). Any conceptual scheme or representational system which can be ours must be, in its content, such a Constitutive Realism, as a condition of our very existence as experiencers – that is, as apperceptive temporally discursive intelligences – at all. But the problem of correctness remained, now sharpened and focused by a recognition of the essentially *formal* character of the Kantian categorial constraints. There are *many* Constitutive Realisms, and, indeed, we pass from one to another across time, but there is – we are categorially constrained to say – only *one* world. How, then, can the undeniable diachronic variability of our representational systems in their descriptive contents be reconciled with the unavoidable posit that our representations can be correct if and only if they are adequate to this one world?

In Chapter V, I sketched the rudiments of an answer: "the connection between our (collective) espousal of a representational system and its (absolute) correctness is a connection *in prospect* and, for us — embedded as we are in . . . diachronic epistemic processes — no more than a regulative ideal" (Above 115). What there supported this proposal were two further "Copernican inversions" and a *possibility*. The first "inversion" established the priority of epistemology over ontology ("The correctness of our representings is the criterion of their adequacy to the world"); the second, the priority of pragmatics over epistemology. ("That a successor conceptual scheme is more nearly (absolutely) correct than its predecessor(s) consists in its adoption or espousal *as* a successor being warranted or justified.") And the possibility from which we drew our (Peircean) hopes was this: that from a pattern of retrospective justifiabilities we could extract a set of invariant constraints on the process of *succession* (replacement) of conceptual schemes which would demonstrably guarantee something like a commonality of focus or direction for the sequence of such representational systems in their determinate diachronic succession — that, in other words, *justification*, properly understood, would guarantee *convergence*. What remained for us, then, was to secure this possibility as actual — and that, in turn, required that we better understand the notion of justification. And so, in this way, we were brought round to the theme of good reasons and sound reasonings — to the theme of practical rationality — and to the investigations which we have only just concluded.

Let me set the stage for the final movement of this study, then, by sharpening up the problematic a bit. The key points can be set up quite quickly: We want to look at the process of replacing one (predecessor) conceptual scheme by another (successor) scheme. We want to consider what *justifies* such a succession of representational systems. That is, we cast ourselves in the role of experiencers who *entertain* both predecessor and successor schemes and who *ask whether* the replacement of the former by the latter is or was or would be justified as a piece of (cognitive) conduct. What we need to look at first, then, is what is involved in a rational agent's *reflective self-appraisal* of his own conducts as justified or unjustified.

The most important point to be made about such reflective appraisals is that they are conducted *in a context*, against a background of posited beliefs and posited motives. At any time, a rational agent *finds himself* with a set of beliefs — that is, with a specific picture of the world — and with a set of motives — that is, with one or more ends — and his reflective questions of warrant or justification are raised in the context of a family of presuppositions concerning the circumstances which obtain (or, retrospectively, which were *thought* to obtain) and the ends or goals which he in fact has (or, retrospectively, which he then had — that is, which, at the time of the action now being retrospectively, critically assessed, were then his ends). Such a reflective agent, in other words, is attributing to *himself* — if only hypothetically — a practical reasoning of the form (R^+):

(R^+)   (1) ¢ I will achieve E. ¢
(2) My doing X whenever R is the case will facilitate my achieving E.
(3) ¢ I will do X whenever R is the case. ¢
(4) R is the case.
(5) ¢ I will do X. ¢

And he is then adopting a critical stance with respect to this reasoning. What he is asking is: Given certain suppositions, is this specific reasoning (or was it, or would it be) a *sound* practical reasoning?

Within this general framework, what is posited as context and what is subjected to critical scrutiny may, according to our earlier taxonomy of justifications, *prima facie* vary fairly widely. What we need to appreciate next, however, is that, for a *reflective* appraisal of conduct, in spite of this *prima facie* variability, there is, in essence, only *one* question which can be raised — and it is a question of the validity of a piece of reasoning.

On the face of it, according to our earlier schemata, our rational agent's justificatory question could be, for example, either

(a)   whether his conduct was (or would be) justified *in the circumstances*,

or

(b)   whether his conduct was (or would be) justified *given what he believes* (or believed).

But when what is being considered is a reflective (first-person) *self*-appraisal, these two issues amount to the same question. To see this clearly, however, we must sort the cases out according to time.

It is clear, to begin with, that in his *prospective* practical deliberations about *what to do*, a rational agent has no place for a distinction between the circumstances which he believes to obtain and the circumstances which in fact do obtain. Prospective deliberation of this sort simply *posits* a family of circumstances *as* obtaining, and then addresses the question of whether a particular course of action would be efficacious in facilitating the achieving of a given end in *those* circumstances, for such prospective deliberation about what to do is something which a rational agent can rationally undertake only after having first arrived at a settled judgment about his *situation*, that is, about what is the case. His question of whether his doing X is or would be justified, then, is the question of whether his doing X in *those* circumstances would facilitate his achieving his end E, or, to put it more revealingly, the question of whether, given that his motive is to achieve E, the fact that his situation is such-and-such is a *valid* reason for his doing X. In terms of our scheme (R^+), in other words, this reflective prospective question of justification is addressed to what appears as premiss (2) — the *means-ends* premiss.

Nor is this point vitiated if the prospective deliberation in question is *hypothetical* deliberation of the sort characteristic of planning for contingencies. Here, to be sure, no single set of circumstances is *posited* as obtaining. Instead, each of a plurality of possible circumstances is (successively) *hypothesized* as obtaining, in order to raise, for each circumstance, the question of whether various conducts would be justified in that situation. The net effect of these proceedings, however, remains the same. Although the question of justification is now addressed in prospect to each of a *plurality* of practical reasonings on the model (R^+), the *focus* of the reflective appraisal does not vary. For *each* of these hypothetically entertained reasonings, an end — premiss (1) — and a situation — premiss (4) — is fixed or hypothesized as a given, and the question of justification is addressed to the validity of the hypothesized circumstances *as* a reason (condition-logos) for performing some action directed at achieving the hypothesized end. That is, the question of justification is again addressed to the cogency of the means-ends premiss, premiss (2).

The point holds equally if the question of justification is not addressed prospectively to conduct contemplated but retrospectively to actions performed. Here there can be a difference between (a) and (b), for what our agent *now* believes to have been the circumstances in which he acted may differ from what he *then* believed his situation to be. But this difference, too, does not affect the focus of his reflective appraisals. Here, too, both end and situation are posited — whether as having obtained (b) or as having merely been *thought* to obtain (a) — and the reflective question of justification is again addressed to the issue of validity. It is again the question of whether, given *that* end, *that* (posited) situation was (or would have been) a valid reason for engaging in the conduct which actually occurred. Here, too, in other words, the focus of our reflective rational agent's self-appraisal remains on premiss (2), the means-ends premiss of a (self-attributed) instance of the general scheme of practical reasoning (R^+).

In a *reflective* (first-person) self-appraisal of an action (whether performed or merely envisioned), then, what is at issue is the obtaining or not obtaining of the relevant *means-ends connection* between the particular conduct and the motivating goal in circumstances posited, hypothesized, or — more generally — represented as obtaining (having obtained, having been thought to obtain, likely to obtain, etc.). This question, however, as we noted near the close of the preceding chapter, is at base one of the validity of a (causal) inference — and, since such inferences are, as was argued earlier, themselves *performances* (that is, cognitive conducts), in the last analysis, the justificatory question is a question of whether certain representings are or are not *authorized* (that is, may or may not be done).

But authorized by what? By the communal norms! For the question of whether *q may be inferred* from *p* can only be the question of whether *one may infer q* from *p* — and this "impersonal" 'one' is precisely the collective 'we' of our agent's community. To ask whether my doing X in situation R would (or did) facilitate my achieving E, in other words, is to ask whether one may infer (an increased likelihood of) my achieving E from a premiss which represents me as doing X when R is the case. And this question, in turn, is precisely the question of whether the principle of permission which authorizes a representing of the conclusion on the condition of a representing of the premiss is among (or, more realistically, may be derived from) *our* principles of objective consequence — that is, those principles of the material logics of space, time, and contents the consilient conformity to which constitutes a particular conceptual scheme as collectively *our* conceptual scheme.

And now we have arrived at the crux of the matter. For the deontic conduct normatives — the principles of permission, prescription, and prohibition — which I earlier argued give the *sense* of claims of semantic relations and semantic appraisal are nothing but the communal norms of our present discussion. To put the point most compactly:

what *one may do*	is	what *we will allow*,
what *one may not do*	is	what *we will prevent*,

and

what *one must do*	is	what *we will insist upon*.

Now these stark idioms of communal conduct regulation suggest a degree of cold-blooded calculation and the deliberate taking of steps which, of course, is foreign to the point I wish to secure. The allowings, preventings, and insistings upon at stake here are not matters of posting "Inference Forbidden" notices or of punishing cognitive malfeasance by public whippings or incarceration. The behavioral constraints to which I advert are rather enforced more subtly, through the *double* action-guiding force of communal norms, operating primarily in the learning situation on beings who are only potentially members of our rational community and who become full-fledged rational agents by acquiring appropriate propensities to respond to *corrective activities* on the part of mature community members acting from (in obedience to) such communal norms. One becomes a member of such a rational community by learning to *check* one's individual representational practices against the collective practices of the community and to *modify* one's individual representational propensities to bring them into consilience with those of the community – *and* by learning to teach others to do this. To take a crude, formal, example: The communal motive to *prevent* inferences which are "affirmings of the consequent" gives rise to derivative plural intentions to *bring it about* that others do not affirm the consequent – and thereby to a diverse and multi-dimensional set of training and corrective practices in virtue of which the behavior of beings not yet members of the community is shaped (i) to avoid affirmings of the consequent and (ii) to avoid them *because* "one may not affirm the consequent" and (iii) to *themselves* engage in the very training and corrective practices vis-à-vis others in virute of which they themselves came to acquire the behavioral propensities (i), (ii), and (iii).

Stripped of its dramatic content, then, the point about a rational agent's reflective appraisal of his conduct at stake here comes to this: An agent's conduct is *justified* – on the supposition of certain beliefs and motives – if it is (was or would be) the outcome of a *reasoning* which conforms to and is sanctioned by the collective inferential norms of the community to which, as a rational agent, he necessarily represents himself as belonging and which, in consequence, are *his* inferential norms as well – that is, are constraints to which his inferential behavior conforms *because* they are constraints to which they (his community) *will* conform (and will enforce) and because he is (i.e., represents himself as being) one of them.

That is what a retrospective justification comes to for the individual. But our problem concerns not the individual but the community. What we must do, finally, then is to see how these insights can be brought to bear on the communal question of the replacement of conceptual schemes. And that brings us, at last, to the final movement of our response to the original skeptical problematic.

CHAPTER VIII

EXPLANATORY REALISM:
THE CONVERGENCE OF CONCEPTUAL SCHEMES

The upshot of the preceding chapter is that the existence of rational agents as such — of intentional agents with the further capacity for reflective self-attributions and self-appraisals presupposes the ability to engage in *means-ends* reasonings and to *check* such reasonings against a family of communal norms of inference. Since such means-ends reasonings are *causal* reasonings, however, the communal norms of inference at issue here must be norms of *material* as well as formal inferences — that is, they must be (deontic formulations of) principles of a chronologic, an arena-geometry, and a material logic of contents (time, space, and causality) collectively constituting a determinate conceptual scheme or representational system. Briefly put, the existence of any rational agent presupposes the existence of a *community* of such agents possessing a *shared world-picture*, a community whose conceptual scheme constitutes some specific, determinate Constitutive Realism.

Now our problem concerns just this shared world-picture. It is, we have observed, subject to diachronic variability. There is a *communal* conduct at stake here. It is *our* (collectively) *adopting* some such determinate conceptual scheme — and, in particular, our adopting it as a *replacement* for some prior representational system. What we need to understand is how *we*, collectively, can be justified in replacing one conceptual scheme by another and how *we*, collectively, can rationally appraise such a conceptual change ("paradigm shift") *as* justified or unjustified.

Such a collective appraisal would, of course, be a communal *self*-appraisal. And this immediately precipitates a crisis. If we adopt the model of reflective appraisal derived from our investigations of an *individual* agent and attribute to ourselves, collectively — if only hypothetically — a pluralized practical reasoning of the form (R^+) into the soundness of which we might inquire, it is difficult to see what could serve as a check on the self-attributed means-ends reasoning implicit in premiss (2) of the scheme, as the communal norms of our shared world-picture served as such a check for the individual rational agent. But this view of rational (self-) appraisal as requiring the (retrospective, hypothetical) (self-) attribution of such a practical reasoning is, alas, the only understanding of the notion of *justification* at which we have been able to arrive. I propose, then, to press forward with this view of justification-as-

EXPLANATORY REALISM   171

practical-reasoning with the hope that, in the end, the problems of adapting it to the question of the justification of collective or communal conducts will not, after all, prove as insurmountable as they appear from our present vantage.

In the case of a conceptual change or "paradigm shift", then, our replacing some predecessor conceptual scheme (or shared world-picture) C1 by another, successor, scheme (or world-picture) C2, will be *justified* in the event that we can retrospectively attribute to ourselves a *sound* practical reasoning which, in first approximation, takes the form:

(C^+1) (1.1) ¢ *We* will achieve E. ¢
  (1.2) *Our* doing X whenever R is the case will facilitate our achieving E.
  (1.3) ¢ We will do X whenever R is the case. ¢
  (1.4) R is the case.
  (1.5) If R is the case, then replacing C1 by C2 (i.e., adopting the material inference principles of C2 as our communal norms of material rationality in place of those of C1) is a case of doing X.
  (1.6) ¢ We will replace C1 by C2. ¢

What we would need to know, of course, to make this more than idle symbol-mongering, is what specifically is "E" here, and what is "R", and what is "doing X".

It is easiest to discern something of the form of an answer to the last of these three questions. We want to view the replacement of C1 by C2 as an instance of a general diachronic *practice* of conceptual change. To do this, however, we must find a justificatory argument which rests on certain *general features* of C1 and C2. To put the point differently, what will be crucial to determining a practical reasoning of the form (C^+1) as *justificatory* will be our representing C1 and C2 as standing in some *relation*, given that R, and thereby representing our specific replacement of C1 by C2 as an instance of a *kind* of conceptual change which arguably facilitates our achieving the relevant end E. If we call the relation at issue here "S" – while remaining temporarily non-commital about what it might in fact *be* – then our doing X will be our adopting conceptual schemes which stand to their predecessor(s) in relation S, when R is the case. We thus arrive at the slightly more detailed scheme:

(C^+2) (2.1) ¢ We will achieve E. ¢

(2.2) Our adopting conceptual schemes which stand to their predecessor(s) in relation S whenever R is the case will facilitate our achieving E.
(2.3) ¢ We will adopt such conceptual schemes whenever R is the case. ¢
(2.4) R is the case.
(2.5) If R is the case, C2 stands to C1 in relation S.
(2.6) If R is the case, replacing C1 by C2 is a case of adopting a a conceptual scheme which stands to its predecessor(s) in relation S.
(2.7) ¢ We will replace C1 by C2. ¢

Now it may appear that we have accomplished little here beyond exchanging an "X" for an "S", but, as we shall soon see, by giving the notion of "doing X" some internal structure in this way, we have, in fact, opened a door to coping with what, a short while ago, appeared to be an intractable problem — the problem of our means-ends premiss, here premiss (2.2).

In terms of the scheme (C^+2), the problem can be stated thus: (2.2) purports to state a means-ends connection. But means-ends connections are *causal*, and the representation of any causal connection presupposes a conceptual scheme. Here, however, we have *two* conceptual schemes at stake — and *neither* can be appealed to in support of (2.2). For we have a dilemma: If we take (2.2) to be warranted by the material inference principles of C1, the putative justificatory argument is self-defeating; but if instead we take (2.2) to be warranted according to C2, the argument is question-begging, for it is our adoption of C2 which is intended to be justified by this sort of argument in the first place.

Here, at last, we have stumbled across the final stronghold of Transcendental Idealism. If we take the first horn of the dilemma, we shall have to abandon the entire idea of a *justified* change of conceptual scheme. We shall find ourselves then saying, with Rorty:

... "the world" will just be the stars, the people, the tables, and the grass — all those things which nobody except the occasional "scientific realist" philosopher thinks might not exist.

"Truth" in the sense of "truth taken apart from any theory" and "world" taken as "what determines such truth" are notions that were ... made for each other. Neither can survive apart from the other.

"The world" is either the purely vacuous notion of the ineffable cause of sense and goal of intellect, or else a name for the objects that inquiry at the moment is leaving alone. (*WWL*: 662–3)

But if we take the second horn of the dilemma, then, once again, the notion of *justification* becomes empty, for *any* conceptual scheme may be "justified" in this question-begging fashion. We shall then see ourselves as saying, as Stroud put it,

... that a certain experience, say an experience of an *F*, is made possible by, and hence legitimizes, our employment of the concept of an *F*,

and it would follow that,

since every concept is such that possession of it makes possible experiences of things as falling under that concept

no conceptual scheme could *fail* of legitimacy. (*TAEN*: 109–10)

And so, in this way, our original epistemological problematic has once again come home to roost. We need, it appears, a *tertium quid* – a "supervenient" or "privileged" conceptual scheme to warrant our citing the replacement of C1 by C2 *as* a means to our (collective) end *E*. But such a *tertium quid* is precisely what, as we have already repeatedly seen, we cannot have. *Any* conceptual scheme is in principle defeasible in its descriptive content (although it must be a Constitutive Realism in its form). So any conceptual scheme is, in principle, replaceable by another. If such a replacement requires, in order to be justified, that a sound practical reasoning of the form (C^+2) be (retrospectively) available to us, it would thus seem to follow that no such replacement *can* be justified. The locus of variability in our conceptual schemes will remain a locus of arbitrariness. We must then give up the notion that one conceptual scheme can provide a better – i.e., more nearly absolutely correct – "picture of the world" than another – for this 'better' gets its sense from the notion of justification – and so we must give up, too, the notion of "the world" as well – for, as we have also seen, this notion of the world gets *its* sense from that of the limit of an increasingly better sequence of systems of representation. Transcendental Idealism *vindicatus est*. Or so it seems.

And is there any way to escape from this dilemma? I think that there is. What we must do is call into question the presupposition which gives rise to it: that the means-ends connection posited in (2.2) is a *causal* connection. For not *all* means-ends connections *are* causal. And, indeed, isn't this one of the lessons of our earlier Kantian ruminations? Some means-ends connections are not causal but *constitutive*. Employing a representational system answering to the constraints (R1)–(R8) is *analytically* a means to the end of achieving a determinate and non-arbitrary unitary diachronic synthesis of representations, if that is the aim of an *experiencer*, that is, of an individual who is a temporally discursive and apperceptive intelligence. And, indeed, just that *must* be the *overriding* end of such a being, for its achieving that end is precisely equivalent to its very existence *as* an experiencer. It is in the having of such a determinate unitary diachronic synthesis of representations that being a temporally discursive and apperceptive intelligence *consists*.

And this shows us how we must proceed in the present case. What we need to do is to so instantiate our 'E', our 'S', and our 'R' that our adopting conceptual schemes which stand to their predecessor(s) in relation S whenever R is the case is *analytically* a means to our achieving E. And, if this instantiation is not *itself* to be simply arbitrary, there is one further constraint: The overriding end E which figures in this practical reasoning must be — as in the case of an individual experiencer — a *non-optional* end, that is, an end which is similarly a condition of *our* (collective) existence *as a community of rational beings* (rational agents).

But we are already in a position to say what *that* end must be! Recall our discussion of the Neo-Realists' Club. The existence of a community *consists* in its members severally acting under the constraint of *communal norms* — each representing himself as a member of the community (as one of us) and doing what he does because that is what (a member of) the community will do (what *we* will do).

Now the community at issue here is not a discussion group but a rational community, and the conducts to be shaped by the communal ends in the having of which the existence of *such* a community will consist will not be luncheon gatherings but reasoning conducts. They will, indeed, be precisely *justificatory* reasonings, that is, reasonings of the form (R^+), for it is the ability and propensity of an agent to engage in such reasonings *and* in appraisals of such reasonings (both reflectively and in the third-person) by virtue of which that agent is a *rational* agent and, thus, a member of a rational community. But the ability to do this, we have seen, presupposes that the agent in question be biperspectival — and that is just to say that he individually operates under a fundamental overriding constraint of bringing *his* world-picture into consilience with the determinate *collective* world-picture of the community to which he belongs (by virtue of representing himself as belonging to it, and, in consequence, modifying his representational propensities under the constraints of communal norms). For there to *be* such a determinate collective world-picture, however, is just for the representational activities of members of the community to be constrained by a determinate set of *communal norms of representation* — and that is nothing but a *conceptual scheme* in precisely the sense in which we have been discussing the succession of conceptual schemes.

The upshot of this line of thought is that the *having* of a determinate (collective) conceptual scheme is exactly in what the very existence of a rational community *as* a rational community consists. To *have* a conceptual scheme is to operate representationally under the (deontic) constraints of a family of communal norms (of inference). Such communal *norms* — which are principles *regulative* of representational conducts — are, however, communal *motives* — and our having them is therefore *constitutive* of our collective existence as a community of rational agents. It follows that to have a determinate conceptual scheme is a non-optional end for a rational *community* (for *us*) in exactly the way that having a representational system answering to (R1)–(R8) is a non-optional end for an individual experiencer. And now we can perhaps see that there may well be some appropriate circumstances R and relation S for which *our adopting* conceptual schemes which stand to their predecessor(s) in relation S whenever R is the case is *analytically* a means to this end — for *adopting* conceptual schemes of a certain kind *can* be analytically a means to *having* conceptual schemes of a certain kind, and the end in question here just is the end of our having a determinate communal conceptual scheme.

In fact, having thus isolated the pertinent *overriding* communal end as that of having a determinate communal conceptual scheme, we are in a position to say in some detail what circumstances R and relation S must be. For, to begin with, R must be circumstances which *call for* a revision of our communal conceptual scheme — and that is to say that they must be circumstances in which the extant (to-be-predecessor) conceptual scheme *breaks down*. To see what this amounts to, we must have another look at the relation of a conceptual scheme or representational system to experience.

Here, the first point to be noted is that we *find ourselves* with experiences. There is a passive element in experience. Our evolving diachronic world-picture evolves in the face of something — and that something is not entirely up to us. Now it must immediately be granted that the experiences with which an individual *does* find himself are a function, in part, of the experiences with which he *can* find himself — and this, in turn, depends upon the conceptual scheme or representational system which, at the time of his experience, he *in fact has*. Every experience is a *taking* (all perceiving is "perceiving *as*"), and what an individual finds himself taking it to be the case will depend, in part, on the descriptive concepts with which he is equipped. An experience (perceptual taking), to put the point naively, is a representational response to a non-representational stimulus — and the responses which an individual can make to some stimulus are limited, *ab initio*, by the *system* of responses available to him, that is, by his behavioral (representational) repertoire. Every experience thus will, in fact, be *structured* according to the descriptive contents of some conceptual scheme, say C1, which is, *de facto*, the conceptual scheme of that experienc*er* at that time.

But while every experience is thus necessarily *structured* in terms of the descriptive contents of some conceptual scheme, it does not follow that every experience will automatically *cohere* with the diachronic world-story — equally structured according to the descriptive resources of that scheme — already endorsed by the individual experiencer. For, as we saw specifically in the case of our Empirical Idealist, George, the inferential development of some experience according to the material (and formal) principles constitutive of that representational system may eventuate in a breakdown of the *determinateness* of the conceptual scheme (C1) in terms of which the experience itself is structured. To put the point compactly, an individual experience with which one finds oneself may have incompatible (material) *consequences* or have (material) consequences incompatible with some other representing already endorsed. Such an experience I shall call a "(C1)-anomaly", and I shall say that it cannot be afforded a "determinate explanatory accommodation" in the evolving world-picture structured by the descriptive resources of the representational system C1.

What is thus true of an individual representer, however, can equally be true of a rational community, for at any time such a community *collectively* endorses an evolving diachronic world-story structured in terms of the descriptive contents of a determinate *communal* conceptual scheme in the having of which the very existence of that community *as* a rational community consists. Of course any experience must be *someone's* experience — and a community can have experiences (collectively) only in virtue of its members having experiences (individually). Thus a finer-grained account here must see the emergence of experiences which are anomalous vis-à-vis the *communal* conceptual scheme as a matter of the *availability* of such experiences to (any) individual *members* of that community, on the condition of the performance by those members of certain *actions* themselves described according to the representational system of the community relative to which the resulting experiences *are* anomalous. In plain language, the existence of *communally* anomalous experiences consists in the specifiability of a *repeatable experiment* the performance of which eventuates in individually anomalous experiences.

It is in the emergence of such anomalous experiences that the circumstances R consist. Conceptual change is *called for* when we *find ourselves* with experiences which cannot be afforded a determinate explanatory accommodation in the evolving world-picture constructed in accordance with the descriptive resources of our extant communal representational system. And this, in turn, tells us what is wanted of a *successor* conceptual scheme, and thus, what we are to put in our schematized practical reasoning to stand as the relation S between successor and predecessor(s).

Briskly, a *justified* successor scheme must restore lost determinateness. As we saw in the case of George's ϕ, ψ, and Ω, there are a *variety* of ways in which this might occur. The one which is of particular interest here, however, is one which did not there loom large in our deliberations: It *may* be the case that determinate explanatory accommodation of such predecessor-anomalies can be achieved only when those experiences are reconceived (re-described) in terms of a *wholly new* set of descriptive concepts — that is, on the condition that we collectively adopt a wholly new set of communal norms of representation (responsive and inferential propensities and constraints).

In doing this, of course, we undertake to reconceive as well our entire *prior* world-story — that vast preponderance of experiences which *were* afforded determinate explanatory accommodation in terms of our extant (predecessor) communal conceptual scheme. And if determinateness of the *whole* is to be restored, these predecessor *successes* must *also* be afforded a determinate explanatory accommodation within the world-picture structured according to the descriptive resources of the new (successor) scheme when reconceived according to the descriptive concepts of the new representational system. The new (successor) scheme, in brief, must not only supply us with an account of why its predecessor broke down where it did break down, but also with an account of why its predecessor succeeded as well as it did where it did succeed — that is, of why our *prior* takings of the world to contain, say, $X^1, Y^1, Z^1, \ldots$ allowed us to develop a determinate picture of a world which we *now* take to contain, say, $X^2, Y^2, Z^2, \ldots$ to the extent that they in fact did. It is this *double* accountability of a successor conceptual scheme to its predecessor(s) — to both predecessor anomalies and predecessor successes — which constitutes the relation S between successor and predecessor to which our justificatory reasoning (C^+2) adverts. C2 stands to C1 in relation S, given R, just in case R is the occurrence of experiences which are C1-anomalies and

C2 affords a determinate explanatory accommodation *both* for these C1-anomalies *and* for C1-successes as well. A conceptual scheme C2 which stands in this (complex) relation to another scheme C1, I shall say, *qualifies* as a successor of C1 with respect to R. And now, finally, we are in the position fully to flesh out our skeletal practical reasoning (C^+2). What we arrive at is this:

(C^+)   (1^+)   ¢ We will have a determinate communal conceptual scheme (i.e., a conceptual scheme which affords determinate explanatory accommodation for those experiences structured in terms of it with which we find ourselves.) ¢

(2^+) Our adopting conceptual schemes which qualify as successors whenever we find ourselves with experiences anomalous vis-à-vis our extant (predecessor) scheme(s) (analytically) facilitates our having a determinate communal conceptual scheme.

(3^+) ¢ We will adopt a qualified successor scheme whenever we find ourselves with predecessor-anomalous experiences. ¢

(4^+) $A_1, \ldots, A_n$ are experiences with which we find ourselves but which cannot be afforded determinate explanatory accommodation within (our extant communal conceptual scheme) C1.

(5^+) C2 qualifies as a successor to C1 with respect to $A_1, \ldots, A_n$.

(6^+) Replacing C1 by C2 is a case of adopting a qualified successor scheme upon finding ourselves with predecessor-anomalous experiences.

(7^+) ¢ We will replace C1 by C2. ¢

On the understanding of rational conduct justification at which we earlier arrived, the communal act of replacing one collective representational system (C1) by another (C2) – that is, the collective adoption of one set of material inferential *constraints* on representational conducts (communal norms of representation) in place of another – can be rationally judged to be justified only if the community can reflectively attribute to itself a *sound* practical reasoning which has as its conclusion a (communal) intention to effect such a replacement, and in which that replacement is *correctly* represented as a means to some communal end. I propose that (C^+) is the scheme of a practical reasoning which answers to precisely these specifications.

There are two key issues concerning this proposal. The first addresses the end itself. We are, you will recall, looking for a way of securing an *original* epistemic legitimacy, but any such practical reasoning could establish at best only the result that the conduct represented in its conclusion is justified *relative to the end* represented in its leading practical premiss. And this is indeed so. But while the justification established here is, in that sense, a *relative* justification, it is not an *arbitrary* justification, for the cited overriding communal end is not an optional end, but rather a condition of the very existence of the community as a rational community, as the having of a determinate individual conceptual scheme was a condition of the existence of an individual experiencer as an experiencer. The Kantian strategy of legitimization by embedding thus replicates itself at the level of the community.

The individual experiencer is committed to the project of constructing a determinate diachronic world-story as a condition of his existence as an apperceptive, temporally discursive intelligence at all, and that his representational system embody the specific (formal) categorial concepts yielded by the constraints (R1)–(R8) – and thereby validate the corresponding synthetic *a priori* judgments as true of the represented world – turned out to be an analytic consequence of this necessary commitment. Similarly, a rational community is collectively committed to the *policy* of adopting qualified successor schemes in the face of emerging (predecessor) anomalies as a condition of its existence as a rational community – of its being in the "logical space" of epistemic *appraisals* at all – and the legitimacy of replacing some specific representational system by some specific other (that is, of some specific "paradigm shift") can be retrospectively secured as an analytic consequence of this necessary (collective) commitment. The individual experiencer must have the concept of a world to *be* an experiencer, and he can have a determinate concept of a world only if it is the concept of a Kantian world – i.e., only if his representational activity answers to the Kantian categorial constraints (interpreted at a suitable level of generality). Analogously, a rational community must have the concept of justification to *be* a rational community, and it can have a determinate concept of justification only if it is the concept of justification by qualification – i.e., only if its *collective* diachronic representational activity answers to the constraint of adopting *qualified* successor schemes in the face of predecessor anomalies. The key difference here, of course, is that where the argument conducted at the level of the individual addressed the *form* of a representational system and thus yielded a set of *a priori* constraints on any *single* conceptual scheme – a set of principles *constitutive* of the concept of a world as that which is represented – the argument conducted at the level of the community addresses the *appraisal* of representational systems with regard to the adequacy of their descriptive contents and consequently can yield only a *regulative* principle, a constraint on the abandonment of one conceptual scheme in favor of another, that is, on the *process* of conceptual change — since, to put the point somewhat perversely, the adequacy of a family of descriptive contents does not depend only upon there *being* one world but also on what that one world is *in fact like*.

The second issue concerning (C^+) concerns not the end but the argument. In order for (C^+) to succeed as a piece of justificatory reasoning, it must be a *sound* practical reasoning. But is (C^+) the schema of a sound practical reasoning — and, more importantly, can (C^+) be *reflectively appraised as* a sound practical reasoning by a community which collectively (hypothetically and retrospectively) attributes such a reasoning to itself without *either* begging the question of justification *or* presupposing some "external" "transcendental" critical point of view? The answer turns on (2^+), (4^+), and (5^+) — and the answer is "Yes"! For since (2^+) is an *analytic* means-ends premiss, it can itself be reflectively appraised as correct on the basis of purely *formal* communal norms, without presupposing the correctness of either C1 or C2; and (4^+) and (5^+), while contingent, demand no "external" or "transcendental" resources for their validation but only the representational resources of C1 and C2 (respectively) themselves. That a representational system does or does not afford determinate explanatory accommodation for a family of representings structured in terms of its constraints is something which is manifested wholly *within* the system itself, and its determination does not presuppose the correctness of that system but only, so to speak, its *mastery*. A reasoning of the form (C^+) is thus *necessarily retrospective* — available to a rational community only when both failed predecessor C1 and qualified successor C2 are available to that community — but when a rational community *can* thus retrospectively attribute to itself a practical reasoning answering to the scheme (C^+) following some "paradigm shift", the conceptual change enjoined by the conclusion (7^+) of that reasoning *is* thereby shown to be (i.e., to have been) justified in a manner free from both question-begging and "transcendental" presuppositions.

With the reconstruction of the retrospective communal justificatory reasoning (C^+), we have at last arrived at a final resolution of our initial epistemological problematic. For the requirement that a successor conceptual scheme *qualify* by affording determinate explanatory accommodation both for predecessor-anomalous experiences and for predecessor successes in order for its adoption to admit of (retrospective) justification exorcises the last remnant of arbitrariness from our collective epistemic practices. This double accountability of a successor scheme to its predecessor(s) secures the requisite convergence. It allows us to make non-vacuous sense of the notion of a diachronic sequence of representational systems tending toward a *limit*, and thus allows us to make sense as well of the notion of a conceptual scheme which embodies an *absolutely correct* representation of the one world. The crucial point, however, is that, precisely *by* invoking the notion of a limit, this double accountability of qualified successor schemes allows us to do all this from *within* the evolving diachronic sequence of representational systems itself, and thus without the positing of some epistemic *tertium quid* or "external", "transcendental", point of view. The last element of my argument which yet remains to be set out, then, is the making good on all of these claims.

The requirement that a successor scheme afford a determinate explanatory accommodation for (its redescriptions of) predecessor *successes* guarantees that "the appearances" will *always* be "saved". Indeed, the expression "saving the appearances" is particularly apt here, for the descriptive successes of the predecessor system(s) are "saved" by a qualified successor precisely *as* appearances. A qualified successor scheme offers a re-description (re-conceptualization) of the one world which its predecessors laid claim to describe. The legitimacy of this predecessor claim itself lay in its determinate integrative success. The predecessor system(s) supplied a set of content-concepts and a material logic of contents which allowed the integration of experiences *thus conceived* into a coherent unitary diachronic world-picture embodying a determinate diachronic mathematics of number and intensity, of how many and how much. *Ex hypothesi*, however, this synthesis has now been broken by the emergence of anomalies. What a qualified successor scheme thus supplies is a new set of content concepts and a new material logic of contents (and perhaps of space and time as well) which allows the integration of experiences thus *re*-conceived into a new determinate unitary diachronic synthesis, now, however, successfully incorporating the (redescriptions of) experiences anomalous under their predecessor conceptualizations.

Most importantly, however, the new synthesis supplied by the successor scheme incorporates as well the (re-descriptions of) experiences previously afforded determinate explanatory accommodation under their former (predecessor) descriptions. In particular, this implies that to each "place" (arena-location) and time to which the predecessor scheme assigned (i.e., represented as containing) contents of determinate magnitudes, the successor scheme *also* assigns (possibly completely different) contents of (possibly completely different) determinate magnitudes. Now the predecessor scheme embodied some specific "material logic of contents". And this is just to say that at least *some* representings of contents of determinate magnitudes at a place at a time which were formulable in terms of the predecessor resources served as premisses for material inference principles authorizing the representing of (possibly distinct) contents of determinate magnitudes at the same (or another) place at another (or the same) time.

Let us call the representing of contents of determinate magnitude at a place at a time a "co-ordinate content ascription". What the predecessor's material logic of contents amounts to, then, is a set of principles licensing the representing of some co-ordinate content ascriptions as *determinate functions* of others – and this, in turn, imposes a *determinate relational structure* on the set of all such representings, both actual and (since the material inference principles authorize the representing of their conclusions as necessary relative to their premisses) possible as well. I shall call this *structure* of co-ordinate content ascriptions (or any of its isomorphs resulting from a re-coordinization admissible under the system's chronologic and/or arena-geometry, or from admissible mathematical transforms of the functional relationships imposed by the system's material inference principles) the "Content-Ascriptive Skeleton" (C-A Skeleton) of the predecessor system. It is this C-A Skeleton which *is* (the core of) the determinate diachronic synthesis achieved by the predecessor scheme – and it is fundamentally this C-A Skeleton into which the (thereby) predecessor *anomalies* would not determinately fit.

Now any successor scheme will, necessarily, also embody a family of co-ordinate content ascriptions – that is, representings of *its* contents as having determinate magnitudes at *its* arena-locations at times. Furthermore, since successor-representings will *also* be governed by some determinate material principles of inference, these ascriptions will *also* give rise to a C-A Skeleton, a structure which is (the core of) the new diachronic synthesis (world-picture) projected by the successor scheme. The key question which we need now to address concerns the *relations* which must hold between these successor ascriptions and their resultant C-A Skeleton and those of the predecessor scheme. What can we say about these relations, on the assumption that the successor system *qualifies* as a successor to that predecessor scheme?

Well, to begin with, it is clear that the co-ordinate content ascriptions projected by the successor scheme cannot *all* match one-for-one those projected by the predecessor, for in such a case the predecessor anomalies, which were the experiential *raison d'etre* for conceptual change in the first place, could equally be afforded no determinate explanatory accommodation within the ostensible successor system – a conclusion incompatible with the hypothesis that the successor is a *qualified* successor. The natural proposal, then, is that the successor scheme preserve, not the co-ordinate content ascriptions of its predecessor *per se*, but rather the structure of functional relationships among these ascriptions which was imposed by the material inference principles of the predecessor. That natural proposal, in other words, is that the successor scheme preserve the *C-A Skeleton* of its predecessor, and that it do this precisely by *including* (an isomorph to) that mathematical structure within its own, new C-A Skeleton.

In more traditional terms, what this proposal amounts to is exactly the Hempelian view of explanation as deduction. The C-A Skeleton of a successor scheme will contain (an isomorph to) the C-A Skeleton of its predecessor just in case the universalized conditional counterparts of the nomological (material) principles of the predecessor can be represented as *formal* (deductive) consequences of those of the nomological (material) principles of the successor. The successor scheme (theory), on this view, explains the "laws" of its predecessor by entailing them. And now we have reached a critical juncture. For what we must next understand is that this proposal, too, will not do.

The reason it will not do is that it collapses into the previous proposal. Indeed, what the emergence of anomalies shows us is precisely that the laws projected by the extant (to-be-predecessor) conceptual scheme *do not* (literally) *obtain*. What we want of a successor scheme, then, cannot be that it *explain those laws* — for to "explain a law" is to supply an account of why the law *does* obtain, of why the law is correct, and, *ex hypothesi*, in the present case, the predecessor laws are *not* correct. What we want of a successor scheme is that it explain the *success* of those predecessor laws. And this requires that it supply an account, not of why they obtain (for they do not) but of why they *seemed* to obtain (even though they did not).

What is fundamentally wrong with the Hempelian proposal is that it posits a degree of independence between *descriptive contents* and *laws* which is wholly illusory. On the Hempelian view, it makes sense to suppose that the *same* content-concepts might enter into *different* nomological (material) relationships and, conversely, that the relations of co-occurrence and succession of *distinct* contents could be governed, in whole or in part, by *identical* laws.

But we have seen, in contrast, that any representational system is *constituted* by its material (and formal) inference principles. Descriptive content-concepts are not given by or read off of experience — with the question of the nomological relationships obtaining among them then remaining a matter for further, wholly independent, discovery and adjudication — but rather *consist in* the families of deontic principles which *are* their "material logics". Descriptive content-concepts are brought *to* experiences, to which they may then prove to be adequate or inadequate – but the only measure of such adequacy is the continuing explanatory accommodation of such experiences within the evolving determinate diachronic synthesis continually being constructed in accordance with the representational constraints of the total conceptual scheme. To recur to one of our simple examples, the difference between a twache and an overlapping twinge-and-ache is not *phenomenological* but rather *nomological*. It is a difference in synchronic and diachronic arithmetic and, as such, wholly constituted by the differing "material logics of contents" which govern twache-representings on the one hand and twinge-and-ache representings on the other. Any difference in contents thus entails a difference in C-A Skeletons as well, and it follows that the second proposal will not do. A putative successor which preserves the C-A Skeleton of its predecessor intact also (necessarily) fails to *qualify* as a successor.

But if neither the co-ordinate content ascriptions nor the C-A Skeleton of a predecessor scheme is preserved by a qualified successor, how does such a successor supply "an account of why its predecessor succeeded as well as it did where it did"? How does a qualified successor scheme afford a determinate explanatory accommodation for its predecessor's descriptive successes? I have already given the rudiments of the answer: It explains them *as appearances*.

But the crucial thing to see here is that, not only does the successor scheme explain the contents of its predecessor as apparent contents, it explains the *laws* of its predecessor as (merely) *apparent laws* as well. And what this amounts to from our present perspective is not the incorporation of (an isomorph to) the predecessor C-A Skeleton within that of the successor, but rather the availability within the successor system of conceptual resources adequate for the representation of a *close approximation* to the C-A Skeleton of the predecessor – that is, adequate for the construction of concepts of *apparent* contents, the interrelationships among which *would*, were they *actual* contents, give rise to a C-A Skeleton *near enough* to being an isomorph to that of the predecessor scheme. What comes to the same thing, the successor scheme must contain the resources for the construction of concepts of apparent contents which, *on some counterfactual assumption* – approximating to the situation posited by the successor scheme as actual, and specifiable in terms of its (new) descriptive resources – *would be* the contents posited as actual by the predecessor (that is, would result in a C-A Skeleton which was a *true* isomorph to that arising from the predecessor.)[1]

It is by thus supplying the resources for the construction of such "counterpart content-concepts" *as appearances* that a representational system earns the balance of its credentials (beyond those accruing from the accommodation of predecessor anomalies) as a *qualified* successor. For it is in this way that a successor scheme affords an explanatory account of the integrative successes of our predecessor takings, without however itself authorizing their endorsement as correct takings.

And from these observations the sought diachronic convergence of successive representational systems follows — for while there need be no literal sharing of content-concepts between predecessor and successor systems, the *policy* of adopting only *qualified* successor schemes in the face of emerging anomalies guarantees that the mathematical structure of each predecessor system (as reflected in its C-A Skeleton) is preserved *in approximation* by each successor. The appearances are continually saved *as appearances*. And since *as appearances* the laws and contents of a predecessor scheme are *retained* within its successor, they remain to be explanatorily accommodated — still as appearances — within any successor of that successor, and so cumulatively through the whole open-ended diachronic sequence of successive conceptual schemes. It follows that, as the various world-pictures projected by successive representational systems across time become increasingly detailed and refined, the magnitudes of the "correction factors" needed to adjust predecessor-appearances to successive successor-posited actualities will themselves, necessarily, continually diminish. And it is here, in the *literal* convergence of the mathematical structures embodied in the C-A Skeletons of successive representational systems, that we find, at last, the resources for speaking sensibly — although at one remove, as it were — of the conceptual schemes themselves as converging across time to an *ideal* limit, a conceptual scheme which embodies an absolutely correct representation of the one real world.

That there need be — and typically is — no literal sharing of content-concepts and laws between predecessor and successor allows for as full a complement of "theoretical incommensurability" as Feyerabend, Kuhn, *et al* could desire. Successive conceptual schemes will be "incommensurable" in the quite literal sense of standing in no *deductive* relationships — the claims of the successor, sharing no content concepts in common with those of the predecessor and consequently, on that account, being incapable of either contradicting or being consistent with those predecessor claims. But the present view does justice, too, to the undeniable fact that science (for the policy of adopting only qualified successor schemes just *is* the method of science) is somehow *cumulative* as well. "Incommensurable" successor and predecessor may be, but "incommensurability" is not *irrelevance*. That predecessor and successor stand in no *deductive* relationships does not preclude them from standing nevertheless in some more elaborate *formal* relationships. That the C-A Skeleton of the successor incorporate a close approximation to that of its predecessor is, indeed, one such formal relationship. It is formal in that, although not itself a deductive relationship, it is a relationship which can be explained in terms of deduction. It is not the deduction of the laws of the predecessor from those of the successor. But it *is* the deduction of *counterparts to* the laws of the predecessor (its C-A Skeleton) from the laws of the successor *on a successor-specifiable counterfactual assumption*. It is a deduction of counterpart laws framed in terms of the concepts of *apparent* contents which are themselves *formally* specifiable within the representational system of the successor.

The concept of a representational system which stands as the limit of such a diachronic process of retrospectively justifiable conceptual scheme replacements is, then, one to which we can give sense. But it is important to add that to *thus* give sense to the notion of an ideal representational system is not to *describe* any realizable conceptual scheme, for we can give sense to that notion from our irrevocable perspective as embedded within these evolutionary processes *only* by invoking the notion of a limit. It is, therefore, a purely regulative ideal, admitting of specification only indirectly, in terms of the description of those epistemic *conducts* which, if – *per impossible* – carried to an ideal limit, would give rise to it.

We may, of course, say of it that it would be a representational system which is ideally adequate to the world which it represents, which corresponds to or fits the world, or which pictures the world (absolutely) correctly, but such characterizations would, in an important sense, be idle. For, as we have already seen, the *sense* of such claims of ontological adequacy or absolute correctness is itself given only in terms of the notions of the succession of conceptual schemes and retrospective collective justifiabilities constitutive of the very diachronic process which we have been describing.

It is tempting to suppose that we could do better than the *mere* evocation of the concept of a limit here. Could we not, for example, say that the ideally adequate conceptual scheme is one which not only *would* not stand in need of replacement but one which *could* not? Would it not be precisely a conceptual scheme which *could* admit of no anomalies?

The answer, surprisingly, is that this is something which we cannot sensibly say. It is just because we are dealing here with a limit concept that the distinction between 'would' and 'could' upon which this description ostensibly rests proves to be purely illusory. To say that a conceptual scheme *could* admit of no anomalies is to say that every *possible* experience conceptually structured in terms of that scheme's descriptive contents would admit of determinate explanatory accommodation within that scheme. But there is no reading which can be given for this use of 'possible'. If we take it to be purely formal ("logical possibility"), adverting only to the total set of experiences formulable in terms of the descriptive resources of the scheme, the claim is demonstrably false — for no determinate scheme could explanatorily accommodate two simultaneous ascriptions to a single location of one content but of differing numerical intensities, both of which would be, however, so to speak, "well-formed" experiences. If, on the other hand, we take 'possible' here to be relativized to the inferential constraints constitutive of the scheme itself ("nomological possibility"), then the claim, while now indeed true, becomes empty. It fails to provide the desired differentia separating the limit scheme from any other for the simple reason that *any* representational system trivially affords an explanatory accommodation for experiences thus compatible with its own explanatory principles.

There is no course remaining for us, then, but to endorse here, too, our earlier conclusion that the *sense* of ontological and epistemological claims is given only in terms of the pragmatics of justification. To say that an ideal limit to the diachronic process of replacement of predecessor conceptual schemes by qualified successors *exists*, in other words, can only be to say that the process itself is, in the specified sense, a *convergent* process — to say, that is, that "the appearances" *are* necessarily continuously saved. And to say that there is but one world will then be simply to affirm that a convergent, non-arbitrary, determinate process of conceptual evolution of this sort is both *possible* and, indeed, for such beings as we in fact are, *non-optional* as well. That there is but one world, then, as we had hoped, turns out to be a claim which is (arguably, *a priori*) *true* — but it turns out, too, to be a rather different truth than we might have originally suspected. For, in the last analysis, the claim that there is but one world emerges, surprisingly, as a claim about us — about the kind of beings which we are, and about the kind of conducts which are therefore mandatory for us as a condition of our very existence as beings of that kind.

Since that is perhaps one surprise too many, it is appropriate to conclude this work by drawing back and looking at some of its results from a wider perspective. It is to this effort, then, that I turn in my next, and final, chapter.

CHAPTER IX

RETROSPECT: THE END OF A MYTH AND THE FUTURE OF A DISCIPLINE

The conclusions at which we have arrived are likely to satisfy neither the Transcendental Idealist nor the Criteriological Realist. The former is likely to insist that, for all that I have said, my "one world" remains ultimately ineffable; the latter, that it is, in the last analysis, incognizable. And both will, of course, be quick to point out that these are, interestingly enough, the very failings on the basis of which I have earlier so vigorously castigated their philosophical views. Despite several hundred pages of close argumentation, there is likely to remain the stubborn conviction that to conclude *thus* that there is but one world, while insisting at the same time that we are able to speak *a priori* of the world only in purely formal and regulative terms – while insisting, that is, that we cannot *a priori describe* that world, specify its laws and its contents – is nothing but an empty gesture, the pointless positing of yet another "Something, I know not what". My notion of the world, it will be said, is still "the purely vacuous notion of the ineffable cause of sense and goal of intellect" (Rorty: *WWL*, 663) – and thus no genuine notion at all.

But by now it *should* be clear that, as objections, such comments fall wide of the mark. The world of which I speak is not some ineffable, incognizable something, but the very world in which we all move and act – and a world of which our collective inquiries *necessarily* give an increasingly detailed, coherent, and refined picture. To say as *I* say that there *is* such a world – and only one such – is not vaguely to gesture at what is only problematically sayable or knowable. It is rather to speak of the living *conducts* which are our sayings and our knowings.

To say that there is but one world is to say of these conducts that they are more than wheels spinning in emptiness – and necessarily so. It is to say of them that they are determinate and non-arbitrary, and that the world-pictures in which they successively issue are, necessarily, successively better pictures, pictures which we are successively justified in adopting, and pictures which are successively more adequate to what is passive in the accumulating experiences to which they are all accountable – and all this for the simple reason that *only* this is what 'better' and 'justified' and 'adequate' *can mean* for such beings as we are.

That there is but one world, that we are justified in so believing, and that we are justified as well in the belief that our successive conceptual schemes embody increasingly correct and adequate pictures of that world are thus not, on my view, *problematic* claims at all. What I have argued, rather, is that their truth emerges *analytically* from a proper understanding of justification and correctness and adequacy – and of who *we* are. For the indispensible central thrust of my argument has been that the pragmatic notion of justification, of the legitimization of (cognitive) *conducts*, is prior to both that of ontological adequacy and that of epistemological correctness, and that the roots of such *pragmatic* warrant or legitimacy, in turn, lie in our natures as temporally discursive, apperceptive intelligences – in the *ends* of conduct which are non-optional ends for such beings as we are, by reason of being the ends in the having of which we are *constituted as* the beings which we are, as sayers and as knowers – that is, as rational beings.

To impute to me, then, the thesis of a world ineffable and incognizable is to misperceive my reasonings and to misread my conclusions. And yet, even in the face of all correctives, the impulse to such an imputation is likely to persist – and with it, a certain lingering malaise, the feeling that, for all that has been said, we have not *yet* come to grips with the authentic core of the problematic with which we began. If we are to achieve a full closure on our problematic, then, this malaise, too, must be confronted. And that brings us around to our beginnings, and to some reflections on the nature and the history of our enterprise.

To read this work as culminating in acquiescence to the ineffable and the incognizable is to read it through the lens of a myth which lies at the heart of our history – the Myth of Mind Apart. The Myth is a polymorphic one, but its central element is the supposition that the world is a thing which is ontologically alien to us as we are, to us as representers and as knowers – a thing which stands somehow outside us, and which challenges us to bring the inner life of our thinkings into harmony with it.

This myth admits, of course, of diverse elaborations. In its most optimistic form, the Myth of Mind Apart welcomes the world as a collaborator. The world *gives* itself to us, and our project is then to set what is given in an order which mirrors the essences of the giver. In its most pessimistic variant, the Myth despairs of a world which is closed to us. We are abandoned to a solipsistic consciousness in which all diversity is necessarily self-engendered appearance and thus, ultimately, merely illusion. *Our* world becomes not a thing given but a thing made, and all that it remains open to us to mirror then is our own essence as its makers.

The Myth of Mind Apart is a Platonic myth. That is why it lies at the heart of our history. It is embodied in the very question with which our history begins: What is the relation between the ideal or conceptual order and the real? The question is a perennial preoccupation of our discipline, but the question rests upon a thesis: that these are two orders, and not one. And that thesis is the Myth of Mind Apart.

For the ideal order *is* the real, not in the false sense that "the world is Idea", but in the sense that our representings *of* the world are at the same time doings *in* the world. The world is not a thing apart from us as we are, but we are both *in* the world and *of* it — and our thinkings are episodes of its own determinate diachronic unfolding. As representers and as knowers, we are within the world as *evolved organisms*. And whatever principles govern the inner life of our thinkings are *necessarily* the principles according to which the world as a whole evolves simply because our inner life is an integral part and aspect of that determinate evolution. What follows from this, of course, is that there can be no *question* of a harmony between the conceptual and the real as something *to be achieved*.

In a deep sense, in fact, just this is what seminal thinkers of our century have, each in his own way, already been telling us for some time: Dewey, by his sense of cognition as practice; Wittgenstein, by his directing us back to the broader "forms of life" in which our words are necessarily embedded; and Heidegger (so I am told), by his vision of the history of philosophy as the growth of Being. And what should immediately strike us now is that, along with his rejection of the Myth of Mind Apart, each of these thinkers has in his own way announced, as well, the death of philosophy as we have known it. So this, too, is a question which must be finally faced.

Now this book stands as testimony that I have not also come to serve as a pallbearer at the funeral of my calling. Arguments, not aphorisms, are what I have had to offer. Philosophy remains for me in essence what it was for Plato — a movement of the Logos — and its own history is still its only universal language (a truth better understood by Heidegger than by Dewey, and one for the temporary misplacing of which in the west Wittgenstein must assume more than a little responsibility).

But if, with the abandonment of the Myth of Mind Apart, philosophy can remain the same in essence, it is equally true that it cannot remain the same in substance. For with the recognition of the unity of the conceptual and the real, it must now, in the end, be the task, not of an autonomous philosophy, but of science — the systematic working out of the only pattern of conceptual evolution which is possible for us — to tell us what, in the end, the world is, and what *we* are, and thus what relations can and do obtain between us and the *balance* of this world which has given rise to us and which, for well or for ill, has us *in* it as knowers of it.

If the conclusions for which I have argued in this book are correct, then what must change in philosophy is not its manner of coming to grips with problems but rather its sense of what is problematic. For once the relationship of the ideal order and the real is grasped as that of evolved part to evolving whole, we can no longer meaningfully engage The Challenge of Skepticism or The Problem of Our Knowledge of the External World. Once the necessary processes of conceptual evolution are seen as integrative, holistic, and (in Peirce's sense) abductive, we can no longer significantly frame The Problem of Induction or The Problem of the Reality of Theoretical Entities. Once the pragmatics of conduct and the rational justification of conduct are understood as prior to the notions both of ontological adequacy and of epistemic correctness, we can no longer feel challenged to adjudicate between Realism and Idealism or between Rationalism and Empiricism. And once the very nature of apperceptive cognition is appreciated as essentially involving an irrevocable appeal to communal norms of conduct, we can no longer be exercised by The Problem of Other Minds or even The Question of the Relation of Fact and Value. For all these great and classical puzzles are only icons of the Myth of Mind Apart.

And with the abandonment of all such icons, does there yet remain a proper task for an autonomous discipline of philosophy? Of course there does. For, even after all demythologizing, there remains the grand project of understanding ourselves, of understanding what it is to be a doer and a knower — now not in a false and problematic separation from the world which gives rise to us and in which we move and think, but instead as elements of the dynamic unity which we and the balance of that world collectively are. There remains the grand project of bringing our rational practices under rational survey, of seeing ourselves not only as we are and as we have been but also as we might become, and of coming in the end to command an articulate overview of what it would mean to realize the *arete* of personhood and of what stands in the way of such a realization. There remains, in other words, the grand project of self-knowledge.

And this, too, is undeniably philosophy — for it is what philosophy was even *before* Plato. Before Plato there was Socrates. And if, with Socrates, we should come to call the quest for an authentic self-knowledge *philos sophia*, the love of wisdom, and so undertake to read our history anew as episodes in the conduct of *that* search, then there is surely no-one who can justly accuse us of being false to that heritage which is, in the deepest sense, the discipline of philosophy.

APPENDIX I

NOTES

CHAPTER I

[1] Kant's *full* theory of experience is, of course, significantly more complicated than this. Its closest contemporary analogue is, perhaps, a recent advertisement, which informs us that "Before you ever see the picture, the Colortrack system grabs it, aligns it, refines it, sharpens it, tones it, and locks the color on track". Similarly, Kant offers us the receptive sensibility, the productive imagination, the *re*productive imagination, and the active understanding which toss, pummel, maul, pound, and shape various sensory and conceptual "raw materials" into a full fledged perceptual taking. For my present purposes, it suffices to eschew detail, and to pick up the story rather late in the game.

[2] This, of course, is the philosophical ancestor of what Strawson calls "descriptive metaphysics". But Strawson's point of departure is the supposed fact of our possession of the relevant concepts themselves, while, for Kant, this is a *conclusion* derived from the fact of certain experiences and inextricably intertwined with the whole of his general theory of experience. Strawson himself advances no theory of experience – and this, as we shall shortly discover, makes a considerable difference to his ability to cope with diverse forms of epistemological and ontological skepticism.

[3] Nor, for that matter, of what *ought to be* – an observation which is the point of entry to another cluster of problems.

[4] The line of argument and approach to the Cartesian texts which follows was suggested by my colleague Richard Smyth.

[5] One typically does not stop to ask at this point: And what's wrong with contravening logic anyway? But this is, in fact, an entirely legitimate question. After all, if one is going to need to appeal to what is "obvious according to the light of reason" at this point to secure the epistemically unchallengeable privileged status of logic, it is hard to see why one shouldn't appeal to it rather earlier on, and save oneself a lot of awkward intervening bad argument. Descartes presses his skepticism to the point of including as dubitable and, hence, not certain such beliefs as that a square has four sides and that 3+2=5. But surely, if such "self-evident" or "definitional" truths as these are not immune to Cartesian doubt, then neither should Descartes remain sanguine about *what follows from what*. When things have gone this far, in other words, not only need he defend the indubitability of '*cogito*' and '*sum*', but '*ergo*', too, is in jeopardy. And on this topic, we find, Descartes offers us no help at all.

[6] On this understanding, the central thesis of skepticism takes the form of a *negative existential* claim of the following sort: There is *no* reason to suppose that there is a connection between espousal and correctness for our beliefs. This observation is important, for it provides "transcendental arguments" with something more do than the purely negative job of demonstrating that this-or-that specific *alternative* to our customary conceptual scheme – e.g., a Humean sense-datum alternative – is self-defeating (or, for some other reason, indefensible). That transcendental arguments are indeed limited to

193

this role of individually defeating in sequence each of a (potentially inexhaustible) sequence of proposed concrete alternatives to our customary conceptualizations has been urged at length by Rorty (*VTA*). If, however, the substance of the skeptical challenge takes the form of a negative existential claim of the sort which I have sketched above — and I would argue that Kant, in fact, so understood the challenge posed by Cartesian demonaic skepticism — then a piece of transcendental argumentation acquires the *positive* function of actually *supplying* a reason for supposing that a connection of the desired sort in fact obtains. The significance of these observations will become clearer as my investigations proceed.

[7] For another, rather more naive, attempt to argue non-constructively for the existence of "criteria" — now in connection with the "Problem of Other Minds" — see Malcolm, *WPI*. The equivalence of such "criteria" to Kant's synthetic *a priori* — to be noted in a moment — perhaps stands out more clearly here than in Strawson's work, despite the self-consciously "Kantian" orientation of the latter.

[8] The class of problematic judgments includes, in fact, those positing the existence of anything independent of our representations and, in particular, those projecting a pluralist ontology of multiply qualified particulars. The basic problematic of empiricism is thus, indeed, equally the basic problematic of realism, in the sense of the term 'realism' which contrasts with 'idealism'. I shall hope to convince you of this in detail in the next chapter.

[9] For another route to the same conclusion, in connection with Strawson's alternative position, see my *SSSN*.

[10] Russell, after agonizing long over the question in connection with the "Problem of Induction", opted for the second horn of the dilemma.

[11] These notions of "*a* world" and "*the* world", of course, are centerpieces of the dialectic of "realism and idealism" which will be our central theme in succeeding chapters. Of the two, the notion of *a* world is relatively the less problematic. I need it here only in a limited sense — roughly, as the "intentional object" of an *experience* which itself has a certain structure (to be elucidated in a moment). As our brief dip into Cartesian waters already suggests, however, we shall, in some sense, need to *earn* the right to speak of *the* world. As my title indicates, I intend to do so — but, for now, my counsel can only be patience. I note the question here only to assure the reader that I do not propose to evade the complex of problems which it embodies but, indeed, precisely to confront them.

[12] Even if such an experience is *possible*, one may obviously still wonder whether it is in any sense *necessary*, and, if so, how. The answer — Kant's and mine — is that it *is*. The details, however, will need to wait until Chapter III.

CHAPTER II

[1] Bennett, I think, gets the distinction wrong. He holds that an extensive magnitude is a magnitude which something has by virtue of its having *parts* (*KA*: 168). If one takes this to mean "virtual parts", then it is an error only in that it takes a magnitude to be something which a thing *has* rather than something which a thing *is*. But Bennett compounds the error, for he takes the part/whole distinction *literally* and, as we have seen, at this level of conceptual representation, things do not literally have parts.

² I shall have occasion to recur to the example of pains later. It is the best and clearest example of an "idealism" which we have.

³ The reader may well have some reservations at this point as to whether the division between realism and idealism which I have sketched here in fact answers to any recognizable historical dispute or indeed, whether the position which I here characterize as "idealism" is one which anyone has ever occupied (or would be interested in occupying). The worry, I think, is a legitimate one, but the issue is complex, and I should like to postpone it for the moment. I will, however, return to the question later at some length. See below pp. 59ff.

⁴ Why anyone would *want* or *need* to be a realist remains, of course, to be discussed. It will be the central topic of my next chapter.

⁵ I now drop the cautionary quotation marks, on the understanding that the cash-value for any talk about "movement" or "position" is to be understood in terms of the regularities of co-occurrence and succession which I have just been describing. There is, in fact, also a *third* interpretation of β-changes which is possible and which further supports the conclusions I am about to draw. It will, however, be easier to formulate it in the next Chapter. See below, p. 67.

⁶ Thus Kant: "If coming to be out of nothing is regarded as the effect of a foreign cause, it has to be entitled creation, and that cannot be admitted as an event among appearances, since its mere possibility would destroy the unity of experience". (A206 = B251; cf. A186 = B229) To put the point in a way which brings out its "idealistic" implications: there would be no determinate distinction between such a creation and a mere (auditory) hallucination.

⁷ This is what Strawson missed. For an elaboration, see my *SSSN*.

⁸ What I am talking about, of course, – the paradigm from which my model derives – is the "lights in the sky", and so the original "Visual Plane" was, in fact, a "Visual Hemisphere". My flat, rectangular Visual Plane is adopted only as a concession to this flat, rectangular paper upon which I must conduct my expositions.

⁹ Why "*outer*"? Thereby hangs a long and convoluted tale. The distinction between "inner" and "outer" has so far not figured in our investigations in this chapter, nor will it. In my next chapter, however, it will become my central concern – and it is there that I will tell that tale.

¹⁰ This unravels the puzzle of "absolute" *versus* "relative" space (and time). The representation of phenomenological regularities under the aspect of modality (as necessary or impossible) is logically prior to *both* the relational *and* the absolute (arena) modes of representation of space (and time). The modality is preserved, however, in the presentation of spatial (and temporal) relations as having their formal properties – symmetry or asymmetry, transitivity or intransitivity, and so on – themselves *necessarily*. It is preserved, in other words, in the necessity of the fundamental propositions of topology and geometry – and this is an observation which will prove of some importance in the next chapter.

There is an exegetical point to be made here as well. Kant's commitment to a Euclidean geometry for space has long been the center from which a variety of facile and simplistic critical attacks have been mounted. The "functional" and "modal" interpretation which I have provided for the notion of a "form of outer sense", however, shows not only that Kant is not entitled to his Euclideanism, but, more importantly, that he does not need it. What is substantively correct about Kant's discussions of space as the form of outer sense, in other words, is wholly compatible with the introduction of Riemannian or hyperbolic geometries, and even with the radical reconceptualization of our world's arena as a unitary Minkowskian space-time inaugurated by relativistic physics.

[11] This is what Strawson senses dimly in his talk of "feature-placing sentences" (*IND*, 202ff.) But Strawson fails effectively to isolate the representations of a Minimal Core from those of a Realist Core (that is, he does not locate the proper place of the dimension of time) and so he erroneously imports concepts from the latter into the former (e.g., "cat-feature"). In consequence, he is able to give no more than a hand-waving account of the relations between, and the conceptual transition from, an ontology of stuffs and an ontology of qualified particulars. Interestingly, Bergmann never discerns an ontology of structured stuffs as a live option. When he comes to Strawson, in consequence, he completely misses the point and accuses Strawson (in *SO*) of proposing an ontology of *facts*.

[12] Descartes was then, to this extent, right about "the real wax". What we are exploring, in fact, is an observation which goes back to Plato and even to Parmenides: that the "real" is that which does not change.

[13] This is a requirement binding on *discursive* intelligences as such. A discursive intelligence is a being who can represent a plurality (a manifold) only by representing its elements *as* in relation to one another. That we are, *in fact*, such discursive intelligences is one of Kant's fundamental insights. But Kant is prepared to entertain the notion of a wholly non-discursive intelligence – an "intuitive understanding" or, equivalently, an "intellectual (non-sensible) intuition" – so this remains an observation of fact and not one of necessity. See Bx (note), B71–2, B135, B138, and B149.

[14] In A: The general principle of the analogies is: All appearances are, as regards their existence, subject *a priori* to rules determining their relation to one another in one time. (A177)

[15] In A: All appearances contain the permanent (substance) as the object itself, and the transitory as its mere determination, that is, as a way in which the object exists. (A182)

[16] In A: Everything that happens, that is, begins to be, presupposes something upon which it follows according to a rule. (A189)

[17] In another way, the example of the ship is very much ill-chosen. It is not, in fact, an example of the kind of alteration which needs, and thus which receives, a *causal* explanation. Kant is candid about this later, in a parenthetical sort of way:

It should be carefully noted that I speak not of the alteration of certain relations in general, but of alteration of state. Thus, when a body moves uniformly, it does not in any way alter its state (of motion); that occurs only when its motion increases or diminishes (B252, note).

[18] Indeed, it is entirely possible to see in Kant's *Third* Analogy – the "Principle of Coexistence in accordance with the Law of Reciprocity or Community" – a prefiguring of Einstein's analysis of simultaneity in terms of causal connectability.

CHAPTER III

[1] This, however, is not *all* we are. We are also beings who lack an active intuition, that is, whose manifolds are given *passively*. We *find ourselves* with experiences. This fact is

not especially important in the present context – although I make tacit use of it – but it becomes *very* important later in the story, when we return to the epistemological theme of justification, and I shall advert to it explicitly then. See below, page 175ff.

[2] This characteristically empiricist coherentism reemerges properly situated in the universal *fallibilism* which Peirce makes a centerpiece of his pragmatism. Although Kant's "Refutation of Idealism", as I shall argue, constitutes an adequate response to the challenge posed by Berkeley's views, his own "transcendental idealism" leaves him open to the challenge of Hegelianism. Only the pragmatic turn finally resolves the classical dialectic of realism and idealism and thereby ultimately defuses the threat of skepticism perennially perceived as lying in empiricism's fallibilism.

[3] For elaboration, see Baier, "The Place of a Pain".

[4] And now I am able to make good on my earlier promise (p. 31) to cite a third, problematic, interpretation of β-changes in our Auditory Model. The β-change

$$T_i^j \Rightarrow T_i^k \text{ while } M_a \text{ remains constant } (j < k)$$

could also represent the approach of a T_i of intensity $k-j$ and its overlapping a stationed T_i of intensity j. Unless loudness were somehow necessarily "quantized" and could not vary, then, admitting β-changes into our Auditory Model would render its *synchronic* counts of its things indeterminate in exactly the same way that the number of coincident pains here becomes indeterminate.

[5] Operating thus with twinges, aches, and twaches, we might come to think of twaches as "between" twinges and aches – as orange is between red and yellow – and proceed to elaborate an entire theory of "primary" and "secondary" pains, "pain mixing", and the like.

[6] Logic, in consequence, emerges as a particular prerogative of *discursive* intelligences. Representations employing the apparatus of logic can be thought of as *recipes* for constructing a sort of all-at-once, "Bradleyian" representation of the *unitariness* of a manifold which *we* can only encounter *as* a manifold and whose unification is for us, so to speak, a task. Consider, by way of analogy, the all-at-once representation of spatial distances and relationships embodied in a *map* as contrasted with a *table* giving the distance and direction between each pair of cities on the map. The table is, in a similar way, a recipe for drawing the map, and embodies the apparatus of logic precisely in the implicit 'and's connecting its successive entries. For an earlier attempt along these lines, see my *LR*: Chapter VII.

[7] This, as we shall shortly see, turns out to be the crux of the matter. It is the crux of several other matters as well – among them the thesis that "incorrigibility is the mark of the mental", for the ideality of George's things is their being "mental" (their *esse* is to be *N*-represented) and the indefeasibility of George's primary *N*-representings in accordance with the PriDoPri is their "incorrigibility". But more on this later.

There are two more remarks which should be made here. The first concerns the historical antecedents of the line of argument which I have just employed. They are, of course, Hume's reasonings on causation. My (C) and (S) are just his "constant conjunctions" and "regular successions"; and my denial of them the status of "analytic truths" in George's conceptual scheme parallels Hume's argument that they are not "necessary connections".

The second remark concerns something which I have *not* imputed to George. I have *not* supplied him with any concept of *correctness* for his own representings nor, indeed, with any apparatus of (semantic, logical, or epistemic) *appraisal* at all. Were I to do so, in fact, we would soon discover indeterminacies and arbitrarinesses with a vengeance! That, indeed, is the leading topic of my *next* chapter. Here, however, I intend to hew closely to more Kantian lines.

[8] In B: That which cannot be thought otherwise than as subject does not exist otherwise than as subject, and is therefore substance.

A thinking being, considered merely as such, cannot be thought otherwise than as subject.

Therefore it exists also only as subject, that is, as substance. (B410–11)

[9] The reason that they do not — or not often — happen to *us*, of course, is that we are *not* idealists. *Our* synthesis is highly evolved and highly stable, at least at its commonplace center. Even our "idealistic" pain discourse is firmly wedded to — and thus stabilized by — our conception of pains as located in, and caused by damage to, regions of our organic (material, empirical) body.

[10] There are thus *many* ways for George to *bring off* a determinate unitary synthesis at t_2 — many forms which his "Material Logic of Contents" might take. He could, for example, resolve

1. That only ϕ's and ψ's (twinges and aches) are real; all Ω's (twaches) are merely apparent; or
2. That only Ω's (twaches) are real; all ϕ's and ψ's (twinges and aches) are merely apparent; or
3. That ϕ's, ψ's *and* Ω's (twinges, aches, *and* twaches) are real — but each sort of content is suitably *quantized*.

Which of these — or perhaps other — strategies would *best* serve the overall project of synthesis, however, depends on the details of George's experience. It is not something which can be determined from our standpoint *a priori*. Once again, our Kantian considerations determine only the most-general (categorial) *form* of any representational system possible for us. It must be ("from within") a Realist Core. The specific empirical *content* of a world-picture, however, is a function of the particular experiences with which a subject finds himself, and thus depend crucially on the passive element in experience, the contributions of the receptive sensibility. This theme will recur, with increased significance, later in our inquiries — when we return to the topic of the *succession* of conceptual frameworks or representational systems.

[11] But that is not the best way to think about pains. See my "Speaking Lions".

CHAPTER IV

[1] Our current neo-Hegelian critic has a name, by the way. In fact, he has three: Rorty, Davidson, and Putnam. See, respectively, their *WWL*, *VICS*, and *RR*.

[2] The affinities between our present project and the general problematic of epistemic justification developed in the first chapter should now be transparently clear. There we sought an original legitimacy as here we seek an original correctness. Indeed, they are really the same project, for the connection which we want is a connection between justification and correctness. We do not, after all, want to be epistemically justified in judgments which are incorrect. We will never get knowledge that way.

NOTES

CHAPTER V

[1] But don't we change our minds (collectively) about the world? Isn't the picture of the world projected by our current sophisticated scientific conceptual scheme radically different from that projected by the conceptual scheme of, say, our ancient Athenian precursors? The answer to both of these questions is, of course, yes. Our collective practices are not static but dynamic. They evolve across time. How they evolve, under what constraints, and how their diachronic evolution affects questions of correctness, warrant, and justification will be the central themes, in fact, of the balance of this book. But there is a (categorial) core of any conceptual scheme which can be ours which does not thus evolve. It does not, because it cannot. And it is this categorial core which is *definitive* of Constitutive Realism. Precisely this is what I established in my earlier chapters. The fact that, in *some* respects, we do (collectively) "change our minds" about the world is thus not a fact which bears upon what is presently in dispute between me and the Transcendental Idealist. These are good questions. Indeed they are! But they are not relevant to what is currently the point at issue.

[2] And, of course, there are layers upon layers of agreements in practice within this one — allowing us to work with various handwritings and typefaces for inscriptions and with differences of volume and accent for utterances. Thus, when I wrote *"the* design 'KLOOP'" a moment ago, I was trading on the fact that, as we ordinarily put it, 'kloop', *'kloop',* 'KLOOP', *'KLOOP',* 'kloop', 'KLOOP', 'KLOOP', and so on all consist of "the same letters in the same order".

[3] Indeed, having introduced this much catholicity into our notational devices, we can extend the semantic idiom to behaviors even of *non*-human intelligences — overt behaviors which, like our covert behaviors, are not *literally* tokening conducts at all but which occupy places in their overt behavioral economy parallel to the places occupied in our own by tokenings.

CHAPTER VI

[1] Since what I have been calling 'quasi-representations' already exhibit the *intentionality* characteristic of representations proper — they are "about" or "stand for" other states of affairs, and they are "useable *in absentia"* — one can wonder at this point what the *difference* between quasi-representations and representations proper might be. What *more* is required to transform a quasi-representation into an authentic representation? As I am using the term 'representation', the gist of the answer is: systemic embedding. Representations proper stand in (broadly) logical relations not only to occasioning stimuli and occasioned macro-behavior but also to *each other*. It is by coming to be caught up in a complex (normatively characterizable) network of connections among themselves that a *collection* of quasi-representations can become constituted as a *system* of representations properly so called. For an elaboration of this point, see my book, *LR*, and the (more recent) essay *LRPN*, The relevant ontological observation here is that the difference between quasi-representations and authentic representations is *not*, on this account, a difference of ontological kind, but merely, so to speak, of degree. Thus we remain free, is desired, to find ourselves *as* representers *in* the world.

² For some additional detail concerning language-learning in its relation to the propensities for those representings which are perceptual takings, see *LR*, Chapter III, especially pp. 43ff.
³ And, presumably, to be explained in a parallel way — by appeal to the fact that humans are complex bio-physical systems of a certain sort which evolved in a certain environmental setting.
⁴ A trick which Paul Churchland taught me to pull off on a clear night in Winnipeg.
⁵ That is, roughly, that doing X when R is the case causally necessitates, if not E itself, then some other outcome O, relative to which the achieving of E becomes more probable. For what to make of statistical or probabilistic talk in connection with causal laws, see my *LR*, Chapter V, especially pp. 77–83.

CHAPTER VII

¹ This 'I' is, in an important sense, still "paralogistic". That is, it does not, as yet, advert to a *thing*, a structured stuff. It *ascribes* representings to subjects *as* (mere) subjects. In contrast to our earlier conclusions, however, the 'I' here is no longer on that account alone empty or idle. Since it now has an operative term of contrast, it now has a job to do as well. It *selects* the subject(s) of a representing from an indefinite multiplicity of possible such subjects. And, although it selects that subject simply *as* the subject of *that* representing, where subjects can *differ* in their world-pictures this is no longer a vacuous principle of selection.

The point of requiring that the collective 'we' be included among the possible subjects to which a representing can be ascribed is precisely to make possible the *normative* dimension of rational appraisal — for only such a first-person-plural point of view could be one which is *both* "external" to the individual subject's 'I' *and*, nevertheless, *binding* on the subject as a norm or standard of correctness (by virtue of his representing himself as necessarily a member of the community at which this 'we' gestures).

For additional detail, see my "Apperception".

CHAPTER VIII

¹ For some relatively straightforward examples drawn from the history of science, see *LR*, pp. 60–66.

APPENDIX II

BIBLIOGRAPHY

Baier, K., 'The Place of a Pain', *Philosophical Quarterly* **14** (1964), 138–150.
Bennett, J., *(KA)*, *Kant's Analytic*, Cambridge University Press, London, 1966.
Bergmann, G., *Meaning and Existence*, University of Wisconsin Press, Madison, 1960.
Bergmann, G., *Logic and Reality*, University of Wisconsin Press, Madison, 1964.
Bergmann, G., *Realism: A Critique of Brentano and Meinong*, University of Wisconsin Press, Madison, 1967.
Bergmann, G., *(SO)*, 'Strawson's Ontology', in *Logic and Reality*, pp. 171–192.
Berkeley, G., *(TD)*, *Three Dialogues Between Hylas and Philonous*; C. M. Turbayne, ed.; Bobbs-Merrill Co., Inc.; Indianapolis and New York, 1954.
Chappell, V. C., ed., *(PM)*, *The Philosophy of Mind*, Prentice-Hall, Inc., Englewood Cliffs, 1962.
Davidson, D., *(VICS)*, 'On the Very Idea of a Conceptual Scheme', *Proceedings of the American Philosophical Association* **17** (1973–4), 11ff.
Descartes, R., *(MED)*, *Meditations on First Philosophy*; L. J. Lafleur, trans.; The Library of Liberal Arts, Bobbs-Merrill Co., Inc., Indianapolis and New York, 1960.
Hume, D., *(ENQ)*, *Enquiry Concerning Human Understanding*; L. A. Selby-Bigge, ed.; Clarendon Press; Oxford, 1894.
Hume, D., *(THN)*, *Treatise on Human Nature*; L. A. Selby-Bigge, ed.; Clarendon Press, Oxford, 1888 & 1896.
Kant, I., *(CPR)*, *Critique of Pure Reason*; Norman Kemp Smith, trans.; Macmillan & Co. Ltd., London, 1929; St. Martin's Press, New York, 1958.
Long, D., *(PTQ)*, 'Particulars and Their Qualities', *Philosophical Quarterly* **18** (1968), 193–206.
Malcolm, N., *(WPI)*, 'Wittgenstein's *Philosophical Investigations*', *Philosophical Review* **LXIII** (1954), 530–59.
Putnam, H., *(RR)*, 'Realism and Reason', *Proceedings and Addresses of the American Philosophical Association* **50** (1977), 483–98.
Rorty, R., *(VTA)*, 'Verification and Transcendental Arguments', *Nous* **5** (1971), 3–14.
Rorty, R., *(WWL)*, 'The World Well Lost', *Journal of Philosophy* **69** (1972), 649–66.
Rosenberg, J. F., *(LR)*, *Linguistic Representation*, D. Reidel Publishing Company, Dordrecht, 1974.
Rosenberg, J. F., *(LRPN)*, 'Linguistic Roles and Proper Names', in *The Philosophy of Wilfrid Sellars: Queries and Extensions*; J. Pitt, ed., D. Reidel Publishing Co., Dordrecht, (1978), 189–216.
Rosenberg, J. F., *(SL)*, 'Speaking Lions', *Canadian Journal of Philosophy* **VII** (1977), 155–60.
Rosenberg, J. F. *(SSSN)* 'On Strawson: Sounds, Skepticism, and Necessity', *Philosophia* **8** (1978), 405–19.
Rosenberg, J. F. 'Apperception', unpublished Xerox.

Russell, B., (*ORUP*), 'On the Relations of Universals and Particulars', in *Logic and Knowledge*, R. C. Marsh, ed., The Macmillan Co., London and New York, (1956), 103–24.

Sellars, W., (*AE*), 'Abstract Entities', *Review of Metaphysics* 16 (1963), 627–71; reprinted in Sellars, *Philosophical Perspectives*, Charles Thomas, Publishers, Springfield, 1967.

Sellars, W., (*LTC*), 'Language as Thought and Communication', *Philosophy and Phenomenological Research* 29 (1969), 506–27; reprinted in Sellars, *Essays in Philosophy and Its History*, D. Reidel Publishing Company; Dordrecht, 1974.

Strawson, P. F., (*IND*), *Individuals*, Methuen & Co., Ltd., London, 1959.

Stroud, B., (*TAEN*), 'Transcendental Arguments and 'Epistemological Naturalism' ', *Philosophical Studies* **31** (1977), 105–115.

Wittgenstein, L., (*PI*), *Philosophical Investigations*; G. E. M. Anscombe, trans., The Macmillan Company, London and New York, 1953.

INDEX OF NAMES

Baier, K. 197n3
Bennett, J. 194n1
Bergmann, G. 45, 196n11
Berkeley, G. 6, 15–6, 25–6, 57, 59ff.

Chappell, V. C. 13
Churchland, P. 200n4

Davidson, D. 198n1
Descartes, R. 6, 10–11, 13, 16, 25–6, 59–60, 76–7, 193n5, 196n12
Dewey, J. 190
Dick 162–3

Euclid 54, 195n10

Feyerabend, P. K. 185
Frege, G. 105

George 57–9, 65ff., 91, 111, 121–5, 176–7, 197n7, 198n10
George-robot 74–5

Hegel, G. W. F. 16, 57, 197n2
Heidegger, M. 190
Heisenberg, W. 54
Hempel, C. 183
Henry 159–61
Hume, D. 4ff., 13, 15–6, 53, 75, 77, 147, 197n7

Jane 162–3

Kant, I. 3ff., 15ff., 26–7, 31, 41, 43, 45ff., 59, 63, 75–7, 85–6, 109, 113–4, 158, 179, 193n1, 195n6, 195n10, 195n13, 195n17, 195n18
Kemp-Smith, N. 47
Kuhn, T. 185

Lobachevski, N. 54
Locke, J. 4, 6, 15, 45, 59ff.
Long, D. 45

Malcolm, N. 194n7

Newton, I. 54

Peirce, C. S. 62, 191, 197n2
Planck, M. 54
Plato 8, 45, 55, 62, 189, 191, 196n12
Putnam, H. 198n1

Rembrandt 98–9
Riemann, G. 54
Rorty, R. 172–3, 188, 194n6, 198n1
Rosenberg, J. F. 98–9
Russell, B. 45, 194n10

Schroedinger, E. 54
Sellars, W. 118, 121, 164
Smyth, R. 193n4
Socrates 1, 55, 191
Strawson, P. F. 14–5, 22, 41, 45, 193n2, 194n10, 195n7, 196n11
Stroud, B. 16, 173

Wittgenstein, L. 94, 103–4, 106, 190

INDEX OF SUBJECTS

Analogies of Experience 46ff., 196n14
   First Analogy (substance) 48–50, 196n15
   Second Analogy (causation) 49–54, 196n16
   Third Analogy (coexistence) 196n18
'analytic truths' 71, 73–4, 78–9, 122, 197n7
   See also: indefeasibility, necessity
anomalies 176ff., 181ff., 186–7
Anticipations of Perception 26, 48
apperception 75ff., 86
   See also: 'I', self
appraisal 91–2, 168
   and deontic principles 126ff., 168–9
   reflective 165ff., 180
   terms of 117, 120ff., 198n7
appraisal theory 129, 141–4, 151–5
arenas 42–3, 46, 55, 66, 73, 78, 86, 195n10
   See also: form of outer sense, space
attribution theory 129, 142
Auditory Model 22–3, 27–8, 29ff. 42, 54, 197n4
Axioms of Intuition 26, 48

beliefs 138, 144, 150
biconditionals 94–6, 110, 112–3, 116–7

C-A Skeleton 182ff.
causation/causes 5, 8, 50ff., 130, 137, 154
   vs reasons 129, 131–4
   See also: necessary connection, relations of objective consequence
certainty 10ff.
change 27, 196n12
   in the Auditory Model 27ff., 197n4
   in the Visual Model 34ff.
   vs alteration (in Kant) 49

changes
   α-, β- 28, 39ff., 41, 197n4
   Π-, Σ-, Θ- 34–41
   of color 44ff.
   of ontological consequence 31, 36, 39, 42, 44, 49
   of position 30ff., 34
   of shape and size 34–6
   real *versus* apparent 32, 37–41, 44, 49
chrono-logic *See*: material logic of time
cognition 6, 45, 85
coherence 60, 84, 86, 107, 145, 175, 197n2
communal
   ends 159ff., 174–5
      vs common ends 159–60
   motives 159, 163, 175
   norms 158ff., 168–9, 170, 174–5, 180
community 104, 126, 156, 158ff., 168–9, 200n1
   constitution of 161ff., 174–5
   locus of semantic correctness in 104ff.
   rational 169, 174–5, 179
   See also: non-vacuous 'I', 'one', 'we'
concept empiricism 6ff., 19–20
concepts 57
   categorial 7, 8ff., 16, 19–20, 55
Conditional Theories 14, 17
consilience 105ff., 117, 125, 145, 156, 158, 169, 174
Constitutive Realism *See*: Realism
Content-Ascriptive Skeleton 182ff.
contents 22ff., 43–5, 65
   descriptive 114, 180, 183ff.
   See also: form, things
convergence 115–6, 165, 181, 185–7
coordinate content ascriptions 182ff.
'Copernican revolution in philosophy' 7, 53, 113, 165

INDEX OF SUBJECTS

correctness 89ff., 103, 110, 124ff.
  absolute 113ff., 116–7, 164–5, 173, 181, 186
  agreement in 94, 100
  concept of 91, 124–6, 156, 189, 197n7
  conditions of 91ff.
  locus of 104, 113, 117
  of Constitutive Realism 110–1
  of labels 93
  original 100, 198n2
correspondence 61, 88ff., 186
counting rules 28–9
  idealist 37, 58, 69
  realist 28–9, 31–3, 38ff., 41
creation and annihilation 31, 38, 44, 49, 195n6
criteria 11, 14ff., 194n7
  of correctness 89, 104, 113
Criteriological Realism *See*: Realism
Criteriological Theories 14–5, 17

descriptive metaphysics 14–5, 193n2
discursiveness 57, 65–6, 68, 72, 196n3, 197n6
  See also: synthesis
double accountability of successors 177, 180–1
double action-guiding force of norms 163–4, 169

embedding 17ff., 179
  See also: transcendental deduction
empirical deduction 4–5, 9
empiricism 12ff., 60–1, 130, 191, 197n2
  problematic of 16, 20, 113, 116, 173, 194n8, 198n2
ends 148–9, 151ff.
  non-optional, overriding 174–5, 179, 189
  See also: means-ends connections, motives
environment
  as evolutionarily selective 116, 131, 135, 139, 141
  vs things 22ff., 43, 48, 65, 76
  See also: evolution

epistemic first principles 10, 20
  See also: original correctness
epistemic legitimacy 3ff., 16ff., 164–5, 189
  original 9ff., 178–9, 198n2
  See also: justification, warrant
evolution 18, 115–6, 131, 134–7, 139–41, 147–8, 155
  See also: teleological explanation
experience 19–20, 85, 175
  in Kant 6ff., 19–20, 45–6, 85, 193n1
  veridical *vs* non-veridical 60ff.
experiencers 110, 121–2, 127, 130, 164
  fundamental project of 121, 127

fallibilism 197n2
form
  categorial, mathematical 114, 179, 198n10
  of inner sense 46, 55, 78
  of outer sense 41ff., 52, 54, 78, 86, 195n10
  real *vs* apparent 32, 49
  vs contents 22ff., 43–5, 65, 114
formal being 11, 61
formal logic 70ff., 130, 197n6
functionalism (in biology) 17ff.
  See also: evolution, teleological explanation

'I' 75ff.
  'I think' 76, 107
  non-vacuous 107, 126, 148, 155ff.
  paralogistic 76ff., 200n1
  See also: community, 'one', 'we'
Idealism 28–9, 58ff., 191
  Berkeley's 59ff.
  Empirical (George's) 78ff.
  Transcendental 109ff., 172–3, 188, 197n2, 199n1
  See also: counting rules
ideas and impressions 4–6, 19, 59, 75–7
incommensurability 185–6
indefeasibility 10, 71, 74, 79, 84, 197n7
  See also: 'analytic truths', certainty, necessity
inner sense *See*: time

INDEX OF SUBJECTS

(INT) 144, 151
intelligence
    as concept-using 57, 65
    of behavior 139–41
intentional action 144ff., 149, 156
    vs rational action 160–1
    See also: teleological behavior

justification 60–1, 114ff., 146, 165, 173, 198n2
    as practical reasoning 126ff., 151–5, 166ff., 169, 170–1, 178ff.
    of behavior 143–4
    of successor schemes 177ff.
    prior to correctness 117, 187, 189
    prospective *vs* retrospective 114–5, 166–8, 180
    See also: epistemic legitimacy, warrant

'kloop' 93ff., 117, 199n2

labels 92–4, 104
limits 115, 185–7
logic *See*: formal logic, material logic
logoi 132ff., 155
    See also: reasons

magnitudes 26ff., 194n1
    See also: contents, qualities
mass terms *See*: contents
material logic 69–74, 83–4, 122, 130, 145, 151, 154, 168, 181ff.
    of contents 74, 83–4, 181ff., 184, 198n10
    of Idealism 79
    of location (arena-geometry) 73–4
    of time (chrono-logic) 69–74
means-ends connections 151–2, 154, 167–8, 170, 172–5
    analytic 174–5, 180
    causal *vs* constitutive 173–4
memory 65, 81–3, 101–3
Minimal Core 27, 43–4, 65, 196n11
motives 144ff., 148
    botanized 148–9
    vs beliefs 150
    See also: ends, volitions

Myth of Mind Apart 189–91

N-representations 65ff., 77, 82–3
necessary connection 5, 16, 33, 41, 48–9, 85, 130, 197n7
    See also: causation, material logic of contents, relations of objective consequence, regularities
necessity 8, 15, 32–3, 40, 47, 70–1, 85
    See also: 'analytic truths', indefeasibility
needs 132, 134–7
Neo-Realists' Club 162–3, 174
non-vacuous 'I' *See*: 'I'

objective being 11, 29, 61, 63
'one' 124, 158–9, 168–9
    See also: community, 'we'
one world *See*: world
other minds 13, 191, 194n7
outer sense *See*: space
'outside perspective' 109ff., 112, 130–1, 142–3, 152–5, 157–8

pains 13, 29, 59, 61, 63, 66–8, 82–3, 85–6, 195n2, 197n5, 198n9, 198n11
Paralogisms of Pure Reason 76–7, 198n8
particulars and universals 43ff.
part *vs* whole 23–4, 194n1
perception 6, 26, 137, 145–6, 200n2
permanence 31, 33, 39, 47ff.
    See also: substance
practical reasoning 126ff., 150–1, 156
    attributed 151ff., 161ff., 178ff.
    self-attributed 166ff.
    communal 171ff.
Principle
    of Dominance of Primary Representings (PriDoPri) 73, 80, 84
    of Idealism 81
    of Non-Coincident Indistinguishables (Pri-NCI) 67
    of Non-Overlapping Contents (Pri-NOC) 68, 79–88
principles
    constitutive *vs* regulative 48, 179–80

deontic 123ff., 156, 168
epistemic 10, 20
normative *vs* summative 74, 79
of objective consequence *See*: relations of objective consequence of permission 3, 123, 168
Private Language Argument 104
problematic
    Kantian 3–4, 9–10, 13, 16, 19–20
    of empiricism 13ff., 16, 20, 113–4, 116, 173, 194n8, 198n2
pseudo-questions 1
(PUR) 139
purposive behavior *See*: teleological behavior

qualification (of successor schemes) 178–80, 182–5
qualities
    of particulars 43–5
    primary *vs* secondary 25–7
    vs contents 23, 26
    See also: contents, magnitudes
quasi-representations 137–9, 144, 199n1
quotation marks/quoting 77–8, 118ff.
    behavioral 118–9
    of thoughts 120

(R1)–(R8) 33–4, 38–40, 43, 84–6, 164, 175, 179
    See also: Realist Core
rational action 157ff., 160–1, 174–5
Realism 28–9, 31–3, 43, 55–6, 58ff., 109, 191
    Constitutive 87, 89ff., 109–13, 164, 170, 173, 199n1
    Criteriological 89ff., 93, 103, 111–3, 116, 188
    Empirical 109
    Locke's 61ff.
    See also: counting rules
Realist Core 43–4, 48, 54–6, 58, 75, 84–6, 109, 112, 196n11, 198n10
    See also: (R1)–(R8)
reasons 128
    as logoi 132ff.
    for behavior 139ff., 151ff.

valid 154, 167–8
vs causes 129, 131
Refutation of Idealism 86, 197n2
regularities 30ff., 34ff., 40–1, 47–8, 52–3, 74, 195n5
regulative ideals 115, 165, 188–9
    See also: convergence, limits
relations
    of consilience 105
    of location 66, 72
    of objective consequence 53ff., 90, 154
    of temporal order 68, 72
rules 47–8, 50
    of inference 72, 168–9, 175
    See also: principles

self 5, 8, 75ff., 86, 130, 157ff.
    -appraisals 165ff.
    Humean 75, 84
    See also: apperception, 'I'
sensibility 6, 193n1
sets 138ff.
skepticism 10, 13ff., 60–1, 191, 193n2, 193n6, 197n2
    Cartesian demonaic 13, 87, 115, 164, 194n6
space 26, 38–9, 41, 52, 54, 86, 195n10
    See also: arenas, form of outer sense
structured stuffs 43–5, 200n1
    See also: things
substance 25, 31, 33, 39, 47ff., 54, 76
    See also: permanence
synthesis 6, 9, 19–20, 46, 181, 198n10
    See also: experience
synthetic a priori 3 ff., 15–6, 19–20, 179, 194n7

T-representations 65ff., 77, 82–3
(TEL) 134, 144, 150–1
teleological behavior 17ff., 129, 131ff.
    tropistic 17ff., 131–3
    want-directed 135–7
    purposive 139ff.
    intentional 144ff.
teleological explanations 17ff., 131ff., 137, 141

See also: evolution
teleological equation 132, 134ff., 144, 150–1
tense 65, 68
   vs time 74ff.
things 22ff., 43–5, 48, 65ff., 76
'third way'/*tertium quid* 16, 20, 114, 173, 181
time 26, 46, 48ff., 55, 68–70, 78, 195n10
   material logic of (chrono-logic) 69–74
   vs tense 74ff.
   See also: form of inner sense
transcendental deduction
   in Kant 3ff., 16ff., 19–20, 26–7, 45ff.
   strategy of 16ff., 19–20
   See also: embedding, empirical deduction
Transcendental Idealism *See*: Idealism
'trinting' 97ff., 117
(TRO) 132
tropisms *See*: teleological behavior
'twaches' 67–8, 82–3, 184, 197n5

understanding 6, 193n1

universals 43ff.

virtual parts *See*: part *vs* whole
Visual Model 22–3, 34ff., 42, 44, 55
volitions 145ff., 149–50
   See also: motives

(WAN) 135
wants 135ff.
   See also: needs
warrant 11ff., 15–6, 19–20, 60, 127–8, 144, 189
   evidential 12–3, 20
   logical 4, 12, 19–20
   See also: epistemic legitimacy, justification
'we' 21, 56–7, 85, 87, 109, 158ff., 168, 189, 200n1
   See also: community, 'I', 'one'.
world 19–20, 87ff., 92, 107, 112, 172, 194n11
   unity of 112, 115–6, 128, 164–5, 187, 188–9

PHILOSOPHICAL STUDIES SERIES
IN PHILOSOPHY

Editors:

WILFRID SELLARS, Univ. of Pittsburgh and KEITH LEHRER, Univ. of Arizona

Board of Consulting Editors:

Jonathan Bennett, Alan Gibbard, Robert Stalnaker, and Robert G. Turnbull

1. JAY F. ROSENBERG, *Linguistic Representation*, 1974.
2. WILFRID SELLARS, *Essays in Philosophy and Its History*, 1974.
3. DICKINSON S. MILLER, *Philosophical Analysis and Human Welfare*. Selected Essays and Chapters from Six Decades. Edited with an Introduction by Lloyd D. Easton, 1975.
4. KEITH LEHRER (ed.), *Analysis and Metaphysics*. Essays in Honor of R. M. Chisholm. 1975.
5. CARL GINET, *Knowledge, Perception, and Memory*, 1975.
6. PETER H. HARE and EDWARD H. MADDEN, *Causing, Perceiving and Believing*. An Examination of the Philosophy of C. J. Ducasse, 1975.
7. HECTOR-NERI CASTAÑEDA, *Thinking and Doing*. The Philosophical Foundations of Institutions, 1975.
8. JOHN L. POLLOCK, *Subjunctive Reasoning*, 1976.
9. BRUCE AUNE, *Reason and Action*, 1977.
10. GEORGE SCHLESINGER, *Religion and Scientific Method*, 1977.
11. YIRMIAHU YOVEL (ed.), *Philosophy of History and Action*. Papers presented at the first Jerusalem Philosophical Encounter, December 1974, 1978.
12. JOSEPH C. PITT, *The Philosophy of Wilfrid Sellars: Queries and Extensions*, 1978.
13. ALVIN I. GOLDMAN and JAEGWON KIM, *Values and Morals*. Essays in Honor of William Frankena, Charles Stevenson, and Richard Brandt, 1978.
14. MICHAEL J. LOUX, *Substance and Attribute*. A Study in Ontology, 1978.
15. ERNEST SOSA (ed.), *The Philosophy of Nicholas Rescher: Discussion and Replies*, 1979.
16. JEFFRIE G. MURPHY, *Retribution, Justice, and Therapy*. Essays in the Philosophy of Law, 1979.
17. GEORGE S. PAPPAS, *Justification and Knowledge: New Studies in Epistemology*, 1979.
18. JAMES W. CORNMAN, *Skepticism, Justification, and Explanation*, 1980.
19. PETER VAN INWAGEN, *Time and Cause*. Essays presented to Richard Taylor, 1980.
20. DONALD NUTE, *Topics in Conditional Logic*, 1980

CPSIA information can be obtained
at www.ICGtesting.com
Printed in the USA
FSOW04n0833030917
38334FS